Books are to be returned on or before
the last date below.

LIBREX-

D1428742

# The Future
# of Class
# in History

*What's Left of the Social?*

GEOFF ELEY & KEITH NIELD

The University of Michigan Press   *Ann Arbor*

2010   2009   2008   2007     4   3   2   1

*A CIP catalog record for this book is available from the British Library.*

Library of Congress Cataloging-in-Publication Data

Eley, Geoff, 1949–
      The future of class in history : what's left of the social? /
Geoff Eley and Keith Nield.
            p.      cm.
      ISBN-13: 978-0-472-09964-1 (cloth : alk. paper)
      ISBN-10: 0-472-09964-7 (cloth : alk. paper)
      ISBN-13: 978-0-472-06964-4 (pbk. : alk. paper)
      ISBN-10: 0-472-06964-0 (pbk. : alk. paper)
      1. Social classes.   2. Social history.   3. Postmodernism.
4. Historiography.   I. Nield, Keith.   II. Title.

HT601.E44     2007
305.5—dc22                               2006020161

# PREFACE

This book has a long prehistory. At the height of the great social history enthusiasm of the 1970s, on the eve of the first signs of what we now call the "cultural turn," we published an article in *Social History* called "Why Does Social History Ignore Politics?"[1] In that essay we raised concerns about the ways in which the contextualizing ambitions of social historians were tending to leave diminishing space for the analysis of politics. Inside the general aggrandizement of social explanation associated with the Marxisms and other materialist sociologies of the time, we could also detect what Richard Johnson had recently called a new "culturalism."[2] Inspired by the influence of Edward Thompson, by Raymond Williams and his linking of culture to "structures of feeling" and a society's "whole way of life," by the early forms of cultural studies, and by cultural anthropologies of the kind associated especially with Clifford Geertz, social historians were increasingly moving toward a kind of "cultural materialism." Yet while vitally enriching our understanding of the bases of social solidarity and difference, the new attentiveness to culture had the effect of further reducing the space for analysis of politics per se. In writing our 1980 article we wanted to call attention to that problem. Without either disavowing the important gains of social history and its insistence that politics be socially contextualized or seeming to suggest that older forms of political history might be restored, we wanted to widen the space for thinking about politics creatively. Our preferred strategy for doing so involved working with the ideas of Antonio Gramsci, whose reception had become such a powerful motor of discussion among the Left in Britain at the time.

Although our intervention seemed to annoy many people and was occasionally cited in their footnotes, we drew disappointingly little response in print.[3] As it happened, our particular proposals for thinking the "social," the "cultural," and the "political" productively together became rapidly superseded by more extreme insistence on the autonomies of politics, which eventually severed the latter from social analysis altogether. During the mid-1980s, the authors of those further-going critiques turned increasingly to linguistic analysis and theories of discourse, whether taking avowedly Foucauldian directions, preferring literary-theoretical or formally "deconstructive" approaches, or searching for the construction of meaning in everyday life. Interestingly, the most fervent and influential advocates of these new directions saw them in serious conflict with the earlier goals of social history, demanding that those be set entirely and unsentimentally aside. The new "linguistic" or "discursive" approach to history was invariably approached in *contradistinction* to that earlier social historiography, for which "Marxist" also became an interchangeable term.

By the turn of the 1990s, the landscape of discussion among left-tending historians had decisively changed. Of course, all of this was also happening amid profound transformations in the contemporary social and political world—embracing deindustrialization and post-Fordist transition, capitalist restructuring and class recomposition, the crisis of social democracy and the collapse of Communism—and the new culturalist perspectives were no less in dialogue with these political changes than the earlier social histories had been in their own time. Many diverse political conclusions might be drawn, across a wide range of centrist or radical choices. But one especially salient consequence of these developments, politically and intellectually, both inside the discipline of history and across the human sciences more generally, seemed to be a new skepticism, uncertainty, or lack of confidence about the concept of *class*.

Whether in its political or its historiographical and broader intellectual dimensions, this was a momentous development. For roughly a century between the later nineteenth and later twentieth centuries, the centrality of class for social analysis and political understanding had been axiomatic for most of the Left. Likewise, for those of our own generations of historians inspired by the social history wave of the 1960s and 1970s, "class" had been hardly less than a master category. So when we were invited to a general stock-taking conference entitled "Historical Perspectives on Class and Culture" organized by Robbie Gray at the University of Portsmouth in September 1993, we decided to talk directly about this new crisis of class-based analysis and understanding.[4] Moreover, while we had often mused about returning to our 1980 article, precisely because of the silence surrounding it, the intervening climate could scarcely have been more changed. Rather than versions of "the social" subtly overwhelming the space and efficacies of "the political," as we had argued in 1980, the social was seen either as a complex *effect* of the political sphere, now reunderstood in Foucauldian terms of governmentality, or else as a separable domain that was appealed to, targeted, imagined, and variously constructed by political actors but that certainly no longer explained or determined their actions in the way social historians had wanted to suppose. In our Portsmouth paper, baldly titled "Classes as Historical Subjects," we set out to recuperate some of the earlier social-historical ground of research and discussion. We wanted to do so not out of nostalgia or from a belief that past historiographies might be salvaged intact to serve as a source of straightforward illumination. Nor were we regretful about the cultural turn or opposed to the new forms of understanding it permitted. We were not trying to turn the clock back or to go "back to the future," as one of our critics subsequently joked. The theoretical and political challenges of the 1980s and 1990s were entirely unavoidable, we thought, and so was the import of the contemporary changes in the actually existing worlds of capitalism.

Rather, we wanted to see whether the grounds for collaborative conversation across the polarized differences between social and cultural historians might be renewed. After a long period in which the class concept had been subject to largely destructive critique, we wanted to offer some sustained reflection on its sustainable uses today—historiographically, theoretically, politically. In choosing this particular ground, we are also seeking to intervene in the wider debates among social historians and cultural historians about how history should best be practiced. We hope that our book furthers not only the more immediate debates about class per se but also much larger discussions in the discipline. It goes back to the paper we presented at the 1993 conference, which itself reflected the much longer collaboration we have described, focused around our common involvement in the journal *Social History*. In the meantime, we have also produced, separately and together, a variety of writings further developing our ideas.[5] In particular, this book should be considered a companion volume to Geoff Eley, *A Crooked Line: From Cultural History to the History of Society* (Ann Arbor: University of Michigan Press, 2005), which develops complementary arguments on a more general historiographical front.

We would like to thank the various audiences to whom we presented parts of our arguments over the years. The ideas in our 1993 paper for Robbie Gray's Portsmouth conference were anticipated in commentaries delivered in 1990 at two earlier conferences, one organized by James Retallack at the University of Toronto in April and titled "Elections, Mass Politics, and Social Change in Germany, 1890–1945" and the other organized by Lewis Siegelbaum and Ronald Grigor Suny at Michigan State University in November and titled "The Making of the Soviet Working Class." The arguments were then further developed in a panel at the Washington, D.C., meeting of the German Studies Association in November 1993; in a lecture at SUNY—Stony Brook in April 1994; in a plenary talk to the Sixteenth North American Labor History Conference at Wayne State University in October 1994; and then in a variety of settings ever since. Most memorably of all, at the very end of the process in February 2005, we presented the book's arguments to a wonderful seminar of faculty and graduate students at the University of Michigan's newly created Institute of Historical Studies. We are each hugely indebted to the extraordinary intellectual community that the University of Michigan provides, both in the history department itself and in the university's larger culture of interdisciplinary collaboration.

We owe far too much to the intellectual advice and inspiration of far too many friends to be able to record those debts comprehensively. But for critical readings and discussions over the years, and for the brilliance and acuity of their own thinking on the subject of class, we would like to thank especially the following: Talal Asad, Lauren Berlant, Janet Blackman, Mònica Burguera, Kathleen Canning, Jane Caplan, Dipesh Chakrabarty, Dennis Dworkin, Kali Israel, Robin Kelley, Alf Lüdtke, Gina Morantz-Sanchez, Sophie Nield, Sherry Ortner, Sonya Rose, Bill Rosenberg, Roger Rouse, John Seed, Bill Sewell, Lewis Siegelbaum, Peggy Somers, Carolyn Steedman, George Steinmetz, Ron Suny, and Dennis Sweeney. In its final stages the manuscript was read by Andrew August, Jessica Dubow, James Epstein, and Sonya Rose, to whom we record our enormous appreciation. Pete Soppelsa helped prepare the final manuscript for production. Among editors Jim Reische showed once again that he provides the gold standard.

While these days the difficulties are mitigated by e-mail and fax, the conditions for writing together, particularly across continents, are rarely very easy to achieve. Usually we managed it at least once or sometimes twice a year, if only in a railway station or a hotel room. But the opportunities had to be improvised, snatched from the other parts of professional and personal life, often at short notice, requiring much support, forebearance, and understanding from the ones who share our lives. So to our respective partners, Gina Morantz-Sanchez and Ortrud Nield, go the final, most heartfelt, and foundational thanks.

# CONTENTS

# I. INTRODUCTION

## PICTURING CLASS

Let us begin with two photographs, each on the jacket of a programmatic volume. The first book is *Bringing Class Back In: Contemporary and Historical Perspectives,* edited by Scott McNall, Rhonda Levine, and Rick Fantasia (Boulder: Westview Press, 1991); the second is the volume *Class,* edited by Patrick Joyce for the Oxford Readers (Oxford: Oxford University Press, 1995). The imagery of the first refurbished a classical cluster of meanings at a time when "class" was already under fire—not only among historians but also in the wider public sphere, as changes in the social world of production seemed to be undermining the efficacy of class forms of understanding. A crowd of workers is shown at a mass meeting, presumably for a strike or some other trade union event: they are cheerful, militant, proletarian; manual workers; all men. The second photograph shows a sour and haughty old lady glaring from the window of a first-class railway compartment of a British train: she is upper class, privileged, possibly on the way to Ascot, a Buckingham Palace garden party, or a society wedding. The first photo displays the collective strength of the working class, a visual manifesto of class-political agency, an embodiment of class consciousness, a celebration of the mass. The second image conveys a very different idea—not the collective strength of an organized social force, but the individualized arrogance of power, in the splendid isolation of wealth. The two representations could hardly be more contrary. What is going on?

During a time of massive structural change in the "real world" of class, in which former certainties were starting to break apart (between the mid-1970s and the later 1980s), certain iconoclasts began arguing for the diminished usefulness, even the obsolescence, of class-analytic approaches to understanding the social world. Such discussions also addressed the class-centered concerns of the socialist political tradition, which during the 1980s entered its protracted contemporary crisis. The tones were often apocalyptic. "Socialism is Dead," the sociologist Alaine Touraine declared. "Farewell to the Working Class," echoed the radical social theorist André Gorz.[1] Reeling from the disappointments of the 1970s and the electoral disasters of 1979 and 1983, British socialists also began a root-and-branch review of established forms of class-political thinking, from the given model of the party to the automatic assumption of "the leading role of the working class."[2] Reflecting on British deindustrialization, the radicalism of Thatcher's attack on the postwar settlement, and the changing sociology of the working class, they concluded that "the world has changed, not just incrementally but qualitatively," and that out of the contemporary restructuring a new kind of social order was being shaped—one "characterized by diversity, differentiation, and fragmentation, rather than homogeneity, standardization, and the economies and organizations of scale which characterized modern mass society."[3]

We are closer now to what might have produced the imagery on our two books. The power of the workers' collective agency in the first photograph, declaring the activism of a collective subject aiming for change, the future inheritor of the good society, is replaced by the purely individualized image of class as a status, in the protected physical spaces of great wealth and privilege. The meanings of these two pictures are also figured through gender. The complete absence of women in the first representation of working-class collective agency is replaced by the arrogance of the female presence in the second image, where the old lady concerned gazes balefully out, possibly onto the kind of plebeian manifestation pictured by *Bringing Class Back In*. Class is gendered masculine where workers are exercising agency, feminine where class signifies privilege, parasitism, and moneyed power. Thus collective action confronts the self-centered individualism of entitlement in an all-too-familiar way.

The image of the old lady is removed from politics and agency. It offers an image of privileged passivity. In picturing the new valencies of class in this way, Joyce (or his designer at Oxford University Press) turns away from collective imagery altogether, rejecting archetypes and other representations of the mass or the ordinary majority of workers. The Oxford Reader also divorces class sharply from economics and production. It seems uninterested in class as a force in politics. In fact, in Joyce's selection of readings there remains little trace of workers in collective motion at all. Workers organizing themselves at the point of production, going on strike, mobilizing in communities, joining socialist parties, confronting employers, or challenging the state are entirely missing from the book. Instead, "class" functions abstractly and impersonally as an analytical tradition, a discursive structure, and a linguistic term. After the first three sections on usages of class by social theorists and historians, Joyce opts exclusively for this approach, finding class in dominant structures of meaning beyond popular agency or control—with sections titled "The History of the Social," "The Hermeneutics of the Social," and "The Language of Class." Not much sign of workers demanding their rights here.

This framing of class is surprisingly ethnocentric too, omitting questions of national difference, empire, race, and immigration entirely. This is surprising, for the postmodernism advocated by Joyce rejects older forms of class-centered analysis by seeing identity shaped in other ways, and so it seems strange to find neither race nor the wider politics of recognition among his selections. For it is not only the challenge of *theory* that destabilizes older notions of class (the story emphasized by Joyce) but a powerful set of contemporary social histories as well, including the eruption of "race" into the very centerground of politics. At a time when European labor markets are becoming not only *feminized* but visibly *racialized* or *ethnicized* as well, the tried and true iconography of the skilled white male worker becomes not just the repetition of old exclusions but also a serious distortion of how the working class is currently being made. In his selected readings, Joyce gives no access to these issues. Yet Stuart Hall, Paul Gilroy, and others have insisted that British identity—and the "Englishness" at its heart—has become structured around powerful assertions of racial difference, coming partly from the imperial past and partly from the postimperial tensions of Britain's decline, which both center national identity around an unspoken "whiteness" and marginalize the presence of blacks and other people of color.[4] Work by David Roediger and others has been changing the parameters of U.S. working-class history in this same respect.[5] Monographs are slowly beginning to appear for other parts of Europe too.[6]

Now let us introduce a third book cover, this time from the volume edited by John R. Hall called *Reworking Class* (Ithaca: Cornell University Press, 1997). Here the design is composed from two lithographs, one superimposed on the other. The smaller of the two, "Domestic Workers" by Claire Mahl Moore (1936), shows the drudgery presupposed by bourgeois good living, as two menial workers scrub the kitchen floor against the background of a dinner party while a third person, presumably the lady of the house, looks brutally on. The second, much larger picture, "Home Front Assembly Line" by Jolán Gross-Bettelheim (1940), shows workers in a classically Fordist plant, probably producing munitions. It presents the mass worker of the more celebratory versions of "modern times," epitomized by the Diego Rivera murals in the Detroit Institute of Arts: muscular, concentrated, applied to the heavy machine, marching in formation, surrounded by the monolithic greyness of the plant. *This* juxtaposition is interesting. It reverts to certain well-established progressive conventions for its images of both "the mass" and "work," yet it disrupts them in other ways. For in both pictures, the workers are entirely women.

### FEMINIST CRITIQUES

These three images say something about the contemporary discomforts of class. During the past decade or so, feminist critiques of the gendered conventions of class analysis came powerfully to fruition. After the pioneering critiques of the 1970s, the challenge of women's history became most effectively realized by arguing for gender as a necessary category of analysis. In various areas feminist approaches made much progress among the profession at large, if not in quantitative extent, then certainly in the power of the key interventions. We are thinking here of the history of political thought, of a substantial genre of writing about the nineteenth-century British and North American middle class, of work on late twentieth-century popular culture, and of histories of social policy.

In labor history, on the other hand, older conventions seemed more resilient. For a long time, the growing volume of women's history left them broadly intact. Even loosely or pretheoretically understood as anything involving women workers, gendered divisions of labor, masculinity, family relations, sexualities, and so forth, gender concerns entered the field of vision of the premier journal for labor history, *International Labor and Working-Class History,* only with a commissioned intervention by Joan Scott, "On Language, Gender, and Working-Class History," in 1987. For some years further on, gender perspectives in the journal then remained fitfully confined to incidental recognition or occasional empirical treatments, dealt with mainly as one aspect of a topic among others.[7] In another emblematic example, Ira Katznelson and Aristide Zolberg's benchmark 1986 edited volume *Working-Class Formation,* gender was entirely missing from its concerns, although some contributors (Michelle Perrot, Alain Cottereau, Mary Nolan) occasionally noticed women workers.[8]

By 1990, on the other hand, in an intended flagship volume of labor history in the United States, edited by J. Carroll Moody and Alice Kessler-Harris, two of the eight essays addressed gender, Mari Jo Buhle's "Gender and Labor History" and Kessler-Harris's "A New Agenda for American Labor History: A Gendered Analysis and the Question of Class."[9] Several benchmark volumes appeared in the 1990s, either collectively establishing the centrality of gender to the study of work and the working class—Ava Baron's edited *Work Engendered* (1991), Laura Frader and Sonya Rose's *Gender and Class in Modern Europe* (1996)—or integrating gendered perspectives into their framework, as in Lenard Berlanstein's *Rethinking Labor History* (1993), which took stock of the French field.[10] By the 1990s, Joan Scott's generalized challenge was also inspiring further theoretical responses, grounded in the first full-scale particular studies, for which Kathleen Canning's *Languages of Labor and Gender* held an impressive and prominent place.[11] In his introduction to the reader *Class,* Joyce acknowledges the force of these developments.

> Feminism has offered as great a challenge as any to the sovereignty of class in social theory, sociology, and history. Feminist theory—and feminist political practice—has offered a new subject for analysis, and new conceptions of identity for our understanding, in the shape of gender.[12]

Yet on the other hand, only six of the forty-seven readings Joyce assembles for his anthology are by women, and only four present a feminist view. As we observed, the cover image to *Class* presents the opposite of a female worker, and the peculiarly abstracted quality of this par-

ticular illustration suggests the difficulties still of registering the difference feminist critiques have made for perceptions of the overall problematic. As Lewis Siegelbaum and Ronald Suny remarked in their framing of a pioneering volume on Soviet working-class formation published
in 1994, empirical research could sometimes lag behind the broader perspectives a field wanted to pursue. Soviet specialists could begin their
own discussions with benefit of gains already registered elsewhere. But
the surface of a gendered analysis was barely scratched in the practical
analyses of the eleven excellent contributions to this book, which
explored aspects of class identities for a variety of circumstances between
the 1870s and World War II.[13] In this case, theoretical consciousness was
outrunning the field's immediate ability to deliver.[14]

The Oxford Reader *Class* could not use the same excuse, because historians like Baron, Canning, Rose, and Scott had been changing the
terms of discussion—in theoretical debate, but also in the practice of
research—for over a decade. This returns us to the heavily abstracted
quality of Joyce's selections, where class resides in a repertoire of social
theory rather than ethnographically or in the extraordinarily rich social-
historical literatures on this or that particular working class. Joyce
approaches class via the classics of sociological theory (from Marx and
Weber to Bauman, Touraine, Bourdieu, and Giddens), via Baudrillard
and Castoriadis, via Foucauldian governmentality, via "the hermeutics of
the social," via Thompson and other general historians, as well as via
recent debates about the "languages of class." Within this theoretical
framing, feminists, with the exceptions of Joan Scott herself, Donna Har-
away, and Denise Riley, are mainly absent.[15] So too are case studies of
actual groups of workers or the many particular social histories one
might describe or invoke, like the fine studies of factory paternalism
Joyce himself conducted once upon a time.[16]

## HISTORIANS AND THE DEMISE OF CLASS

Joyce is far less interested in how gender changes class analysis on the
ground, in fact, than in moving us to a place where such older-style social
histories no longer matter. "Class" turns thereby into a "discourse," or a
"narrative principle," a way of organizing "stories of past and present."
Furthermore, those stories are taken to be misleading. For Joyce, class is

a hardened construction of "relatively recent origin," projected back onto earlier times ("imaged back upon the past") and thereby "distorting" them, obscuring the forms of understanding actually operative, like the categories of "citizens" or "people" Joyce deployed in his own studies of Victorian Britain. The construction of these retroactive "views of class" is what should be focusing historians' attention, according to Joyce. They should be looking behind the dominant languages to find "new actors and new narratives" to replace the old class-based interpretations, which contemporary social change (the "postmodern condition"), politics (the end of Communism), and epistemological progress (postmodern theory) have all discredited.[17] Joyce would like us to theorize the terms of identity, rather than trying to complicate the everydayness of class relations through social histories of the workplace, neighborhood, and home. This is an irony familiar to feminists. Women workers finally arrive on the pages of social historians, and the theorizing of class promptly migrates elsewhere.

These terms through which Joyce chooses to enframe the subject of class in his *Reader* pose our problem starkly enough. Thus on the one side of the divide are the social histories of class generated in great profusion between the 1960s and 1980s, heavily influenced by Marxism, but at all events indebted to one form of materialist sociology or another, summarized by Joyce as "the classical tradition." Though tracing their own origin back to the fundamental workings of the economy and its social relations and to the associated working-class experiences of exploitation, these understandings of class now stand unmasked by Joyce as mere representations, as an elaborate discursive formation, which may have possessed compelling purchase in politics until recently, but which can now be shown for what it really was. From our wiser and more skeptical vantage point, "class formation" or "the rise of the working class" thereby transmutes into one of those grand constructions postmodernists have become so adept at laying open and breaking down.

In the process, the working class of history becomes just a particular kind of story told about the past, a mere projection, the narrative ordering of past time for the validating of a particular kind of collective identity. Social histories of the working class may have claimed to be grounded in the intensively researched evidence of the archives, to have captured a main truth of the development of capitalist societies, and to have defined the principal direction of progressive politics during the later nineteenth and most of the twentieth centuries, but this was a telling of history that could only remain partial, self-interested, and also exclusionary. Like all such powerfully centered narratives, its own claims for itself required the silencing and marginalizing of others, a slighting or displacing of all those actors and stories not easily assimilable to the main terms of the account. With benefit of the critiques of knowledge associated with the "linguistic turn" since the 1980s, Joyce and other critics now claim, we can now push behind these social histories to find the other narratives they served to obscure.

On the other side, accordingly, are the new cultural histories encouraged by the linguistic turn and the "discursive approach to history."[18] Such studies approach the primary meanings of class not via the methods of social history, even if these remain part of the wider methodological tool kit, but through the languages, imagery, and representations that identified and shaped class historically, for these alone (it is now argued) can give us access to its presence. Indeed, in this newer literature, class appears mainly as an object of critique—as something to be deconstructed, as only one possible identity or locus of investigation among many. Class formed only one nexus of significant relations, practices, and meanings among a larger and more dispersed array of sites and connections defining an individual's place in the world. Centering our attention overridingly on a traditional understanding of "class" per se, according to this view, does violence to the fragmented and particularized bases upon which people actually seek to negotiate some workable coherence for their social and cultural lives.

At another level, of course, class also figures among the rhetorics of political life, but not as a direct expression of any underlying or objective interests. Instead it appears again as one term among others in the mobile and contingent play of political appeals and affiliations. In other words, class ceases to provide the social historian's archimedean point, from which all other questions might be viewed. At most, its place in the overall web of a person's or a community's relationships can be approached ethnographically, via the languages of subjectivity, or through some other form of microhistorical investigation.

This clashing of rival approaches—class as a materialist sociology or social history versus class as a consequence of discourse—preoccupied left-tending historians for much of the time between the earlier 1980s and mid-1990s. Among social historians of Britain, for example, the resulting debates began in response to an essay by Gareth Stedman Jones on the languages of class in Chartism. They soon resonated with related controversies among British Marxists and other social theorists over how best to theorize the relationship between the building of alliances in politics and the bases of interest and identity in society. These in turn drew powerful momentum from conflicts in the Labour Party, dramatized in especially spectacular and embittering form through the great miners' strike of 1984–85. By the end of the 1980s, the particular disagreements about class had passed into the generalized political and theoretical debates surrounding the "New Times" agenda of the network based around the magazine *Marxism Today*. That gathering critique of class politics then received urgent additional impetus from the global political changes associated with the Eastern European Revolutions of 1989, the dissolution of the Soviet Union in 1991, and the end of Communism. The damaged confidence of a class-analytical tradition of social history was certainly connected to this broader crisis of the political traditions of socialism, for which class had always provided the fixed and primary referent.

The rhythms and extent of these debates about class varied country by country, and national field by national field. Among historians in the United States, for example, although again in some national fields more than in others, the so-called cultural turn had won widespread endorsement by the later 1990s, forcing older-style labor historians in particular on the defensive, whereas in Britain the balance of advantage was rather reversed. To be sure, the practice of labor history on the basis of an older-style class analysis, invariably invoking the influence of Edward Thompson but anchoring itself securely in the cumulative historiographical achievements of the 1960s and 1970s, did not cease. But outside an older generation of practitioners some previously common standpoints became harder to find. Historians of the working class became far more hesitant about connecting their particular social histories to the broader patterns of national political history or larger-scale questions of societal stability and change. They backed away from the earlier self-confident ambition of rewriting the national story or composing accounts of the development of the whole society, which had driven social history's popularity twenty years before. Along with the new doubts about "class" came receding interest in other generalizing terms previously vital to the search for an overarching account of social and political development, including concepts of capitalism, crisis, the state, forms of domination, and the associated models of structural change and determination.

The social historian's commitment to making structural connections across different levels or spheres of a society's development receded markedly from view. "Social explanation" in that structuralist sense fell into some abeyance, even into disrepute. After one set of generations had insisted so aggressively during the 1960s and 1970s on the primacy of social context for an understanding of everything else, including the contours of a society's political landscape and its overall trajectories of development, powerful voices were now heard arguing not just for the autonomy of political history and its independence from forms of social explanation, but effectively—through theories of language and discourse—for its precedence *over* the social, for its power in regulating, mediating, and constructing our very access to any understanding of the social itself. If social historians of the 1970s often downplayed and diminished the efficacy of political actions "from above," therefore, calling instead upon the explanatory ascendancy of popular agency "from below," advocates of "the discursive approach to history" now reversed the signs. In the process, an older disconnection between "politics" and "society" became surprisingly reinstated.[19]

The particular debates about class thus connected with a much broader upheaval in historical studies beginning in the 1980s, namely, the turning away from social history toward cultural history, which itself was part of a more general crisis of social explanation across the disciplines in the human sciences. Over the longer view, this shift was momentous. Our own lifetime as intellectuals—as historians—has been shaped by two great movements of innovation between the 1960s and the present. If the first of these involved the discovery of social history, then the second produced the "new cultural history," and both shared a complex and intimate relationship to the surrounding political climates of their respective times. Despite the radical contrariness of each moment, and the bitterly fought-out differences they frequently mobilized, each reflected the desire for greater democratic inclusiveness within history as a discipline and a profession, an inclusiveness through which previously hidden and suppressed histories could be recognized and previously marginalized groups could be welcomed into the historians' ranks. If social historians had stressed material life, class, and the history of society, their culturalist successors emphasized meaning and the forms of perception and understanding that people construct and display, but each brought a radical broadening of the historian's accepted agenda. Over this thirty- to forty-year period, accordingly, the practices and subject matters of history as a discipline became quite dramatically pluralized.

Yet the movement between social history and cultural history was not an uncomplicated progression. There were some losses as well as the necessary and indisputable gains; and the shift happened only through embittering disagreements, whose destructive fallout made the desirable commonalities of purpose much harder to see. For a time, left-tending historians threatened to separate into two sharply defined camps, with some choosing to follow the logics of the new cultural history by taking the linguistic turn, while others defended the hard-won ground of an avowedly materialist or structuralist social analysis. At the height of the disagreements in the late 1980s and early 1990s, generosity and pluralism often seemed in very short supply. Among some of the leading participants civility declined to a dismayingly low point.

Thus the voice of postmodernist advocacy sometimes adopted a peremptory and hectoring timber, in dire and apodictic tones: historians *must* do this; they *cannot ignore* that; they had better recognize the future and move with the times. Such commentary often presented itself as the new, self-evidently persuasive, overpowering logic of the age, the unstoppable direction of contemporary inquiry. It was a truth that could not be opposed, that somehow superseded everything else, everything that came before. Not surprisingly, perhaps, some defenders of established historiographical practice duly replied in kind, drawing upon impressive reserves of closed-mindedness and arrogance. Playing on the wider anxieties provoked by the "culture wars" of the time, a number of prestigious voices raised early warning cries aimed at demonizing the newfangled critiques, calling the profession to arms for the defense of its integrity against the corrosive influence of relativism, postmodernism, poststructuralism, and other foreign ideas.[20]

Difficult and destabilizing questions were definitely in play, which went to the heart not only of the historian's practice but also of the associated wider universe of assumptions about the social and political world and its rules of intelligibility. By calling into question the given epistemologies of social history, as well as some of the implicitly accepted but question-begging theoretical procedures linking social analysis to politics and to matters of consciousness and subjectivity, the new critiques unlocked a set of rather solidly functioning consensual understandings. That is, the debates getting under way during the 1980s opened a badly needed space for discussions that were patently not getting started very easily before. Everything we now summarize under the rubric of the "linguistic turn" or "cultural turn" helped free social history from an impasse of its own making in that way, by suggesting strategies that were not available to social historians inside the given terms of their inquiry. In that sense, the so-called cultural turn was entirely productive and unavoidable.

Nonetheless, the appearance and appeal of a clean and decisive rupture can sometimes be deceptive. There *was* a discourse of self-reflexive and theorized historiography *before* the advent of the various poststructuralisms and postmodernisms that now sought increasingly to wipe the previous slate clean. That preexisting pluralism of practices and discussion, we want to argue, cannot be wished away simply by pronouncing the truths of the new. For edicts of that kind amount to a closure; they allow no space; they forbid continuing intellectual exchange between a complex past and a complex present; they deny creative conversations. They perpetuate the effects of a discursive field already scarred by earlier confrontations. Those effects include anxieties, rage, disappointments, nostalgias, resistances, failures of intellectual generosity, refusals to take the risks of engagement. As we remarked in an earlier commentary on these matter, a theoretical hauteur instructs a redoubt of methodological conservatism, and the latter shouts defiantly back. But between these two then lies a silence, a barrier that can no longer be crossed.[21]

In writing this book, we are hoping to break that silence. We want to offer means, if not of synthesis, then of productive and continuing conversation. There will be some who dismiss this effort as a misguided search for the "middle ground," disqualified from the outset by its fudging of necessary differences. We will also no doubt be accused of wanting to have our cake and eat it too. Others will see in our efforts merely a nostalgia, a futile desire to resuscitate something forever compromised and gone. We will be sharply rapped across the knuckles, we are sure, for wanting to revisit the ground of an earlier social historiography, for thinking that certain aspects of its distinguishing problematics, some of the questions it asked and the directions of analysis it pursued—certain Marxisms and structuralisms, perhaps—might still have something to tell us about the character of capitalism and its social relations in the emergent postmodern and postmaterialist present. We know, of course, that "the questions we have to ask now are necessarily different from those we asked in the 1970s." As should be plain from what follows, we share the commitment of social history's poststructuralist critics to the project of exploring what the best form of those questions might be. But there is still room, we think, for constructive interchange—fruitful traffic, as we shall call it—with social history's earlier, more structuralist register of analysis. To ask for this is more than mere sentimentality. It is not a desire simply to hold on to the past, a hankering for "preservation of the worlds (of social history, working-class movements, and class analysis) we have lost."[22]

Our book is an invitation to further thought. It invites its readers to step outside the given lines of disagreement. But the last thing we seek is a smoothing over of difficulty, in a pretense that problems do not actually exist. We want to find, rather, a space of collaboration, where difficulties can be honestly discussed, wrestled with, and rendered more manageable. For some, the power of poststructuralist critique seems to have foreclosed upon the older kinds of social history altogether, disabling those earlier questions and rendering such terms of inquiry entirely nugatory; the desire to preserve them can then only be a nostalgia, the desire to cling to or keep alive something better left to die. But as any longer perspective of intellectual history should remind us, pronouncements of final and absolute closure of that sort seldom secure lasting vindication. In the intellectual life of a discipline or field of study, finding the ways to continue a conversation is usually better than trying to close it down. If the histories of the past two decades mean that there is no longer any way *back,* then some of the older forms of knowledge may still help us in the project of moving forward. So in light of poststructuralist critiques, we agree, there can be no straightforward return to the kind of social history practiced before, because for all its own strengths and excitements that earlier moment has ceased to be available for reoccupying. But that does not mean there is nothing at all left to recuperate, nothing left to learn.

## THE SHAPE OF THE BOOK

This book began life as a paper titled "Classes as Historical Subjects" written for a conference, "Historical Perspectives on Class and Culture," organized at the University of Portsmouth in September 1993 by Robbie Gray.[23] Within a year or so, mainly in response to the interest of colleagues on either side of the Atlantic, at what seemed to be a propitious moment in the ebb and flow of the fighting among social and cultural historians, we had decided to expand the argument into a small book. Our intention was conciliatory, not because we doubted the importance or productiveness of the substantive disagreements, nor because we lacked combative temperaments of our own, but because we saw grounds for fruitful collaboration across the differences that could allow the maximizing of the strengths on either side. For complicated personal reasons on each of our parts, the completion of the project then became delayed, although in the meantime we aired its arguments in two articles and gave them a variety of outings in seminars and conferences over the years.[24] We also managed to sit down together in front of the computer at least once a year to move the writing forward, if only in the less than ideal circumstances of a hotel room. Otherwise, we relied on the new electronic means of communication. The initial conference paper had materialized from an intense back-and-forth of e-mail and fax, and e-mail remained essential for the later stages of the writing.

To begin exploring the complex field of meanings—historiographical, theoretical, political—associated with the concept of class, we needed to trace the subject's recent intellectual history by looking at how social historians tended to formulate their questions. That in its turn required reviewing, in however elliptical and summary a manner, the circumstances of social history's rise during the 1960s and 1970s, its main intellectual priorities, and the grounds of its remarkable popularity. Accordingly, our first substantive chapter ("Social History and the Discursive Move") considers the intellectual contexts of the respective movements of social history and cultural history during the past half century in the broadest of outlines, centering our attention to a great extent on the influence of the British Marxist historians and the critiques of their work. Here we are only too well aware of the risks, the drawbacks of such a hurried and partial review. No short treatment can ever do justice to the full story, to the rich and variegated histories from which this recent tradition was actually produced in all its transnational, subdisciplinary, and field-specific diversity and range. We would be the first to admit that our standpoint is inevitably bounded in all sorts of ways, not least by the practical limits on our own historiographical familiarity.

After setting the historiographical scene in chapter 2, the next chapter ("A Species of Modernism?") broadens the perspective to take in the wider intellectual debates over social and cultural theory getting under way during the 1980s, commonly summarized beneath the rubric of postmodernism. Postmodernist critiques of Marxism and other materialist sociologies initially proceeded well beyond the hearing range of most historians, marking their greatest impact in the arts and aesthetics, literary scholarship, and the emergent interdisciplinary contexts of cultural studies. By the later 1980s, however, conjoining with the influence of poststructuralist theory, particularly via the accelerating diffusion of the thought of Michel Foucault, and especially among feminists, historians were definitely taking note. During the early 1990s a powerful body of critique, either avowedly postmodernist or else strongly moved by poststructuralist ideas, was being produced among historians per se, decisively shifting the main accents of historical discussion. A small but vociferous avant-garde of explicitly postmodernist historians had formed, but the reach of the so-called linguistic turn and the "new cultural history" extended far more generally across the discipline. In chapter 3 we take stock of the consequences of these intellectual histories, tracing the impact of postmodernist critiques of knowledge on the thinking of historians and teasing out the lasting differences they have made. Through this discussion, we also seek to clarify the character of what came before, as postmodernists concentrated much of their fire against Marxists within the broader social historiographical consensus. To put it another way, we seek to identify the modernism that postmodernist critiques have tended to presuppose.

In chapter 4 ("Materialism and Disavowal: From the Social to the Cultural?"), we move to a detailed discussion of the literatures of social history and cultural history, seeking to explore the limits of usefulness for historians of the new epistemological critique. Rather than attempting any systematic or comprehensive review of the pertinent literatures, we have chosen to do this by focusing on the writings of a few emblematic historians: Patrick Joyce, William Sewell, and especially Joan Scott and Gareth Stedman Jones. We choose these particular practitioners because their works have been especially influential over the period covered by this book, not least on the long-term development of our own thinking. Having stood for the best of the new social history during the 1970s, they exemplified the new directions of the following decades in the most searching and coherent of forms. It should be clear from the terms of this chapter—we certainly hope—that our critiques are predicated on the utmost respect. In common with our colleagues and students in the discipline at large, we remain hugely indebted to the clarity that each of these authors brought to the dilemmas haunting historical studies during the last few decades. But at the height of the controversies surrounding the cultural turn during the later 1980s and earlier 1990s, the challenge could also be extremely polarizing. From our own vantage point, we think that discussions have now reached the point where we can move past those older polemics and begin to move forward in a different way.

Chapter 5 ("What Is the Valency of Class Now?") seeks to draw out the consequences of the culturalist critiques of social history for the purposes of understanding the relationship of class to politics. If we accept the force of those critiques and adopt the "discursive approach to history," what follows for our understanding of "class" per se? In light of our own argument about the continuing importance of a structuralist register of analysis, how might a viable concept of class be reinstated? On the cusp of the early debates leading to the so-called cultural turn, we had ourselves published an earlier article in 1980 that worried about the difficulties social historians experienced in dealing with the autonomies of politics: they tended either to neglect political processes as an area of institutional history that could be left to other historians working elsewhere, or else they subsumed analysis of politics into the superordinate importance of social forces and social determinations. Yet by the 1990s, ironically enough, precisely as a result of the antireductionist logics of the cultural turn, the autonomies of politics had been restored so successfully as to become entirely removed from social explanation. In this final chapter, accordingly, using the ideas of Antonio Gramsci and Michel Foucault, we try to suggest how the relationship between the political and the social, between politics and class formation, might now be rethought.

When we floated the arguments of this book in an article for a forum called "Farewell to the Working Class?" in the journal *International Labor and Working-Class History* several years ago, the commissioned responses were disappointingly defensive. We had wanted to depolemicize an important field of differences among historians by renewing the space for more constructive forms of debate, whereas in the event the divisions between camps seemed only to be confirmed. One group accused us of ducking the issues of capitalism and globalization. They asked "Where's the beef?" and recalled us to the ground of material reality and "actually experienced structures," to class as some had always wanted it understood. Yet by the other group we were mocked for still mourning the cold corpses of Marxism and structuralism, clinging sentimentally to old forms of politics and history that simply no longer worked. With one or two exceptions, unfortunately, the respondents chose not to address our substantive arguments, but rather talked past them, reiterating the mutually confrontational positions each had previously taken up. But inside that imagined space of polemical opposition, we suspect, diminishing numbers of historians were still really listening. For our own part, we will continue trying to pose the questions. We persist in believing that the political formation of subjectivities and the structured consequences of capitalist inequality can both be addressed in the same analysis. There should be ways of combining the poststructuralist critique of knowledge with certain registers of cautious structuralist argument. Both are patently possible. We *do not have to choose.*

## II. SOCIAL HISTORY & THE DISCURSIVE MOVE

### INTRODUCTION

During the excitements of the 1960s when many of us were formed, social history took shape as a particular kind of overarching ambition and polemical claim. It promised the opening up of new empirical areas and the use of social-science methods, but expressed above all a powerful reaction against the dominance in the discipline of political history as it was then mainly understood—that is, as a narrowly defined tradition of inquiry stressing foreign policy, statecraft, constitutions, high politics, administration, and the conduct of government. Social history entailed a fundamental shift of perspective from "state" to "society" in that sense. Whether beneath the slogans of "people's history" or "history from below," with their implicit populism and focus on the experience of subordinate social groups, or through more explicitly Marxist influences or the social-science idealization of "structural analysis," the case was repeatedly made for social explanation—for the analytical priority of social context—if the forms of political development were to be understood. By the early 1970s the dominant form of this ambition, certainly among radical historians, reflected a classical or foundational materialism, taking both Marxist and non-Marxist forms, in which robust notions of social causality, social determination, and social totality carried the day.[1]

For a long time the robustness of those convictions remained more practical than theoretical; that is to say, they stood more as unrefined presuppositions than as the outcome of lengthy conceptual labor. Nevertheless, such convictions sustained the confidence of social history in its disciplinary intent, grounding its widespread belief that questions of power, social relations, and inequality could be rendered intelligible by the use of an ambitious contextualizing analytic. Those questions were to be understood crucially by reference to class, mediated through culture and consciousness. The concept of class served as a master category, no less. It became so integral to the larger practice of social history, we would argue, that its specific purposes and effects have become uncommonly hard to disentangle. In our current contemporary climate of skepticism about the usefulness of class as a category, moreover, it is extremely difficult to separate the loss of centrality of the concept of class in social history from a sense of crisis pervading the field as a whole. The loss is complex, and part of our purpose here is to scrutinize it, to examine its meanings and effects, and to explore some of the implications for how social history can now be done.

At the outset, certain caveats need to be entered. First, the primary referents for what follows will be the capitalist societies of Western Europe and North America during and since industrialization. Where our modest familiarity permits, other historiographies will also be drawn upon. But some major areas crucial to social history's overall achievements during the last fifty years will necessarily be left out, including medieval and early modern Europe, peasants and peasant societies, many aspects of women's history and gender history, and the history of the family and demography, to name only a few. Historical studies in and of large and important parts of the globe will have to go undiscussed. In other words, we are not claiming to offer any comprehensive accounting of social history's trajectories during the second half of the twentieth century. Our discussion is directed less toward social history as an entire subdiscipline than toward those parts of it where understandings of social class supplied a key motive force.

Second, country by country, social history's late twentieth-century rise to popularity followed very different paths. In Britain, for example, after some pioneering studies of the social effects of industrialization earlier in the century, the main sources were economic history, the interest in social policy and social administration descending from Beatrice and Sidney Webb, and a strong tradition of workers' education and popular history identified with the labor movement. The process of institutionalization after 1945—economic history departments at a number of universities, a strong metropolitan nexus at the London School of Economics (LSE), and the Society for the Study of Labour History founded in 1960—delivered some excellent foundations for social history's upsurge in the 1960s, variously encouraged by the great university expansion and cultural radicalism of the time. In Germany, on the other hand, similar earlier twentieth-century starting points, including the historical school of economics, sociological studies by Max Weber and others, and the labor movement histories pioneered by the SPD and later the KPD, had been tragically severed by Nazism and the post-1945 division of the country. So when West German social historians began pressing for change in the discipline, likewise in the 1960s, it was mainly to U.S. social sciences that they looked. In contrast, France was a unique case of precocious institutionalization going back to the influence of Lucien Febvre and Marc Bloch and the launching of the journal *Annales d'histoire économique et sociale* in 1929.[2] After 1945, the creation of a new sixth section for the social sciences under Febvre's presidency at the École Practique des Haute Études endowed social history with exceptional interdisciplinary strength at the center of the social sciences. So while social historians in Britain and West Germany were still carving a place for themselves in the 1960s, social historians in France were reaping the benefits of several decades of institutional growth and prestige.

Each of these varying trajectories sedimented different bases for how class came to be understood in the social history boom years of the 1960s and 1970s. British social historians viewed class mainly from the workplace and the social circumstances of working-class residential living, breaking out of the confining institutional frameworks of the older labor history (trade unions and parties), while retaining its materialist attentiveness to the nuts and bolts of working-class life (wages, working conditions and job rules, skills and deskilling, apprenticeship and work hierarchies, housing and transportation, protests and strikes).[3] In comparison, their West German counterparts had neither the pragmatic materialism of the British economic history tradition nor its impressive Marxist variant to draw upon. Instead, from the 1960s they relied on a remarkably consistent Weberianism for their approach to the working class, complemented by an equally centered political interpretation of the period between the 1870s and 1940s stressing the labor movement's recurring exclusion from legitimate society.

In France matters were more complicated. While the *Annales* tradition encouraged an unrelenting structuralism based on the primacy of demography, price movements, labor markets, economic fluctuations, and the long-term stabilities of social life, a second French tradition emanating from the study of the French Revolution and its legacies privileged a Marxist approach to class. French social history also acquired a heavy Marxist presence from the influence of a strong Communist Party. For those reasons, there was a stronger Marxist presence among social historians of the working class in France than in either West Germany or Britain.[4]

Third, to a remarkable degree the pioneering impetus for social history, from the founding periods in the early 1900s to the big upsurge of the 1960s and 1970s, has always come from *outside* the historical profession as such rather than from within the discipline. This was especially marked in Britain, where the key early contributions ranged from the Webbs' multivolume studies of trade unionism, industrial democracy, and local government, and the many works of the Oxford political theorist G. D. H. Cole on the history of socialism and working-class movements, to a trilogy of books by the radical journalists John and Barbara Hammond on the experience of the laboring poor in the Industrial Revolution. Even the impact of R. H. Tawney at the LSE came as much from his general works like *The Acquisitive Society* (1921) and *Equality* (1931) and from his advocacy for the Workers' Educational Association (WEA) as it did from his academic research on the Tudor-Stuart economy. The same syndrome reappeared after World War II, when a number of social history's key progenitors lacked positions in university history departments, instead working either in schools (George Rudé) or adult education (most notably Edward Thompson and Raymond Williams, but also the Africanist Thomas Hodgkin and a less well-known figure like Henry Collins), or else in another discipline altogether, like the Cambridge economist Maurice Dobb. During the 1970s the pioneers of women's history in Britain also produced their works without benefit of teaching positions in university history departments. This mirrored the early twentieth-century experience of precursors like Alice Clark, Ivy Pinchbeck, Dorothy George, and Barbara Hammond, who then all but disappeared from the historiographical record once the professionalization of academic history supervened.[5]

The main impulse toward social history for these early pioneers was a left-wing interest in the social consequences of industrialization and a powerful identification with the common people, linked to political activism through Fabianism, feminist suffrage politics before 1914, the rise of the Labour Party, and later the more radical dissidence of the Communist Party.[6] In Germany, this relationship to political progressivism was if anything even clearer, aided by the institutional strengths of the labor movement and the flowering of German sociology under the Weimar Republic. In 1933 the disaster of the Third Reich abruptly severed such potentials and scattered them into an Anglo-American diaspora, whence they could be recuperated only several decades later as a result of the internationalizing reach of the post-1960s social history wave. Later in the twentieth century, West German social history was to receive its own injection of energy and creativity from another extramural source, namely, the history workshop movement and the multiform public history flourishing from the late 1970s. The West German impetus for women's history also came from outside the walls of the universities, forced onto the agenda by the new women's movement after 1968.

These comments point to a vital dimension of social historians' treatment of class: it has always resonated with vital political meanings, sometimes implicitly or obliquely, but often directly through consciously expressed political projects of one kind or another. This political dimension is certainly part of our own purpose in this book. On the one hand, we hope to draw out the political implications of the various bodies of work we have chosen for discussion. But on the other hand, we are also guided by a sense of political urgency, a desire to bring the debates among historians into fruitful alignment with the political exigencies arising out of our new twenty-first-century present.

Finally, there is a tendency in recent debates to overgeneralize one's arguments, to exaggerate the influence or prevalence of the patterns and assumptions at issue, and by polarizing the alternatives in that way to force readers into taking sides. In choosing this or that body of literature to concentrate on, however, we do not wish to imply that this is all there is, that its main characteristics may be used straightforwardly to describe the social history field in general, or that a wider assortment of coherent and sophisticated approaches cannot be found. In fact, it is precisely that kind of simplification and polemical conflation we want to avoid.

For example, in focusing on the British Marxist historians we have no desire to suppress the comparable importance of other schools, strands of work, notable individuals, or methodological and theoretical orientations. The influence of J. H. Plumb would need to be foregrounded in any comprehensive accounting of social history's development in Britain, it is clear, as would that of Asa Briggs, whose early studies of Birmingham, more general works like *Victorian Cities* (1963), and editing of pathbreaking local research in *Chartist Studies* (1959) and *Essays in Labour History* (1960) vitally shaped social history's early map of the nineteenth century. During the 1950s an extensive archipelago of activity also defined the prehistory of social history's emergence in Britain, based around George Kitson Clark and Henry Pelling in Cambridge, A. E. Musson and Harold Perkin at Manchester, A. J. Taylor and Briggs in Leeds, F. M. L. Thompson in London, and the economic historians H. J. Habbakuk, Max Hartwell, and Peter Matthias in Oxford.[7] Thus Perkin occupied the first university post in social history at Manchester in 1951, took up the first professorial chair in social history at Lancaster in 1967, and published the key general history, *The Origins of Modern English Society, 1780–1880,* in 1969.[8]

The very elaborate contributions to scholarship associated with these names can all be read for what they say about class, which in its turn cannot remotely be reduced to a common or agreed-upon straightforward set of meanings. Where the scholars concerned placed their conceptual assumptions explicitly on the table—in itself not a particularly common practice—they developed quite divergent standpoints. "Class" was often deployed pragmatically or descriptively, with rarely much direct reference to the competing frameworks available within social theory. In that more exacting theoretical sense, "class" was not a particularly transparent vector of meaning in the early social history writings of the 1950s, nor even universally accepted as the appropriate concept for organizing the analysis of social structure and social relations under capitalism. In these terms, accordingly, Edward Thompson's famous definition of class in the preface to *The Making of the English Working Class* in 1963 amounted to a major departure: it stood out among his fellow historians' writings for the strength and clarity of its explicit claims. Indeed, it helped launch a period of intensive debate, conducted with great polemical verve, and acquiring further momentum from the political radicalism assailing the universities in the later part of that decade.[9]

To our minds, only the relatively short period between the publication of Thompson's *Making* and, say, the appearance of John Foster's *Class Struggle in the Industrial Revolution* in 1974, together with all the resulting debates, marked the real heyday of class analysis among social historians in Britain.[10] During that time possibly the broadest consensus coalesced around the term's usable meanings. Still rarely explicated, but rather taken as a practical armature for the ordering of rich and inventive empirical research, the operative assumptions might be described as follows: class was not a condition or a "thing" but a relationship, defined both by horizontal solidarities (for example, with other workers) and vertical antagonism (against a bourgeoisie); class belonging came fundamentally from one's place in production, if not by a strictly Marxist notation of labor power and surplus value then certainly by one's relationship to work; class was experiential, shaped by consciousness of shared histories and recognizable through the accretions of a common culture; class consciousness was dynamic, produced via the experience of exploitation and political oppression; and, most important of all, class was the necessary starting point for making sense of what was happening to nineteenth-century society as a whole.[11]

These common understandings were certainly not uncontested, and indeed a series of general works by leading historians like Harold Perkin, Geoffrey Best, Arthur Marwick, and John Vincent, who exerted far more institutional power in the British profession than any Marxists at the time, directly disputed the Marxist approach favored by Thompson and Foster.[12] But to a remarkable degree those understandings shaped the languages available for younger people seeking to make themselves into historians. They even composed the common sense of social analysis, delivering a sensibility and an idiom highly distinctive to the 1960s in Britain. They gained enormous momentum from the impact of Thompson's book, which appeared in its Pelican paperback edition in 1968, bristling with a postscript riposte against his critics. The same moment was framed by the appearance of Eric Hobsbawm's massively influential books—first *The Age of Revolution* in 1962, then *Labouring Men* in 1964 (also reissued in 1968), and finally *Industry and Empire* in 1968—which offered an encompassing framework for grasping the emergence of class society under capitalism, with the history of working people at its center.[13]

On this basis "class analysis" supplied the common orientation points for the broad cohorts of students entering the profession during its unprecedented expansion of the 1960s and early 1970s, many of whom were inspired by the cultural and political radicalisms of the time, and who chose disproportionately to work on aspects of working-class formation in the nineteenth century. These were the generations who completed their dissertations and secured their first teaching positions during the 1970s, published their books by the end of that decade, and provided the energy for the Social History Society and new journals like *Social History* and *History Workshop Journal,* all of which were launched in 1976. They also entered their full maturity during the 1980s, when the axioms of social history's youthful years were already being subjected to critique.[14]

The rhythms of these local intellectual histories—our primary illustration is obviously British, but comparable stories can be told about other places too—are crucial to the dynamics of the debates forming our starting point for this book. In reflecting on the story of social history's emergence, it is easy to miss or forget just how short-lived and transient the periods of most intense innovation have actually been. As we already remarked, the time from the appearance of Thompson's great book to the debates surrounding Foster's *Class Struggle and the Industrial Revolution* and the first efforts at critical retrospection in the new organs of *Social History* and *History Workshop Journal* was barely more than a decade. The earliest fissures in the functional "class-historical" consensus crystallizing around the impact of *The Making of the English Working Class* were then opened by two symptomatic debates: one over the usefulness of the concept of the "labor aristocracy," which helped problematize the connections social historians were hoping to draw between changes in class relationships and changes in the polity; and one over the underlying theoretical assumptions holding together Thompson's analysis in *The Making.*[15] Though eventually exhausting themselves via polarizing displays of intransigence, these discussions were crucial in clearing away some ground. Even more crucial in the long run, feminist historians were also radically calling into question the authorizing assumptions of the new working-class histories.

But the temporalities of historiographical change are never straightforwardly supersessionist and linear. Historical work seldom moves forward in a self-evidently improving register of enhanced understanding, allowing earlier problematics to be revised via chains of self-contained and discretely separated debates, each purged of its predecessor's obscurity and error. On the contrary, projects and problematics have a tendency to persist and overlap, interpenetrating and getting in each other's way, jostling and speaking out of turn, in a simultaneity of practices and conversations whose meanings become far messier—but also more rewarding—than the advocates of consistency allow. Historians whose sensibility was shaped in one moment of the discipline's development—including their understandings of pedagogy, their methodological habits, their underlying historiographical commitments, and their sense of what defines a significant project—may continue adding to the corpus of solidly founded and creatively executed scholarship long after the succeeding episodes of critique have questioned their original assumptions and moved the general disciplinary agendas further along, especially if the formative moment in question was as dramatic and inspiring as the 1960s. The resulting complexities are what we want to explore.

## ANGLO-MARXISM AND THE "OLD" SOCIAL HISTORY

For the coordinates of social history's practice in the 1960s and 1970s, the aggregate influence of the British Marxists associated with the Communist Party Historians' Group between World War II and the crisis of 1956 had a particular importance. Besides Edward Thompson and Eric Hobsbawm, these Marxists numbered Christopher Hill, Rodney Hilton, George Rudé, Victor Kiernan, John Saville, Dorothy Thompson, and others, including a precocious schoolboy Communist called Raphael Samuel.[16] If their interests were variously inflected, they formed a definite grouping between the 1940s and the 1960s, directing a key strand of social history toward a stress on "the people," preeminently the working class, their experience, and their culture. Never even remotely hegemonic within the British profession, their work nonetheless set new agendas of historical debate and challenged others. They established a complex framework of assumptions joining elements of Marxist political economy to an empirical focus on the experiences and cultures of the popular classes. That is, they fashioned a distinctive historical discourse whose slate of pertinent questions emphasized issues of class, of consciousness, of human agency, of experience, and of culture. They were never a collective organized around a manifesto, or even (beyond the breaking point of 1956) around a plainly shared political project. Yet by the 1960s their work nonetheless stood for a new and coherent repertoire for social history—not always consistent, not an orthodoxy, but a constellation of interests, an agenda of salience somehow recognizable, while difficult to define in any clear and tightly integrated way.

This grouping was part of a wider network of British intellectuals who came to the Communist Party (CPGB) during the 1930s through the urgencies of antifascism. While some left the party in the early years of the Cold War, it was the larger hemorrhage of resignations during the crisis of Communism in 1956 that ended the group's effective life. Very few of its members had positions at the center of British academic life in Oxbridge or London. University history departments gave them few supports. George Rudé and Edward Thompson were unable even to secure academic appointments until the 1960s, Rudé only by traveling to Australia. Some did their historical work beyond the framework of the discipline, such as the more senior Maurice Dobb, an economist in Cambridge whose 1946 book *Studies in the Development of Capitalism* was at the center of the group's early debates.[17] Others worked in adult education. The group's collective raison d'être was political: a passionate belief in history's relevance for the present, the desire to reach a popular audience, a broader commitment to democratic values. The much older Dona Torr, a nonacademic CPGB intellectual and Marx scholar, who published *Tom Mann and His Times* in 1956, was an important mentor. The group honored her with *Democracy and the Labour Movement,* published in 1954 under John Saville's editorship.[18]

They had originally envisaged writing a social history of Britain capable of contesting official or established versions of the British past. For this purpose, they took as their model A. L. Morton's *A People's History of England,* which had appeared at the height of the antifascist campaigning for a Popular Front in 1938. While as such that project never came to fruition, the career-long oeuvres of several of the group's members effectively marked out such an achievement: for example, the work of Rodney Hilton on the English peasantry, of Christopher Hill on the seventeenth-century English Revolution, of John Saville on labor history, of Dorothy Thompson on Chartism, and of Edward Thompson and Eric Hobsbawm on many aspects of popular history from the eighteenth through the twentieth century. These imposing accomplishments aggregated into the popular democratic counternarrative of British history that the young Communists of the 1940s had aspired to create.

Some members of the group displayed extraordinary international range. Hobsbawm's interests embraced British labor history, European popular movements, and Latin American peasantries, as well as the history of jazz and other popular arts, the changing forms of social protest, and the plenitude of the Marxist tradition. Among his larger interests he recurred consistently to the study of nationalism. No one was more familiar with the diversity of international approaches to how the past can be studied. With the benefit of that breadth, he sought to illuminate the varying forms of social life associated with capitalist industrialization, the changing possibilities of political action, and capitalism's successive transformations into a global system. He engaged those themes in an unparalleled sequence of world histories appearing at roughly decade-long intervals between 1962 and 1994.[19]

Victor Kiernan was another remarkable generalist whose works ranged across a wide variety of grand themes and contexts, including aspects of imperialism, the dynamics of early modern state formation, and the history of the aristocratic duel, as well as more specialized monographs on British relations with China and the 1854 Spanish Revolution.[20] An exact contemporary of Albert Soboul and Richard Cobb, George Rudé pioneered the analysis of the great crowd actions of the French Revolution. More broadly, through *The Crowd in the French Revolution* (1959), *The Crowd in History* (1964), and his collaboration with Hobsbawm, *Captain Swing* (1969), he helped reinvent the social history of popular protest.[21] Two other members of the Historians' Group worked primarily in British history but inspired historians across the globe in Europe, the Americas, and the non-Western world with their examples: Raphael Samuel as the moving genius behind the History Workshop movement and its journal; and Edward Thompson through his great works *The Making of the English Working Class* (1963), *Whigs and Hunters: The Origins of the Black Acts* (1975), and *Customs in Common* (1991).[22]

Thus the Anglo-Marxist historiography consolidating itself during the 1960s showed an ambiguous picture. On the one hand, it was solidly ensconced in a set of distinctively British concerns. Several of its leading voices—Hill, Hilton, Saville, the Thompsons—spoke exclusively the languages of English, let alone British, history. Their broader outlook was intensely focused on national themes, as in Edward Thompson's famous 1965 essay "The Peculiarities of the English" and first book, *William Morris: Romantic to Revolutionary,* which was published on the eve of the crisis in the Communist Party in 1955, or in the convergent works of Raymond Williams, a nonhistorian whose twin books *Culture and Society* (1958) and *The Long Revolution* (1961) marked out cognate terrain.[23] These British concerns were strongest in two areas. One was labor history, whose growth during the 1960s was decisively shaped by the alumni of the Communist Party Historians' Group, especially through the Society for the Study of Labour History, Hobsbawm's foundational essays in *Labouring Men,* and the influence of Saville, shortly to be institutionalized in the multivolume *Dictionary of Labour Biography* which began appearing in 1972. The other area was the history of capitalist industrialization in Britain, most notably through the standard of living controversy between Hobsbawm and Max Hartwell during 1957 through 1963. Here Saville's *Rural Depopulation in England and Wales, 1851–1951* (1957) also provided a critical counterpoint to the mainstream accounts of "English landed society" by G. Mingay and F. M. L. Thompson.[24] Several of the later classics bore on this larger question, including Thompson's *Making* and Hobsbawm and Rudé's *Captain Swing,* as well as Hobsbawm's general British economic history, *Industry and Empire.*

Yet in other dimensions these Marxist historians were the opposite of parochial. Rudé was closely connected to Georges Lefebvre and Albert Soboul in France; Kiernan practiced an eclectic version of global history; Hobsbawm maintained wide international connections, especially with Germany, France, and Italy, but also with Eastern Europe and Latin America. Two other figures, Thomas Hodgkin and Basil Davidson, one in the CPGB and the other not, vitally influenced African history, again from positions outside the academy in adult education and journalism.[25] Hobsbawm interacted with Fernand Braudel and the other *Annalistes,* as well as with Ernst Labrousse, Lefebvre, and Soboul. Hobsbawm and

Rudé each helped transform the comparative study of social protest in preindustrial societies on the broadest of international fronts.

Rudé dismantled older stereotypes of the destructiveness and irrationality of "the mob," using the French Revolutionary uprisings and eighteenth-century urban riots in England and France to analyze the patterning and motivations behind collective action, while replacing loose and lurid descriptions of an undifferentiated rabble with a careful sociology of the "faces in the crowd." Hobsbawm studied the transformations in popular consciousness accompanying capitalist industrialization across a wider variety of settings, beginning with the essays eventually collected in *Labouring Men*. This interest ran partly through studies of Luddism and other forms of labor protest preceding trade unionism; partly through his classic lectures on "archaic" forms of protest in agrarian societies such as social banditry, millenarianism, and mafia, published as *Primitive Rebels* (1959) and the later *Bandits* (1969); partly through work on peasants and peasant movements in Latin America. Hobsbawm's influence was vitally involved in the earliest stage of the conversations among historians and anthropologists. It helped inspire historians into rethinking how the meanings and modalities of political action might be encountered in so-called preindustrial societies, which more accurately meant those societies without a developed parliamentary system, an emergent civil society and the rule of law, or a democratic constitution.

The influence and ambitions of the Anglo-Marxist historians were convened most effectively of all in the form of a new journal, *Past and Present,* launched in 1952 under the subtitle *Journal of Scientific History* (itself an obvious giveaway in light of the reigning ideological climate). Conceived with the aim of keeping dialogue open among Marxist and non-Marxist historians during a period of tightening Cold War conformities, this new initiative could originally count on extremely thin disciplinary support. The first editor and main instigator, the ancient historian-cum-medievalist John Morris, was joined on the board by Hobsbawm, Hill, Hilton, Dobb, and the archaeologist Gordon Childe, who were all Marxists, together with a contingent of distinguished non-Marxists who numbered the ancient historian Hugo Jones, the Czech historian R. R. Betts, the Tudor-Stuart historian D. B. Quinn, and the generalist Geoffrey Barraclough. Six years later, in the interests of furthering pluralism once again, the board was broadened to lessen the Marxist appearance by adding the early modernists Lawrence Stone and John Elliott, the medievalist Trevor Aston, the archaeologist S. S. Frere, and the sociologists Norman Birnbaum and Peter Worsley. At this point, the journal also changed its subtitle, becoming simply *Journal of Historical Studies*. Not coincidentally, these changes followed the political crisis of Stalinism in 1956–57, when a large contingent of intellectuals, including most of the historians with the exception of Hobsbawm, had resigned from the CPGB.[26]

During its first two decades, *Past and Present* made lasting contributions to social history's early formation that helped vitally shape its period of rapid growth. One of these was internationalism, for it brought European work into the English-speaking world, aided by its editors' political networks, direct exchanges with France, and the new Social History Section of the International Historical Congress inaugurated at the Paris meeting of the latter in 1950, which allowed new contacts with a younger *Annales* generation to be made. Second, like *Annales* across the Channel in France, it made the case for comparative study of societies within an overall framework of arguments about historical change, posed at the level of European or global movements and systems. This commitment, which crystallized from the agenda of the CP Historians' Group and the editors' Marxist education, patently informed the journal's recurring thematics, which were also addressed in its annual conferences beginning in 1957. These included early modern revolutions and the general crisis of the seventeenth century, the origins of industrialization, war and society from 1300 to 1600, science and religion, colonialism and nationalism, and so forth. Third, it opened interdisciplinary conversations with sociologists and anthropologists, again encouraged by Marxism's default acceptance of the indivisibility of knowledge, and again paralleling the intellectual culture pioneered by *Annales*. Fourth, social history was perceived at this time in tandem with economics, whether through the *Annales* paradigm and its master category of structures, or through Marxism and the materialist conception of history. In British academic life, as social history became gradually disengaged from the "manners and morals" mode of popularizing (and from the CPGB projects of "people's history"), it became coupled to economic history, registered institutionally in the first independent departments of economic and social history created in some universities during the 1960s.

As it emerged from the pages of *Past and Present,* in other words, "social history" was coming to mean the commitment to understanding the dynamics of change and stability at a level of whole societies. It spelled the ambition to make connections between political events and underlying social forces. From 1947 through 1950, the CP Historians' Group had devoted a series of conferences to the transition from feudalism to capitalism, revolving around a controversy between Maurice Dobb and the U.S. Marxist economist Paul Sweezy and a series of associated questions concerning the rise of absolutism, the character of bourgeois revolutions, the agrarian bases of capitalist development, and the societal meanings of the Reformation. An ambitious two-part article, "The Crisis of the Seventeenth Century," published by Hobsbawm in *Past and Present* in 1954, now prompted the defining discussion of the journal's first decade, whose various contributions were later collected under Trevor Aston's editorship as *Crisis in Europe, 1560–1660.* That debate energized historians of France, Spain, Sweden, Germany, Bohemia, Russia, Ireland, and early modern Europe generally, as well as historians of Britain. It explored the relationship between the political upheavals of the seventeenth century and forms of economic crisis graspable in continental European terms, in what Hobsbawm posited as the final phase of the general passage out of feudalism toward capitalist forms of economy.[27] It built a case for studying the religious aspects of the crisis in their social dimension. It grasped the nettle of conceptualizing the histories of societies as a whole, with profound implications for their future historiographies, as Elliott's article "The Decline of Spain" so vividly made clear. It reemphasized the convergence between *Past and Present* and *Annales,* for Hobsbawm's initial theses could not have been developed without the work sponsored by Fernand Braudel.[28] Above all, the debate proselytized the value of the "comparative method."

This multiform pioneering work clustered around *Past and Present* laid the cumulative foundations for the explicit and large-scale emergence of social history during the 1960s. The journal's longer-term influence also remained very great, although for many years this became heavily accented toward the medieval and early modern eras. Its board had some success in encouraging submissions from other fields, including South Asian and other non-Western histories. But the body of historiography that most interests us here, nineteenth- and twentieth-century studies of working-class history, was far less saliently represented.[29] But when in 1971 Hobsbawm published his stock-taking survey "From Social History to the History of Society," social history in a much wider variety of contexts had already taken off. Out in the wider world of the discipline, the next ten years saw a remarkable expansion and diversification of activity—with regular conferences, international networks, new journals, and new subdisciplinary societies like the British Social History Society formed in 1976.

SOCIAL HISTORY'S ARRIVAL

The tendency we have been describing—"the British Marxist historians," or "Anglo-Marxist historiography," in the accepted parlance—ran through the years of social history's emergence like a red thread. In any case, by the late 1960s it was sufficiently unified to turn into a frequent object of attack, not least from within the Left itself, and sufficiently self-conscious to enter ferocious self-justifications in response.[30] But such palpable influence notwithstanding, its programmatic presence remained muted. Its exponents practiced in an "empirical idiom," where theory and its assumptions seemed somehow anterior to the act of historical study or writing itself, requiring little overt expression. As a consequence, expressions of theoretical perspective and commitment were often pressed to the margin, voiced incidentally or in nonacademic and polemical ways, including via the occasional interviews conducted by younger colleagues during the 1970s and 1980s, so that the distinctiveness of the collective standpoint was sometimes hard to recuperate. During the next two decades, on the other hand, the systematizing of the group's legacy has turned into a small historiographical industry all in itself.[31]

The clearest and most famous example remains *The Making of the English Working Class*.[32] A vast epic of the self-making of the working class, passionately written and archivally based, the book derived its concentration on the cultures, experiences, and political resistances of the working class in the fifty years or so before 1832 avowedly from Marx. Yet the text offered little in the way of a formal theoretical argument, save for sustained polemical assault on the axioms of contemporary economic history, which in its time was certainly resonant enough. Incompletely defined notions of "experience" and "exploitation" did a good deal of the organizing work in Thompson's approach. This powerful centering of class, of its consciousness and cultures, together with the supposed theoretical ineffability of the relations of "being" to "consciousness," left behind a powerful but subtly simplified view of the social constitution of class politics.

Thompson's work also advanced an eloquent counternarrative to gradualist versions of British history as the triumphant march of parliamentary evolution, from which popular uprisings, government coercion, and civil strife—all the rich and turbulent histories of democratic mobilization in extraparliamentary spheres—had largely been banished. Instead of this polite and complacent success story, Thompson sought to reground the history of democratic gains in an epic recounting of resistance against violence, inequality, and exploitation. As he famously put it: "I am seeking to rescue the poor stockinger, the Luddite cropper, the 'obsolete' handloom weaver, the 'utopian' artisan, and even the deluded follower of Joanna Southcott, from the enormous condescension of posterity."[33] His book was also a passionately antireductionist manifesto—attacking narrowly based economic history, overdeterministic Marxism, and static theories of class. For Thompson, class was dynamic, eventuating through history—a relationship and a process, a common consciousness of capitalist exploitation and state repression, all graspable through culture. Through the example of *The Making,* the move from labor's institutional study to social histories of working people thus gained enormous momentum, rapidly encompassing the parts of life that historians of parties and trade unions had rarely found relevant, except in antiquarian and colorful ways—not just the workplace in all its practices and customs, but also housing, nutrition, leisure and sport, drinking, crime, religion, magic and superstition, education, song, literature, childhood, courtship, sexuality, death, and more.

Thompson wrote *The Making of the English Working Class* outside the academy while working in adult education in Leeds. He was active as a Communist until 1956 and thereafter as a New Left spokesman. His restless energies, polemicist's panache, and talents as a public speaker gave him a powerful and compelling charismatic presence. He continued committing himself to a variety of progressive causes during the rest of his life, most prominently during the rise of the peace movement in the early 1980s. He created the Center for the Study of Social History at Warwick University in 1965, the only period in which he held a regular university appointment, directing the center until his resignation in 1971. Thereafter, he withdrew into an independent life, devoting most of the later 1970s and early 1980s to his public political activities. From time to time he accepted visiting appointments in North America and elsewhere. By the later 1980s, he was returning to his unfinished historical works. He died in 1993.

This combination of political principle, professional marginality, and disciplinary radicalism was essential to Thompson's aura. He was undisciplined and unassimilable. Beyond the networks of labor history and *Past and Present,* his great book on the making of the working class was aggressively dismissed by those established historians responsible for constructing the optimistic narrative of the Industrial Revolution as a wealth- and welfare-producing breakthrough to universal prosperity and improvement. Until the early 1960s, that polite and evolutionary consensual view had carried most conventional historiographical opinion before it, reaching out into the wider public and down into the schools. In comparison, Thompson's *Making* seemed a rude and inappropriate intrusion. Its author was widely disregarded as an outsider lacking in credentials, deficient in either the craftsmanship or the decorum of the profession. But his example energized younger generations. It also inspired the reviving Marxisms so central to the developing social history wave.

Around the margins of the British historical profession, Thompson's impact helped two new initiatives to form. One of these was the Social History Group in Oxford between 1965 and 1974. Although situated inside British intellectual life's metropolitan triangle of London and Oxbridge, this initiative received no support from the Oxford History Faculty and its accredited representatives. Its young conveners included the Marxist author of *Outcast London* published in 1971, Gareth Stedman Jones; a specialist on Spanish anarchism, Joaquin Romero Maura; a German historian working on the experience of the working class under Nazism, Tim Mason; and especially Raphael Samuel, who after leaving the Communist Party in 1956 was active at the core of the British New Left while a student in Oxford, before taking a tutor's position at Ruskin, the Oxford-based nonuniversity trade union college, in 1961.

In this distinctly youthful company—Mason and Romero Maura were born in 1940, Stedman Jones in 1942—Samuel was slightly the more senior presence. He provided the driving energy behind the Ruskin History Workshops, which began partly as a challenge to conventional historiography, partly as a wider forum for his own students at Ruskin to present their work. Those students were "worker historians" on trade union scholarships to Ruskin's two-year residential program, whom Samuel encouraged into doing primary research projects, invariably on aspects of their own working-class backgrounds. The annual conferences became a vital engine of the new social history in Britain, starting modestly, but soon mushrooming into large-scale international events. They turned into festivals of the new kinds of historical work, styling themselves as "people's history" by subject matter and identification, appealing to the radicalism of the emergent generations and their self-consciously insurgent élan. The first thirteen History Workshops met at Ruskin itself between 1967 and 1979, before the immediate relationship became broken and future meetings migrated elsewhere. They also inspired a series of pamphlets (twelve in all, 1970–74) and a run of over thirty books from 1975 to 1990, a variety of locally based counterparts, some sustained involvement in various public controversies, including most notably the national curriculum debate during the 1980s, and last but not least the launching of *History Workshop Journal* in 1976.[34]

The second new movement owing some inspiration to Edward Thompson was women's history. While the British pioneers of women's history were moved mainly by the wider cultural and political dynamism of the 1960s, which found most of the key figures still in their twenties, they drew important support from both the earlier Marxist generation and History Workshop's newly emergent milieu: figures like Anna Davin, Sally Alexander, Catherine Hall, and Sheila Rowbotham all shaped their historical interests in direct conversation with the latter, sometimes adversarially, but mainly in collaborative ways. Rowbotham, for one, was also directly mentored by the Thompsons. Moreover, what emerges powerfully from even the briefest review of the emergence of women's history is once again the indebtedness to politics—that is, the evident reciprocities joining the impulse for change in the discipline with the commitment to radicalism in the political sphere. Thus the first National Women's Liberation Conference also convened at Ruskin College in March 1970, after several women historians—Rowbotham,

Alexander, Davin, and others—responded angrily to the belittlement of women's questions at the Fourth History Workshop the previous November. Also partly in consequence, the Seventh History Workshop in May 1973 was eventually titled "Women in History." No less than the impact of antifascism for the CP Historians' Group, in other words, these political contexts of the late 1960s and early 1970s directly shaped the conditions of social history's emergence.

In the course of the 1960s, Edward Thompson's own work had been moving backward in time. His social history of property crimes and the law in relation to early eighteenth-century modalities of political order, *Whigs and Hunters,* and the work of his Warwick students collected in *Albion's Fatal Tree* (both eventually published in 1975), explored the transformations of customary culture beneath the onslaught of a rapidly commercializing capitalism. Two essays, "Time, Work-Discipline, and Industrial Capitalism" and "The Moral Economy of the English Crowd in the Eighteenth Century," appeared in *Past and Present,* whose board Thompson also joined in 1969; a third, "Rough Music," appeared in *Annales.* Two others followed in the *Journal of Social History* and *Social History,* plus a legendary lecture, "The Sale of Wives," that remained unpublished. Finally gathered together as *Customs in Common* in 1993, this work helped transform perceptions of the transition to industrial capitalism, further dismantling the Industrial Revolution's gross causality. Moreover, *Albion's Fatal Tree* argued that crime and punishment should be considered "central to unlocking the meanings of eighteenth-century social history," and a host of exciting new research and publications during the 1970s and 1980s quickly confirmed that claim.[35]

Thompson's influence also quickly became international, offering the main alternative source of inspiration for those unattracted by the social science methodologies and perspectives largely dominating the rise of social history in the United States. *The Making* shaped North American, African, and South Asian agendas no less than studies of class formation in Britain and Europe, while Thompson's later eighteenth-century essays exerted similarly imposing influence, especially "The Moral Economy," which became the object of a retrospective international conference in Birmingham in 1992. More generally, the processes of transnational diffusion and collaboration getting under way during the 1970s impressively internationalized social history through the media of conferences, journals, and translation. In one particularly significant example, Thompson, Hobsbawm, and others of the same generation joined a series of round tables on social history organized by the Maison des Sciences de l'Homme and the Max Planck Institute of History in Göttingen, which convened an exciting assortment of somewhat younger scholars from the English-speaking world, France, Italy, West Germany, and elsewhere beginning in 1978. The successive volumes of essays issuing from those meetings, together with the associated monographs and wider publications, provide a fascinating trace of the trajectories followed by historiographical innovation between the 1960s and now.[36]

So far, we have been telling a mainly British story. A counterpart to Edward Thompson in the United States, and the leading transatlantic interlocutor in the round tables just mentioned, was the Harvard-trained sociologist Charles Tilly, who taught for many years in sociology and history at the University of Michigan before moving to the New School for Social Research in 1984 and thence in the 1990s to Columbia University. His first book, *The Vendée,* published in 1964, was an exciting model of archivally grounded historical sociology, exploring the complex interrelationship between local political affiliations and regional patterns of socioeconomic development during the French Revolution. One strand of his subsequent work then focused on the dynamic reciprocities between capitalism and state-making, extending from an edited volume, *The Formation of the National States in Western Europe* (1975), to his grand survey and summation, *Coercion, Capital, and European States, A.D. 990–1990* (1990), while another strand dealt with the demographic dimensions of proletarianization. But Tilly was known best of all for his sociology of collective action, establishing himself during the 1960s and 1970s as that field's preeminent practitioner. Using the concepts of "contentious gatherings" and "repertoires of contention" to theorize and map the changing bases of popular mobilization in social movements between the early modern era and the present, he tackled successively several centuries of French history and the era of the Industrial Revolution in Britain, publishing in each case countless essays and an imposing book. Moreover, accomplishing those projects presupposed grandiose longitudinal studies and large-scale collaborative research, requiring big resources, large teams, and huge machineries of quantitative production.[37]

In the U.S. context Tilly's influence proved quite as inspiring as Thompson's in Britain and was similarly reinforced by a broader intellectual movement, in this case a tradition of social science history whose resources and prestige far surpassed anything the Marxist historians could muster on the European side of the Atlantic. As William Sewell has argued, the rise of social history under these auspices "effected a profound intellectual transformation in the field of history—in subject matter, in methods, and in intellectual style," producing "a vast double enlargement of the scope of historical study."[38] As Sewell remembers the excitements of this moment, their attractions perfectly mirrored the appeal we have attributed to the Anglo-Marxists in Britain.

First, social history studied categories of people who had previously been ignored by historical scholarship. Rather than political leaders and great intellectuals, who had been the prime objects of previous scholarship, social historians tended to work on the obscure and the downtrodden: servants, workers, criminals, women, slaves, shopkeepers, peasants, or children. And second, rather than concentrating on politics, social history attempted to capture the whole range of ordinary people's life experience: work, child rearing, disease, recreation, deviant behavior, kinship, sociability, procreation, popular religion.

Following this agenda required new questions, new types of sources, and new analytical methods if social historians were to get closer to "the social structures, institutions, and life experiences of millions of ordinary people." A huge amount of the effort—and the inventiveness—of the new social history in the United States thus went into the "systematic use of quantitative methods," which certainly presupposed the privileged infrastructure of large-scale funding available in the U.S. universities (and, it should be remembered, nowhere else), as well as the objectivist promises of rigorous scientific discovery, but which also became inseparable from an emergent generation's radical vision. The anonymous majority of the population notoriously leave few documents behind them, let alone detailed written accounts of their own lives. But to the degree that they were captured in nets of public surveillance, via the registrations of the life cycle, via taxation and conscription, via the census, and then increasingly via policing and the regulative intrusions of investigative bodies, the new social historians argued, often with evangelical zeal, ordinary people could be brought effectively into visibility. Only "by aggregating the rather thin and stereotypic information contained in the records of such encounters between ordinary people and the state," they insisted, could social historians hope "to reconstruct the patterns of their lives."

Underlying this ambition was an "objectivist epistemology" that took the explanatory importance of "social structure" as a necessary given, as an already accredited resource of the social science theory that social historians were seeking to borrow, much as the assumptions behind the materialism of the Anglo-Marxist historiography also remained anterior to its practice. The valency of "social" in this usage implied a strong type of contextualism, a "presumption that social structures were analytically prior to social action," and an image of society as knowable, susceptible to "objective" analysis, and graspable as a whole.[39] In this understanding, as Sewell explains it, "social structures" embraced everything beyond an ordinary individual's immediate agency—namely, "occupational distributions, economic structures, demographic patterns, inheritance systems, urban settlement patterns, systems of land tenure, and the like." These structures were "objective and transpersonal patterns or forces of which actors were at best incompletely aware and which tightly constrained their actions and thoughts." They were also "essentially autonomous from political or intellectual history," constituting at least "the underlying conditions" for the latter and "perhaps even the determinants." In these terms, Sewell concludes, "the rise of social history entailed a redefinition of the very object of historical knowledge, from politics and ideas to anonymous social structures, as well as the discovery of new means of gaining knowledge about this object."[40]

What Sewell leaves out of this account, though, is the macrohistorical understanding of whole societies changing across time, guided by a confidence in developmental models drawn from the social sciences, which was certainly just as vital to the new social historians' sense of their goals in those years. And here Charles Tilly was again the key practitioner, whose grandiose facility with the analysis of long-run and large-scale social transformations fully matched his intensive studies of collective action in the pervasiveness of their appeal. Indeed, it was precisely the *combination* of these faculties that proved so inspiring—not only the prospect of getting closer to ordinary people's experiences, but also the ability to situate these in overarching frameworks of societal change. Moreover, the oversimplified quality of some social historians' references to such larger frameworks should not be allowed to disqualify the contributions made by their particular studies. Sometimes reduced to a Whiggishly unidirectional notion of "modernization," but more commonly articulated via arguments about industrialization, economic growth, nation building, and state formation, the evoking of these frameworks did not prevent social historians from producing nuanced and sophisticated studies located in particular places and times, however perfunctory and talismanic the larger languages of social change might be.[41]

Again, the full flood of the self-confidence of this new social history in the United States lasted for a finite time—roughly from the mid-1960s, when younger generations began their dissertation work amid the largesse of the university expansion and its funding, inspired by the examples of Tilly and others, to the later 1970s, when a series of far-reaching critiques began to appear. During that time there was little serious tension between what might be described as the doubled genealogies of social history: on the one hand, identifying with the people; on the other hand, learning from social science. If in France, for example, this balance was tilted toward the authorizing ideal of a social science–based interdisciplinarity, and in Britain the accent was more toward the class-centered people's history espoused by the Anglo-Marxists, in the United States these elements appeared more as a seamless combination.[42]

What was most memorable about this time was not just the intellectual excitement of changing an entire discipline and the political discovery of a history that mattered, but also the supreme self-confidence and accompanying ambition. No area or type of history seemed immune to social history's transformatory or reconstructive claims. The key to those claims, we have suggested, was a universalizing logic of "social context," with causalities unfolding outward and upward in a classical materialist manner. Some notion of social determination, conceptualized on the ground of material life, whether primarily in relation to demography, political economy, the labor process, class relations, or cultural forms, usually gave social history its consensual tissue of assumptions. This implied a willingness to understand *all* facets of human existence in terms of their social determinations—to "be as much concerned with questions of culture and consciousness as with those of social structure and the material conditions of life," as the founding editorial of the new journal *Social History* put it.[43] Usually some idea of social totality was also entailed. Confidence in that possibility—in the importance of grasping society as a whole, by theorizing its underlying principles of coherence and then demonstrating their efficacy by means of a concrete project— was essential to social history's verve.

## DISPERSAL AND RETREAT

How did it become possible by the end of the 1990s to describe social history as "an intellectual project in crisis"?[44] By the end of the 1970s, it is certainly true, a definite fractiousness had already appeared inside the fold. Various leading voices entered vigorous complaints about how social history was mainly being done, often in the context of a general stock-taking exercise—for example, Elizabeth Fox-Genovese and Eugene Genovese, Gareth Stedman Jones (both in 1976), Lawrence Stone (1977), and Tony Judt (1979).[45] But these were still challenges from *inside* the project, calling on social historians to be the best versions of themselves—to be more ambitious and consistent in their contextual- izing, to show less dependence on the social sciences, to be more coura- geous in developing theories of their own. Moreover, the institution- building aspects of the social history upsurge were still very much in evidence—for example, in the multiplying of new journals, the bur- geoning of subdisciplinary societies, the thickening of international net- works, the recasting of curricula, the creation of new teaching positions, and the rapid accumulation of dissertations. In light of this expansion, debates over theories and methods seemed the normal signs of diversification and growth, evidence of vitality rather than ill health. Only those of a narrow or sectarian disposition might complain.[46]

But rethinking was already under way. In 1980, William Sewell's study of the languages of labor in nineteenth-century France developed an unexpectedly cultural approach to working-class formation for an author so prominent in the new social history. Attached to Charles Tilly in the 1960s under an SSRC Training Fellowship, Sewell was something of a poster child for the union of history and sociology. But a five-year stint at the School of Social Science in the Princeton Institute of

Advanced Study unlocked his earlier intellectual allegiances, beginning in 1975–76 with intensive discussions among a group of symbolic anthropologists and historians assembled by Clifford Geertz. In retrospect, *Work and Revolution in France* seems less of a radical break than is often assumed, containing none of the exclusivist advocacy of linguistic analysis so characteristic of later debates. Its emphasis on the "artisan ethos" was substantively continuous with Sewell's earlier sociologically informed work on the Marseille working class, and now he argued quite moderately for extending the social historian's interest into the analysis of "workers' discourse" in order to enter the "mental universe of ordinary men and women in the past."[47] But Sewell's approach certainly signaled a key disciplinary transition: from focusing on work, migration, marriage, residence, and other quantifiable aspects of workers' material lives, he now called for a very different emphasis on "structures or systems of meaning." For Sewell, the turn to anthropology promised access to questions of human agency foreclosed by the objectivist fixation on social structure: "interpretive methods . . . could restore to history the dimension of meaningful human action that had been marginalized in the new social history."[48]

In the course of the 1980s, it is fair to say, social history surrendered its primacy as the acknowledged source of innovation in the discipline to what became known as the "new cultural history." An eclectic and anthropologically oriented cultural analysis now took its cues from Clifford Geertz, from the pioneering examples of Natalie Zemon Davis and other early modernists, from various mavericks like Carlo Ginzburg, and from a particular reading of Edward Thompson.[49] Another set of influences came from an antireductionist British Marxism, exemplified by Raymond Williams, the Birmingham Center for Contemporary Cultural Studies, and Stuart Hall. It was further extended by the gathering reception of the ideas of Michel Foucault, whose philosophical works *The Order of Things* and *The Archaeology of Knowledge* and highly original treatments of madhouses, hospitals, and prisons were systematically translated during the 1970s, followed by the three volumes of his *History of Sexuality* and various editions of essays and interviews.[50] Finally, the challenges of feminist theory became unavoidable for social historians in the 1980s, whereas the early wave of women's history had been more easily compartmentalized and kept at bay, and the new cultural turn overlaid this development too.

The resulting changes may be variously tracked.[51] Between his early polemical essays of the later 1960s and a series of highly regarded theoretical interventions during the 1970s, for example, Gareth Stedman Jones had come to stand for a "non-empiricist" and "theoretically informed history" that was avowedly Marxist and materialist in social history's common understandings of the time. His *Outcast London* published in 1971 placed him firmly in a lineage with Hobsbawm, Thompson, Saville, and other Anglo-Marxist historians of the working class.[52] He was widely viewed as carrying the torch for the next generation. Then in 1983, apparently out of the blue, he published *Languages of Class: Studies in English Working-Class History, 1832–1982,* proposing a linguistic approach that left the familiar ground of social historians disconcertingly behind.[53] This was followed in 1986 by Joan Scott's article in the *American Historical Review,* "Gender: A Useful Category of Historical Analysis," reprinted two years later in her extraordinarily influential *Gender and the Politics of History,* which presented more elaborate and further reaching poststructuralist propositions.[54] By questioning the assumptions around which social historical analysis had been ordered, reinforced by the more general encroachment of Foucauldian "discourse theory," these and other works radically destabilized social history's recently acquired self-confidence. Social history became one site of a wider ferment of epistemological uncertainty in the humanities and to a lesser extent the social sciences. Unexpectedly, leading voices were questioning social history's underlying materialism, extending even to the determinative coherence of the very category of "the social" itself.[55]

Feminism was at the center of this turmoil. In social history's earlier advocacy, women's history had played no part. When the latter's pioneering works appeared, they were also effectively consigned to a new and discrete subfield, conceptualized via "separate spheres" or subsumed into the history of the family, a pattern only partly broken by syntheses like Louise Tilly and Joan Scott's *Women, Work, and Family,* which appeared in 1978. It was really the turning to gender, as the complex, unstable, and historically variable construction of sexual difference, that made feminist critiques and the gathering corpus of women's history much harder to ignore. Many social historians still continued unawares, of course. But the slowly accumulating studies of gender and work, together with equally rich gendered critiques of social policy and the welfare state, each of which brought historians into thickly populated interdisciplinary fields, created highly receptive audiences for Joan Scott's theoretical intervention. By the early 1990s social historians more broadly were beginning to reflect on their previously unexamined gendered suppositions. Most important of all, field-defining books by Sonya Rose, Anna Clark, and Kathleen Canning pursued those assumptions audaciously into the social history heartland of labor history and working-class formation, making it impossible for work in those areas to be credibly conducted any longer in the old gender-insensitive ways.[56]

The fate of Marxism during this process was especially complex. If it enjoyed a relatively secure and legitimate, even a prestigious, place in the universities of Italy and France, largely accruing from the antifascist legacies of World War II and the presence of a large Communist Party, Marxism was generally a weak and beleaguered presence during the Cold War elsewhere in Western Europe and the English-speaking world. After the student explosions and radicalization of the universities in the late 1960s, this certainly changed. Marxist intellectual work secured firm footholds for the first time in the universities of Britain and North America. The resulting diffusion initially favored various classical versions of Marxist theory, as in Louis Althusser's "anti-humanist" separation of the mature from the young Marx, the more general structuralist stress on mode of production and an economically centered concept of class, the revival of Marxist economics, studies of the labor process inspired by Harry Braverman's *Labor and Monopoly Capital,* or the feminist debate over domestic labor.[57] During the late 1960s and early 1970s, a new generation of students and younger faculty were inducted into the Marxist tradition, and their process of discovery reinstated *Capital* as the starting point, invariably through the small-scale medium of the reading group.

At the same time and despite their classical intimations, these discussions saw themselves as *departures,* as critical advances on an older heritage of orthodoxy and its "economistic" forms of theory. The "base and superstructure" model of social determination, with its assignment of logical priority to the economy and its social relations, came under particular attack. As they intensively worked through the writings of Louis

Althusser and Nicos Poulantzas during the early 1970s, British Marxists opened widening holes in such orthodoxies, through which an army of mainly French influences was then able to march—Lacanian psychoanalysis, Saussurean linguistics, the philosophy of science of Gaston Bachelard and Georges Canguilhem, the aesthetics of Pierre Macherey, semiotics and theories of film, and so forth.[58] The resultant freeing of politics and ideology for "relatively autonomous" analysis, anchored to the economy via "structural causality" and "determination in the last instance," opened the entire domain of the "non-economic" to Marxist view—aesthetics, literature, the arts, theories of knowledge and the disciplines, intellectual life, popular culture, sexuality—in short, "culture," as a convergent strain of British dissenting Marxism was coming to understand it.[59]

The excitement of those days, the sense of participating in a continuous and unsettling drama of revision, deserves to be remembered. In the British context, this was arguably a remarkable generational achievement, which both internationalized (or at least Europeanized) a previously parochial intellectual culture, cajoled it kicking and screaming into an openly theorized mode of exchange, and simultaneously problematized the latter's terms of address. There was also something slightly manic and self-defeating about the rapidity of the progression from one set of intellectual positions to another, as though a path was being laid across difficult and dangerous terrain only immediately to have the ground cut away, so that moving forward became the only choice. This process can easily be given greater unity, coherence, and logical continuity than it displayed at the time (or could ever have possessed), with one move reduced to the rational consequence of another, causally inscribed in the contradictions and insufficiencies that came before. But intellectual histories seldom unroll as rationally as that; and the process of revision was divisive rather than harmonious, managed via conflicts and disruptions as much as by its own unfolding momentum. Here, for example, is Terry Lovell's account of British feminism's trajectory in this period.

The journey begins with Marxist- or socialist-feminist writings (in history, social science *and* cultural studies), seeking to uncover the material conditions of women's oppression under capitalism; it advances with the recognition that certain aspects of that oppression do not yield very readily to Marxist categories and that a more adequate account of feminine subjectivity is required for understanding the ways in which that oppression is *lived,* which might be sought in psychoanalysis rather than Marxism. Then, via Lacan and modern theories of language, the journey continues into the "poststructuralism" and "deconstructionism" whose luminaries include Foucault, Derrida, and Kristeva. Some travellers continue beyond feminism itself, into a "postfeminism" and "postmodernism" which understand both Lacanian psychoanalysis and Marxism to have been mere staging-posts along the way.[60]

In the longer run, such discussions played havoc with the received forms of Marxist and more general materialist understanding so vital to the new social history in its period of arrival. For many, the logic of this antireductionist turn became overpowering, leading to an unanticipated "post-Marxist" destination and the more predictable recriminatory counterreactions from those not comfortable with such an apparent "retreat from class."[61] But what for some has been the feared Pandora's box of uncontrollable heterodoxies remained for others a bottomless bag of tricks, containing not only the antireductionist promises mentioned earlier but also the more daring options of postmodernism and the linguistic turn. By the end of the 1980s, this restless probing of the limits showed few signs of coming to a halt. Shibboleths had fallen one by one. The continuing pursuit of the antireductionist logic, through increasingly sophisticated readings of culture and ideology via Gramsci, Foucault, Voloshinov and Bakhtin, French poststructuralism, cultural studies in Britain, and the still diversifying fields of feminist theory on both sides of the Atlantic, had left the earlier intellectual moment of the 1960s far behind, to the point of bringing the original materialist inspirations badly into doubt.[62]

As the hold of the economy became progressively loosened, and with it the determinative power of the social structure and its causal priorities, therefore, the imaginative and epistemological space for other kinds of analysis also grew. Indeed, for many who went this route, that classical materialist connection became broken once and for all. "Society" as a unitary object—the presumed object of social history—could no longer be sustained. Structural coherence could no longer be derived quite as straightforwardly from the economy, from the functional needs of the social system and its central values, or from some other overarching principle of social order. It was certainly possible to continue placing particular phenomena—an event, a policy, an institution, an ideology, a text—in particular social contexts, in the sense of conditions, relations, practices, sites. But that earlier sense of an underlying given structure was now lost. Social history's axiomatic confidence in a workable idea of social totality, whether Marxist or not, was the major casualty of this long-lasting intellectual flux.

That ideal of grasping *society as a whole,* of writing the history of "whole societies" in Hobsbawm's foundational 1971 notation, on the basis of society's underlying principles of unity—a commitment that by the 1990s was being characterized conventionally as part of the specifically "modern" or Enlightenment project—passed into extreme disarray. For Marxists and others on the left, this was connected to a complex of political experiences, including the long-term numerical decline of the historic working class and its traditions, the crises of Keynesianism, the welfare state, and statist conceptions of socialism, the economic, political, and moral bankruptcy of Communist systems, the catastrophe of the environment and of the old ideal of the mastery of science over nature, and the declining purchase of straightforward class-based forms of political address. Those changes corroded belief in the forward movement of history, while depriving the past of its accustomed narrative order. In Jean-François Lyotard's oft-quoted summation of the consequences of all this, the postmodern moment had arrived, proudly bearing its "incredulity with regard to master narratives."[63] The grand ideals allowing history to be read in a particular direction as a story of progress and achievement, from the Industrial Revolution to the emancipation of the working class, the victory of socialism, and the equality of women, no longer seemed persuasive. All bets were off: "[T]here is no single right way to read history. Indeed, history becomes a narrative without a teleology," a story without an end.[64]

Thus the period between the 1970s and the 1990s witnessed a dizzying intellectual history. We moved from a time when social history and social analysis seemed to be capturing the profession's central ground, and the force of social determinations seemed axiomatic, to a new conjuncture in which "the social" came to seem ever less definite and social determinations surrendered their earlier claims. The road from "relative autonomy" and "structural causality," which seemed the hard-won gains of the 1970s, to the "discursive character of all practices," which became the new poststructuralist dictum of the 1980s, was rapid and disconcerting. The persuasiveness of the antireductionist logic proved extraordinarily hard to withstand, rather like an up escalator with no way down.

But if "society" as a totalizing category was dissolving, did that leave social explanation as such without any role? Too frequently, this question has gone by default. In much historiography, the reception of Foucault and other poststructuralisms has been allowed simply to collapse the distinction between "the social" and "the cultural" altogether, with the latter functioning as a kind of summary description for the entire discursive domain. During the antireductionist agonizing of the 1970s, following one of the key Althusserian leads, the concept of "social formation" increasingly replaced the older conventional form of "society" in the usage of many Marxists precisely to open a place for greater indeterminacy, indicating the complex articulations required among different forms of the economy, different types of social relations, different institutional bases for politics, different cultural practices, and so forth, if the cohesion of specific societies in particular places and times was to be either secured or understood. But in the meantime, that commitment to a complex model of totality has now itself largely dissolved. "Social formation," and hence the bases of interconnectedness, became redefined agnostically as an abstract and peculiarly nonguaranteed theoretical projection, hedged and qualified by severe epistemological cautions—as the aggregate of "discursive practices," as "equivalent to the non-unified totality of these practices," and as "a complex, overdetermined, and contradictory nexus of discursive practices."[65]

Moreover, as Sewell observes, poststructuralist understandings of textuality indebted to Derrida now make "the unreflective realism that underlay social history's evidentiary practices seem utterly naïve," because "all the texts and text analogs we use as evidence must be subjected to an acute critical reading and . . . much of what once passed for direct evidence of past 'realities' might better be thought of as a textual reference to yet another level of textuality." As a result, cultural historians shy away from "referring to social structures, social forces, modes of production, or class relations as facts standing outside of textual logics."

When it comes to dealing with many of the classic questions motivating social historians in their heyday—for example, "the distribution of wealth, the dynamics of industrial development, changing patterns of landholding or employment, demographic structures, or patterns of geographical concentration and dispersion"—this new and chastened level of understanding becomes extraordinarily disabling.[66] Once social historians saw that "reality" could only be accessed linguistically, their materialist footing became unstable and unsure. For if we can only enter and interpret the social world through language—in constitutive theoretical terms as well as the commonsense descriptive ones most would accept—and "the social" is only ever constituted *through* discourse, then what place is left for specifically social determinations at all?

## DOING HISTORY AFTER THE LINGUISTIC TURN

So by 1990, growing numbers of historians were beginning to speak the language of "cultural constructionism." If an interest in cultural anthropology had mediated the first moves in this direction, increasingly reinforced by the ever-more-ramified impact of Foucault, deconstructive literary theory and British cultural studies had also entered the mix, all of which was also translated extensively via feminism. As "race" pervaded social anxieties and political exchange, it also joined gender as a central category of historical analysis, greatly strengthened by the popularity of postcolonial studies. The importance of empire also returned to the domestic history of the metropolitan societies, initially again via anthropology, literary criticism, and cultural studies, exemplified in the widely influential writings of Ann Stoler, Ann McClintock, and Paul Gilroy.[67] Historians gradually responded in kind, mainly by route of gender. Catherine Hall's work was especially notable, moving from the classically social-historical *Family Fortunes* published in 1987 through a series of essays on the "racing" of empire to the publication of *Civilising Subjects* in 2002, which placed images and understandings of the empire at the heart of an argument about the emerging logics of cohesion in Victorian English society. In the future, the centrality of such work could only increase.[68]

Not all such works explicitly took the so-called linguistic turn or disavowed a social analytic. Often, in fact, social history was rather enhanced by attentiveness to language and the cultural histories of representation. The result could be a mobile "culturalism," not indifferent to social analysis or social contextualizing, but far more drawn to the domain of meaning than before. This also eased a rapprochement with intellectual history. It pulled history toward literary theory, linguistic analysis, the history of art, studies of film and other visual media, reflexive anthropology, and theories of cultural representation, thereby throwing open the agenda of possible histories. In 1989, an important programmatic volume of essays, *The New Cultural History,* was edited by Lynn Hunt, but the more important activity was already manifest in substantial freestanding books. Hunt herself was migrating from social history, leaving behind an earlier identity as a Tilly-influenced urban historian of the French Revolution for the wholly culturalist *Family Romance of the French Revolution* in 1992. That was already an increasingly familiar pattern, which counterposed Scott's *Gender and the Politics of History* (1988) with her *Glassworkers of Carmaux* (1974); and Sewell's *Work and Revolution* (1980) with the sociologically derived problematic of his *Structure and Mobility: The Men and Women of Marseilles, 1820–1870,* which appeared only in 1985 but originated long before in the early 1970s. Likewise, the social histories addressed by Judith Walkowitz's *Prostitution and Victorian Society* (1980), which were shaped by the early History Workshop milieu, were now revisited in her *City of Dreadful Delight* (1992), which was profoundly indebted to the new post-Foucauldian and poststructuralist analytics.[69]

This pattern was repeated many times. It scarcely lacked controversy, particularly within labor history, which had long since ramified into an extraordinarily rich social historiography of the working class. In German history, Kathleen Canning's work, which combined gender theory with a critical poststructuralist approach, set the pace, pressing well beyond the thinking of most labor historians in Germany itself. In the French field, Sewell and Scott tended to shape discussion, which was valuably mapped in an anthology edited by Lenard Berlanstein, *Rethinking Labor History,* published in 1993. The reception of Jacques Rancière's *The Nights of Labor: The Worker's Dream in Nineteenth-Century France,* originally published in 1981 and then translated in 1989, but already triggering discussion in the early 1980s, gave particular momentum to the progress of discourse analysis among French historians in the United

States. In British history, debates were especially fierce, as prominent representatives of the earlier social history wave now moved polemically away from doing social history altogether. Patrick Joyce traveled from his early work on the social contexts of factory cultures in Victorian Lancashire, published in 1980, through the broadened culturalism of *Visions of the People,* a major study of nineteenth-century popular social and political values published in 1991, to the theoretically rationalized intellectual history of *Democratic Subjects: The Self and the Social in Nineteenth-Century England* in 1994. The same trajectory was followed by Stedman Jones.[70]

Other new work in the British field by, for example, Robbie Gray, Anna Clark, or Sonya Rose, negotiated the tensions between classical and discursive approaches more creatively.[71] By now, we had come a long way from the context generated by the appearance of *The Making of the English Working Class,* and works such as these impressively condensed the wealth of intervening knowledge, insights, and critiques into a workable basis for taking Thompson's questions further. They took the measure of all the accumulating theoretical discussion without repudiating the underlying commitments Thompson eloquently placed on the table—above all to understanding the relationship between "exploitation" and the production of new subjectivities, which Thompson had so incompletely addressed in his ideas of "experience" and "consciousness." Of course, *The Making* was innocent of any of the skepticism, nervousness, or downright disowning of class analysis that now came to pervade the field, although there were perhaps signs toward the end of Thompson's life that he was coming to a form of that recognition.[72] Above all, Thompson's powerful centering of class around the classical Marxist couplet of "being" and "consciousness" had licensed a highly problematic understanding of the relationship between social history and politics, and it is to that central space of difficulty that we now return.

The simplification lay in the inherent assumption of a class politics grounded in material life and the brute ontologies of capitalist exploitation, handled and mediated in complex ways via cultures that were primarily class-defined. In other ways Thompson was perfectly capable of giving the autonomies of politics their due, even as he saw their indebtedness to surrounding and longer-run dynamics of social change, whose consequences could both enable and constrain. His work contained a powerful indictment of existing histories for equating politics with the parliamentary arena of Westminster and the actions of government while ignoring both the wider public sphere and the popular "counter-theater of threat and sedition" in the crowd and the streets. Moreover, the late eighteenth century saw a new strengthening of the state's coercive powers at the expense of earlier forms of public authority organized primarily in local ways, which also encouraged new initiatives of popular political association in response, best exemplified by the London Corresponding Society. The emergence of a conscious working-class presence between the 1789s and the 1830s, David Mayfield has aptly observed, "was predicated as much on this newly formed public sphere—one in which popular politics took the novel form of *representation*—as on any experience of changed productive relations." In this respect, Thompson's analysis was the opposite of "economistic," and "only the most naïve reading of *The Making* could treat it as a simple narrative of a working class forging an adequate consciousness of its own objective economic circumstances."[73]

But unfortunately, Mayfield goes on to point out, "Thompson's early analysis in *The Making* faltered just where he was so innovative: in his description of working-class political representation." His insistence that the "making" was completed by the 1830s assumes all those practical modalities of representation whose construction would be needed to bind the mainly artisanal radicalism of the 1820s to the still-emergent and far more heterogeneous collectivity of the working class as a whole. The potential solidarities of that larger working-class collectivity—the "sociological" working class already distinguishable by its relationship to production and distribution—remained heavily fragmented by differences of skill, gender, region, religion, and more. "By failing to show how these sectional differences were negotiated," Mayfield argues, "Thompson seems to reintroduce the culturally mediated dialectic between the workers' consciousness and their 'objective' condition as wage earners as the model of class formation at exactly the point where he had displaced it." In common with other critics, Mayfield suggests "that Thompson's inability to eradicate this rather orthodox Marxist dialectic between social being and consciousness is tied to the conceptual vocabulary of 'experience' running throughout his work."[74]

Thompson's own response to this problem was his very idiosyncratic, eloquently explicated, but in many ways profoundly conventional defense of the historian's craft. For him, the historical issues concerning power and social relations, as well as the social and historical constitution of politics and its class inflection, could properly be broached through an empirical practice, an empirical "idiom" requiring no extensive essays into matters of theory as such. That practice indisputably nourished historical readings and reconstructions that count among the finest examples of historical writing of the later twentieth century. Approaches to the past based on those same assumptions and procedures also sustained an immensely valuable and complex historiography, one that held the field of innovation for a generation or more, well past the immediate decade after the publication of Thompson's book. But at the same time, as we have described, those approaches were also the source for the very concepts and practices that after a surprisingly brief ascendancy became so rapidly vacated by social historians during the 1980s, sometimes coolly, sometimes with a polemical flourish. In precisely this gap, between the questions enunciated in Thompson's book and the ground preferred by his latter-day critics, we want to argue, there is a great deal of productive thinking still to be done.

In this book we want to raise the possibility of recovering a viable relationship between politics and class: a recovery that neither reduces the one to the other nor banishes class from the field of determination altogether. We want neither the kind of reduction that restores the justly discarded economistic forms of causality nor the one that makes class purely an effect of language or politics, as a purely discursive construction rather than being locatable in social structures in some analytically useful nondiscursive or prediscursive way. Our discussion addresses itself, in a restrained but firm critique of much widely accepted understanding, to the terms in which discussions of class and culture are tending these days to be formally enframed. If earlier those terms often left out politics or the public sphere as such almost entirely, these days we increasingly encounter the opposite extreme, a tendency to foreground political discourse to the exclusion of *any* explanatory contextualizing in the study of society.

So our question is really this: how are the meanings of class organized or made available at the level of the political culture and the political system, in both national and societywide as well as local contexts and ways?

ity of accurate communication by the use of language, the force of logical deduction, and the very existence of truth and falsehood.[2]

Yet elsewhere in the intellectual landscape, talk of "the postmodern" was clearly afoot. This began in the arts, where critics were increasingly aggregating various formal innovations and aesthetic departures into the framework for describing a coherent contemporary movement, most notably in fiction, poetry, painting, and architecture, but then extending by the early 1980s into film, photography, television, and the full range of the popular arts. Equally significant, an emblematic debate material-ized around publication of the French philosopher Jean-François Lyotard's *The Postmodern Condition* in 1979, which moved Jürgen Haber-mas into a major restatement of Enlightenment principles and their con-tinuing claims.[3] Beyond its specifically philosophical contents, moreover, Lyotard's book also established what became one of the hallmarks of avowedly postmodernist advocacy—namely, a grandiose claim about the overriding but now decisively ruptured historical logic of the epoch since the Enlightenment and French Revolution, counterposing the new predicament of the present against a now superseded "modernity." The meanings of this break were universalized across all the manifold spheres of life.

In this first phase of interest in postmodernism and the transitions it seemed to signify, therefore, there were perhaps two axes of discussion: one in aesthetics and the arts, centered in North America but reaching increasingly across the Atlantic to Britain; and one in philosophy, impli-cating a mainly Franco-German field of differences around the durable validity of the Enlightenment project, but likewise rapidly extending to Britain.[4] Then a key essay by Fredric Jameson boldly historicized these discourses by placing both in a common societal context of the present, finding in them "the cultural logic of late capitalism."[5] This changed the stakes of the discussion. Henceforth it migrated to the ground of what might loosely be called the culturalist left, while intersecting vitally with Marxist and other accounts of contemporary capitalist restructuring. Interest intensified during the later 1980s around three main areas. One concerned the global analysis of contemporary socioeconomic change, usually associated with arguments about a "post-Fordist transition," new regimes of "flexible accumulation," the "end of organized capitalism," or the passage to a "post-industrial age."[6] A second accompanied the early consolidation of cultural studies into a new interdisciplinary field in Britain and the United States.[7] And a third involved a series of specifically feminist critiques.[8]

Each of these discussions flared brilliantly but briefly. Of course, many of their *consequences* have perdured. Contemporary transformations in the organization of capitalism subsumed increasingly during the 1990s under rubrics of deregulation, market reform, and globalization were first extensively theorized in the works of the late 1980s mentioned previously, many of whose active insights certainly remain. The chastening of intellectual confidence in classical Western values of Enlightenment, Reason, and Progress associated with the reception of Lyotard's critique, leading to varying types of skepticism, disavowal, and irrevocable damage, has also remained. Aesthetically and culturally speaking, the distinctive postmodernist conventions—emphasizing irony, pastiche, depthlessness, fragmentation, anachronism, hybridity of forms, the effacement of differences between "high" and "low," playfulness and performativity, and so forth—have now diffused into a general sensibility, becoming arguably part of the cultural common sense. In each of these ways, the fascination for all aspects of "the postmodern" developing during the 1980s left behind a set of lasting rhetorics, which had permeated a "diverse number of vocabularies" remarkably quickly, "spread[ing] outwards from the realms of art history into political theory and onto the pages of youth culture magazines, record sleeves, and the fashion pages of *Vogue*."[9]

Over the longer term, the appeal of arguments about postmodernism also entered academic sectors that had previously been more resistant, including most notably the mainstream of sociology in the United States, where some scholars now began exploring what a "social postmodernism" might mean.[10] Yet in the central territory of cultural studies, discussion had already moved on. Earlier commitments to distinguishing a specifically postmodern *era,* which drew so much of the initial interest, seemed to dissipate, displaced by the new organizing category of globalization and perhaps by a loss of confidence on the intellectual left in the possibility of shaping the political logic of the postmodernism discussion per se. Vast quantities of work still bore the imprint of the 1980s discussions, particularly on film, television, and all areas of visual culture, on

popular reading genres, on fashion, style, and taste, on museums, mon-
uments, and memory, on tourism and traveling, on dance cultures and
performativity, and so forth. Major new specialisms have flourished
under the aegis of cultural studies in this way—race and new ethnicities,
whiteness, sexualities, masculinities, queerness, diasporas, disabilities,
and more.

But as a unifying term aspiring to hold all this together, postmodernism has patently receded, enjoying far less resonance by the end of the
1990s than, for example, "postcolonialism" and "the postcolonial."[11]
Here, the voluminous proceedings of two international conferences held
in Urbana-Champaign in 1983 and 1990 made a telling contrast: if the
first, "Marxism and the Interpretation of Culture," captured the "postmodern moment" at the point of its emergence, with a substantial section
called "The Politics of Modernity and Postmodernity," the second, "Cultural Studies," effaced that category altogether, finding no place for it
among the sixteen thematic headings under which the forty contributions
were grouped, even as the new postmodernist sensibility suffused the
overall occasion.[12]

### POSTMODERN HISTORIES

Yet, paradoxically, just as this wider discussion of "postmodernism" was
receding, historians discovered the term. This could be seen first, perhaps, in the widespread and often ill-informed aversion against the
spread of French poststructuralism and its distinctive rhetorics of theory,
so that by the later 1980s seldom a seminar or conference could pass
without snide remarks against "discourse." Similarly, while some were
certainly taking him seriously, few names could polarize a room of historians as rapidly as Michel Foucault.[13] Amid this gathering contentious-
ness, "postmodernism" became an all-purpose term of disapproval. At
the 1994 American Historical Association Annual Meeting, in a paper
titled "Bismarck in a Postmodern World," for example, Kenneth Barkin
likened the resultant tensions to the gangland enmities of Crips and
Bloods in LA, with scholarly buzzwords ("discourse," "constructed")
standing in for the wearing of colors. He then proceeded to parody the
obscurantism and impenetrable language he attributed to postmodernism, while charging it with out-and-out relativism, nihilism, hostility

to history's evidentiary practices, and "hypersubjectivism," not to speak of a provenance in fascist trains of thought.

> The concept of the universal is rejected; truth is culture-specific. Natural law and natural rights go down the drain. The Enlightenment, we are told, turned human emancipation into universal oppression. Because history is not referential, knowledge is impossible. . . . All consensual standards of truth, justice, and ethics are challenged. . . . Reason, we learn, led to Auschwitz, to environmental pollution as well as to inequality and racism. The concept of objectivity is a device of the powerful to prevent the dispossessed from taking power.[14]

For historians like Barkin, clearly, "postmodernism" spelled trouble. It named a source of endangerment. The discipline was under siege from ideas inimical to history's calling, they seemed to be saying.[15] British historian Gertrude Himmelfarb was especially angry, denouncing postmodern epistemology as a cynical politicizing of history driven by "a denial of the fixity of the past, of the reality of the past apart from what the historian chooses to make of it." Postmodernists, she said, rejected any idea "of an objective truth about the past."[16] But these hostile usages of the term "postmodernism" were hopelessly nonspecific. They lumped together all sorts of disparate views, conflating not only the philosophy of Lyotard and the ideas of Foucault but also a falsely homogenized "poststructuralism" and a range of contemporary trends in the humanities to which historians like Himmelfarb were opposed, including everything from feminism and multiculturalism to types of iconoclasm and playfulness, some of whose participants may have subscribed to recognizably "postmodernist" outlooks, but many of whom did not.

Hostile simplifier in chief was Lawrence Stone. Incorrigibly self-confident in his misunderstandings, yet ever ready with a haughty *pronunciamento* on the defense of history's integrity, Stone published a brief "Note" of breathtaking naïveté in *Past and Present* under the title "History and Post-Modernism," in the text of which he managed never to mention the offending term itself. Instead, he rallied historians to the barricades against three enemies in particular, who presumably composed the threatening postmodernist phalanx: first "linguistics" and especially Jacques Derrida's theories of deconstruction, then "cultural and symbolic anthropology," and finally "New Historicism" in literary studies. Historians needed to pay attention, Stone warned, because as a result of "these rumblings from adjacent disciplines" history was fast "on the way to becoming an endangered species."[17]

To sort out the confusions perpetrated by these overheated interventions, some disaggregating is needed. In fact, most of the ideas excoriated by critics like Stone or Barkin were more aptly considered under the heading of poststructuralism, although that too could easily be inflated into an artificially unified entity. More than any other single text, probably, Joan Scott's 1986 article "Gender: A Useful Category of Historical Analysis" was responsible for opening historians to the possible uses of Foucault and other poststructuralists, although a more general quickening of interest was also unmistakable around that time.[18] Scott focused on the relationship between knowledge and power, on the constitutive role of power for social relations, on critiques of the rationally acting (male) subject of the Enlightenment, on the constructedness and decenteredness of identities, on instabilities of meaning rather than fixities, on the making of meaning via exclusions, and on the necessary incompleteness of the desire for coherence, all in the interests of a putative theory of gender. This also entailed a pronounced *turning away* from earlier structuralisms, in what Jane Caplan called "the refusal of totalization and binarism, the affirmation of decentering and multiplicity."[19] For Scott, this meant a fundamental review of history's epistemological standing.

> Such a reflexive, self-critical approach makes apparent the particularistic status of any historical knowledge and the historian's active role as a producer of knowledge. It undermines claims for authority based on totalizing explanations, essentialized categories of analysis (be they human nature, race, class, sex, or "the oppressed"), or synthetic narratives that assume an inherent unity for the past.[20]

It was this foundational questioning of the historian's practice—or more exactly, of history's relationship to the past—that now attracted the "postmodernist" tag, rather than Scott's more specific proposals for the study of gender, power, and the making of subjectivities. In neither the original 1986 article nor Scott's subsequent book did postmodernism per se figure as an operative category. It was made into one when the stridency of the traditionalist critics clashed with the emergent advocacy of a small number of self-described partisans who started seeing themselves severally as an aspiring avant-garde.[21] Leading voices among the latter numbered the Dutch philosopher Frank Ankersmit; intellectual historian turned philosopher of language Hans Kellner; nineteenth-century British historian Patrick Joyce; U.S. intellectual historian Robert Berkhofer; and two British historiographers, Alun Munslow and Keith Jenkins.[22] By the later 1990s a critical mass of work had accrued, including a notable series of exchanges in the journals *Past and Present, Social History, Journal of Contemporary History,* and *History and Theory,* together with various anthologies and general guides. Then in 1997 two countervailing initiatives brought controversy to a head: a new mouthpiece, *Rethinking History: The Journal of Theory and Practice,* was launched capturing the critical momentum; and Richard J. Evans published a book-length polemic defending history against "the onslaught of postmodern theory."[23]

Where do these developments leave us? Clearly, a sizable body of publication sympathetic to postmodernism has now amassed. Yet the actual numbers of entirely convinced epistemological postmodernists almost certainly remains quite small. Rather few historians have warmed to the purist advocacy evinced by Ankersmit or Jenkins, to the Olympian skepticism of a Berkhofer, or to the polemical incautions of a Joyce. Historians' receptiveness has not been encouraged by the highly abstract terms in which postmodernist advocacy is delivered. Moreover, most of the relevant discussions have been conducted by historiographers, theorists, and indeed nonhistorians by disciplinary affiliation.[24] Whereas the editors of *Rethinking History* and other journals—including the flagship journal of the U.S. profession, the *American Historical Review*—have fostered much experimental writing in response to postmodern historiographical exhortations, the most substantial demonstrations in practice remain those of intellectual historians and historiographers. There materialized very few book-length or monographic examples showing what a postmodern history might mean.[25]

But if the meanings of the postmodernist challenge are to be distilled, we would argue, current advocacy of its most drastic philosophical entailments (which can easily be construed into the absolute relativism, nihilism, and hypersubjectivism alleged by Barkin and Stone) needs to be matched by more workable proposals with clearer connection to what most bona fide historians actually do. For when the postmodern maxi-malists declare history in its given forms to be obsolete, or pronounce the "impossibility" of history in its empirical-analytical mode, they are self-evidently misdescribing present circumstances, in which large quantities of successful, satisfying, and sometimes inspiring historical scholarship continue to be produced and read. In saying this, we have no wish to dis-miss or deflect the importance of questioning the grounds of any of that given scholarship, which the critiques of historiographers like Berkhofer and Munslow have brought under properly searching review. But there is something askew and attenuated—and ultimately ineffectual—in a cri-tique that in its positive outcomes appears to license only a new version of the history of ideas and so far seems only to accumulate in ever more abstruse historiographical strictures against what historians should *not* be able to do.

It thus seems unsatisfying and evasive—and perhaps a little pompously disingenuous—for Keith Jenkins to argue that the characteristics of "postmodern histories" cannot be described in advance of them actually being produced: "For if postmodern histories are 'histories of the future,' are histories 'which have not yet been,' then they are clearly not yet in existence."[26] The proof of the pudding is in the eating, we might just as well say. Postmodernist critiques *do* and *should* make a difference, we believe, both to the manner in which professional historians go about their business and to the ways in which their labors circulate for a wider public. But unless the critics can exemplify these consequences by means of the concrete grappling with particular problems of the past that still forms the mundane justification for the historian's distinct professional existence, then most working historians will simply go about their busi-ness much as before. More to the point, the even larger majority of non-historians in the wider citizenry will find no compelling reason to stop reading or listening to them, or to cease seeing them as the legitimate voice of that distinct profession mainly entrusted with the job of render-ing the past for the wider purposes of the societal and political present. If postmodern historiographers are to realize their ambition—if they are actually to *change* the culture of the profession—then both these fronts need practical attention: not only the given practices of working histori-ans, but also their acceptance by the largest part of the interested public.

History's presence, after all, is to be encountered not only in its institutional order as a discipline, but also in the pedagogies of its societal diffusion via schools, universities, media, party politics, governmentality, and other forms of publicness, and in the subtle, direct, blatant, and disguised articulations between the knowledge that historians produce and the varying contexts of local dailiness and larger national life. Given all these manifestations of history's already constituted presence as a discursive formation, it is simply naive to expect many practicing historians to agree with the drastic epistemological consequences of a full-scale postmodernist critique, whose terms in any case remain legitimately contested and in some cases genuinely problematic. In light of this actual diversity of historical practice, amid which the out-and-out postmodernists remain one of the smaller minorities, we would argue, there are good grounds for trying to begin the conversation closer to the places where intelligent and successful practitioners—including the most self-reflexive and theoretically sophisticated among them—are tending to think. Short of driving one's opponents from the seminar rooms and banning their books, sharp epistemological, theoretical, and temperamental differences will in any case always persist; and whether for practical and "strategic" reasons or for principled ones, some pluralist and respectful acknowledgment of those differences, if only in "a pragmatics of good faith," as we called it on a previous occasion, makes eminently good sense.[27]

## WHAT DIFFERENCE DOES POSTMODERNISM MAKE?

In the interests of such a conversation, accordingly, the following seem to us the usable consequences of a postmodernist critique.

First and foremost, that critique properly problematizes history's relationship to the past, meaning both the particular pasts involved in any historian's investigations and the generic past of previous time. Likewise, it problematizes the past of the discipline per se. In opposing older ideals of objectivity, postmodernists also reject the working assumption they ascribe to other historians that the past is graspable in some accurate, truthful, and putatively authoritative and final way. They dispute, too, the associated belief that the accumulation of knowledge brings us progressively closer to the past's "true view." They also seem to question the efficacy of the historian's accepted evidentiary practices in that regard, namely, the sifting and evaluating of sources, the checking, corroborating, and falsifying of facts, the building of interpretations by inference and argument, and the process of contextualizing all of this in relation to the rest of scholarship. While procedurally necessary to the historian's craft, postmodernists say, these practices are ultimately vitiated by their failure to accept the contingency and partiality of the sources and facts in play, which are less the phenomenal traces of a "real past" waiting to be uncovered or reconstructed than the artifacts of the historian's own design.

In the further unfolding of this argument, unfortunately, there has been much scope for artful misunderstanding, as neither postmodernists nor their enemies show much reluctance to caricature the other's views. Thus postmodernists delight in attacking any naive belief that works of history can directly reproduce or correspond to the real world of the past. They insist that the archive provides no direct access to the past, that documents contain no straightforward transmissions of meaning, and that no originary coherence of those meanings is retrievable by historians, however experienced and skilled. Understandably irked, such "naive" historians then hit back. They accuse their critics of abandoning all sense of a past that actually existed, of making history equivalent to fiction, and of surrendering the ability to distinguish reliably founded interpretations from those that are invented.

People holding the extreme versions of these ascribed standpoints on either side may doubtless be found. But the actual practice of historians reveals a far more complex multiplicity of positions than such a stark polarity allows. For example, the usefulness and probity of the historian's evidentiary practices, indeed their continuing *necessity* if persuasive and reliable histories can ever be written, are far less seriously at issue for most of those embracing the logic of postmodernist critique than the nature of the guarantees those practices are supposed to provide. For rather than allowing historians to reconstruct the past in some objectively truthful way, reflecting its meanings directly, such postmodernists would say, those practices can only do their work of assemblage by means of an active process of construction. Only through *that* process—through the interventions of historians, that is—can the raw materials of the past be made into evidence. By their work of selecting, adjudicating, discarding, and inferring, historians translate evidence into "facts." More generally, they bring order into the plenitude of the past's disorderly traces. There is no order to the past as such *before* the historian begins that labor of producing coherence—unless it derives from the preceding presence of earlier historians, that is, or for that matter from the anterior processes of construction that brought such materials to the archive in the first place.[28]

The best history has *always* presumed some version of this recognition, as opponents of postmodernism have been quick to point out. Yet it seems churlish and self-deceiving not to admit that we owe to postmodernist critiques a far more open, thoroughgoing, and self-aware airing of the problem.[29] Thus between "the past" as the object of study, which historians seek to appropriate in the form of knowledge, and "history" (as the stories, analyses, and representations produced about the past) are interposed two necessary and inescapable barriers: on the one hand, the "archive," or all the stuff and matter that can be turned into "facts" and "evidence"; and on the other hand, the historian's interventions, which impart to that stuff and matter coherent narrative or interpretive form. That is, the past can be made knowable only through an active process of construction, which shapes not only the resulting interpretations, but even the evidence and documentation on which the latter have to be based. This mediating and constructive agency of the historian is managed through language, through the operative analytical categories, and through the entire cognitive apparatus historians bring to their study. The "real past" is not a figment of our imagination, even though the more extreme postmodernists imply that it would make no difference if it was. But *that* past is simply not reachable or self-evident as such. In Munslow's words: "The past did exist, but does not have meaning until the historian writes it as history." Furthermore, given "the absence of a direct correspondence to the reality of the past, the way in which history is interpreted and reported as a narrative is of primary importance to the acquisition and character of our historical knowledge."[30]

Thus postmodernist historians properly insist on the difference between the past traces of an earlier time (the past-as-history) and the labors of reconstruction that inscribe those traces with meaning (history-as-knowledge). The one is never attainable *except* by the mediation of the other, and consequently the knowledge history delivers can only ever be partial, provisional, and decisively prefigured by the historian's complex particularities of outlook. The latter derive not only from the historian's professional standpoint, technical skills and training, and a host of historiographical and disciplinary factors, but also from political and intellectual situatedness, ethical choices, and other forms of subjectivity. This immediately points us to a second and associated consequence of the postmodernist critique, therefore, namely, the serious qualification of the historian's claims to be an "objective" or disinterested observer.

This is partly a matter of the means by which historians bring order to the past, which are always already shaped by conscious and unconscious choices, as well as by disciplinary protocols, practices, and frameworks repeating themselves beyond any individual historian's immediate volition. Accordingly, far more attention needs paying, Munslow argues, to "the full implications of how we prefigure history by trope and emplotment (not to mention argument, gender, ethnocultural, or ideological preferences)." That means facing up to "the consequences of the fact that history is generated through the imposition by historians of a personally chosen narrative form on the past."[31] Recognizing this severely undercuts one of the discipline's classic expectations, Munslow continues, which has always demanded "a necessary distance between knower and known in writing the past-as-history." Even more, it levels "a philosophical challenge to the modernist notion that understanding emanates from a center—the independent knowledge-centered subject which we designate variously as the evidence, or the author, or Man."[32] This challenge scarcely disempowers the author, we might aver, as opposed to providing far more license for authors to put themselves inside the text and thereby acquire for themselves a new and visible centrality. But it does compromise or at least complicate the author's claim to disinterested expertise and objective standing. More important, it opens the way for multiple standpoints. Because the past cannot be definitively reclaimed or reconstructed, and the past's totality is irrecoverable, our access to understanding will necessarily remain "partial, provisional, and to 'some degree idiosyncratic.' "[33]

If we put these first two ideas together—the irrecoverable remoteness of the past (its necessary nonidentity with history) and its fashioning into history by the historian's manufacture of coherence (the writing of "the past" into "history" by the shaping of narrative)—then we get a third consequence of postmodernist critiques, namely, the growing attention now being paid to the specifically literary qualities of historical work. The key early influence here, of course, was Hayden White, whose *Metahistory* argued that all works of history, even when adhering single-mindedly to the rules of evidence, standards of objectivity, and a "scientific" method, are constructed nonetheless around predictable narratological forms, drawing on finite modes of argumentation, types of emplotment, ideological frames, and rhetorical tropes. If White thereby faced objectivist historiography with the moral and aesthetic principles implicitly organizing its own production, literary deconstructionists associated with Jacques Derrida and Paul de Man then radicalized this challenge, separating texts even further from the intentions of authors while opening them to multiple possible readings. Deconstruction pushed the indeterminacy of meanings as far as it could go, that is, to the point of "undecidability."

During the 1990s under Joan Scott's influence, modest and eclectic versions of a deconstructive approach became widely adopted among historians. Ideas of "textuality" encouraged an interpretive approach to historical studies of ever more generalized applicability. History came to be regarded more and more commonly as a corpus of texts made by historians about the past, while the past itself became conceived increasingly in analogous fashion—as an "archive" available for "reading" by the same kinds of techniques. This was where the wider panoply of related influences—"new historicism" and other forms of literary theory, linguistic analysis of various sorts from semiotics to Bakhtin, psychoanalytic theory, film theory, the revival of a textually based intellectual history under the influence of Dominick LaCapra and others, and the burgeoning fields of cultural studies—also came in. Converging in a similar place was the long-running inspiration of Clifford Geertz, whose 1973 essay "Ideology as a Cultural System" had invariably jostled Edward Thompson in the footnotes of those social historians seeking a nonreductionist approach to cultural analysis. As U.S. anthropology negotiated its own linguistic turn during the 1980s, finally, embracing forms of "postmodern ethnography" while cleaving ever more reflexively to the narrative ordering of the experienced world, new collaborations between history and anthropology became added to the mix.

In the course of this reimagining of the discipline, "society" became displaced from its centerground. Indeed, for many whose thinking was influenced by this ferment, history became recentered instead around "texts." Further, this occurred just as everything entailed in the work of interpretation was being called radically into question: the transformation of literary studies during the 1980s under the impact of deconstruction problematized both the very category of the text and the older practices of reading and writing. Moving away from questions of authorial intention and rejecting the chimera of any singular or authoritative interpretation, literary theorists now stressed the text's necessary openness, its multiplicity of attainable meanings. For many historians, too, some modified or pragmatic version of the basic program of deconstruction implied by this development—at its simplest, "a reading which involves seizing upon [a text's] inconsistencies and contradictions to break up the idea of a unified whole"—was becoming commonplace.[34]

This was not incompatible with keeping a due sense of the contextual, as an external realm of significance *beyond* that of the text itself. Indeed, any social historian was likely to heed the continuing claims of externality, at least in the form of Raymond Williams's notion of determination as the setting of limits, or what Derrida called "the diachronic overdetermination of the context" or the "constitutive outside."[35] In gaining the benefit of a deconstructive method, in varying degrees of flexibility or rigor, historians have usually sought to combine it with the two classic modes of contextualizing, which carry the analysis not only *back* to the sites of the text's production, but also *out* to the complex processes that construct and translate its meanings. For an essential part of explaining what any particular text might mean is the task of understanding how it works. Grappling with those complexities requires the very opposite of any narrowly "textual" approach focusing only on language in the esoteric and technical literary sense; rather, one might argue, it calls upon all the well-tried methods of the social historian too. As Tony Bennett put this at an early stage of such discussions, with the characteristic Gramscian inflection of British cultural studies, "The text is a site on which varying meanings and effects may be produced according to the determinations within which the work is inscribed—determinations that are never single and given but plural and contested, locked in relations of struggle."[36] As already suggested, this mode of analysis has been increasingly extended from written texts in the more conventional sense to all manner of documents, and beyond them to practices, relationships, and events as well.

In effect, textuality has become a general form of description for the interpretable world.

Fourth, postmodernists proceed axiomatically from the demise of an older model of causality understood as social explanation. Their thinking breaks decisively with the structuralist analytic of Marxism and other materialist sociologies that, as we saw, were constitutive for the great popularity of social history between the 1960s and 1980s. At the most minimal this proposes a complex and nondetermined, contingent and unpredictable relationship between social conditions and material life, on the one hand, and the production of meaning and profession of ideas, on the other. Culture is set free from economy, politics from social life. Rather than being simply abstractions from social realities that objectively structure the experienced world of practices and beliefs, as "base" supports "superstructure," accordingly, categories like "family," "individual," "state," and "society" need themselves to be treated as constructed and malleable. In this perspective, moreover, such categories are seen to be acting on social circumstances to shape them rather than merely reflecting any pregiven social facts. In the words of two self-avowed sociological postmodernists, those categories should be regarded "as historically emergent rather than naturally given, as multivalent rather than unified in meaning, and as the frequent result and possible present instrument in struggles for power."[37]

Here the lines of postmodernist critique blur toward the broader poststructuralist challenge. The same is true of the fifth point which this immediately raises concerning agency. As we saw, social historians tended to engage matters of agency mainly through studies of collective action theorized in terms of class, grounded in political economy or sociologies of work and community, and linked in the more Marxist notations to theories of class belonging and class consciousness resulting in action. But under postmodernist dispensation, this centering of collective agency around class falls. Agency can no longer be traceable to the materialities of class position and class experience in that way. Possibilities for politics are not to be read off from an account of class and its social relations, however subtle and sophisticated the investigation: continuities of political affiliation can no longer be projected around class as the sovereign actor. Nor does agency conceptualized in terms of class converge to political action in the way social historians liked to presume. Partly, a new constellation of movements, sometimes called identitarian, has emerged from the shadow of the old class-based hegemonies now that the latter's unifying and universalizing claims have dissolved. Partly, the instabilities of the categories associated with the older politics also open a space for imagining political subjectivities differently. If the modern subject was supposedly centered, unified, coherent, rational, and masculine, then its postmodern decentering implies fragmentation, multiplicity, fracturing, and all the complexities inscribed by difference. Cut loose from the old class-derived big battalions, the argument runs, progressive political potentials are now to be found in the margins, in the forms and dynamics of subalternity, in queerness, in minority discourse, and above all in feminism and postcoloniality.

Of course, in principle none of these insights—contrary to the pronouncements and prescriptions of the most extreme postmodernists themselves—precludes continuing to talk about class, political economy, the social relations of production, the social distribution of inequalities, or any other feature of capitalism as an economic system and associated social formation in a variety of ways. Furthermore, those ways will certainly not be restricted to the historiography of how the categories came to be used or the intellectual histories of how they came to be constructed and understood. No less than in the past, they will provide necessary analytical instruments for substantive social inquiry. Reaffirming this becomes especially pertinent in light of the final aspect of postmodernist critique we want to cite, namely, Lyotard's celebrated dictum regarding the end of all grand narratives—that is, his linking of postmodernity to a loss of conviction in the universalizing and progressivist metanarratives of human improvement we take from the Enlightenment. Whether we associate those grand ideas of forward historical movement with specific philosophical-political traditions such as Marxism or liberalism, or with broader ideals like the triumph of science over nature, the rise of the working class, or the emancipation of women, it seems clear that during the last quarter century an older belief in history's directionality has become severely damaged in its persuasiveness.[38] Master concepts such as class or the Industrial Revolution that did vital service for social history in its heyday have likewise now become seriously impaired.

Producing self-consciousness in this respect—making us far more self-aware about the directions and developmental logics we impute to the histories we write and teach in our various national and analytical fields, or about the deeper-set assumptions we bring epistemologically to the understanding of historicity per se—has been one of the most telling results of postmodernist critique. We may doubt the prevalence any more of the simpler versions of that recourse to grand interpretive design. But as soon as we open an undergraduate survey text, peruse a syllabus, or deconstruct the curriculum, or for that matter examine our own practice in the classroom, it becomes rapidly apparent that grand narratological thinking has not been quite so easy to escape. In the more mundane contexts of discussion—in the seminar room or at the dinner table, for instance, or in the bus queue or the bar, and for a favored few of our colleagues in the television studio or the Op-Ed piece—such recourse is exceedingly hard to avoid. Moreover, in the middle range of such thinking, national histories are replete with instances of powerful analytical figures that structure our long-range thinking, shaping the kinds of questions we think to ask and those we don't—like the rise of Nazism, the events of 1933, and the place of the Holocaust in German history, for example, or the rise of the British Labour Party in the early twentieth century, or the breakdown of czarism in 1917, and so forth. Attainment of greater sensitivity to the consequences of such historio- graphical patterning, of the choices entailed by one interpretive design as opposed to another, remains an unqualified good.

On the other hand, the suggestion that we might ever want to forgo the use of large-scale concepts incorporating claims about the character of societal change across time, or that in the diverse practical settings of political, pedagogic, and everyday discourse it could ever be feasible to do so, seems to us a sign of either willful denial or naïveté. We say this not least because in the two decades accompanying the intellectual pop- ularity of Lyotard's critique, a new set of grand narratives has been patently remaking the social and political environment required for the flourishing of really existing capitalism—meaning not just the end of the Cold War, the dissolution of the Soviet Union, the erasure of socialism as a viable political project, and the triumph of neoliberalism, but also the new geopolitical grand narratives of globalization now saturating the public sphere, not to speak of the unfurling of the U.S. Middle Eastern and Central Asian imperium. In light of these destructive consequences, it seems to us, eschewing the use of the large-scale concepts commensurate with any effective contesting of these developments would amount to a shocking abdication.

Here, though, let us not forget the main thrust of Lyotard's own proposal. After all, this was not only advanced to refute the unifying coherence of the great universalizing visions of humanity's rise in the past, or by extension the totalizing claims of any single "great story" in a particular society's official or collective representation of its own past. In principle, we should remember, Lyotard also sought to expose precisely the multiplication of *different* narratives. Although the range of possible histories may display an incommensurable diversity incapable of being gathered coherently into any single all-encompassing story, this insight hardly prevents us from reconstructing their respective logics of development and coherence, or even from arguing carefully but forcefully for the virtues of some of these narratives over others.

### HISTORY AND EPISTEMOLOGY

This exposition of postmodernist thinking has been truncated and episodic, we freely admit, and a far more elaborate exegesis would be needed for each of our points to fall better into place. Much else might be added. Postmodernism's broad intellectual incitements were certainly part of the mix moving historians toward new subject matters, new approaches, and new forms of cross-disciplinary collaboration during the 1990s. Many of the new areas are now very familiar—the turning of gender studies toward masculinity; the flourishing of the history of sexuality; studies of taste, style, and consumption; work on every form of visual culture; histories of leisure, tourism, and entertainment; histories of medicine, psychology, and psychiatry; histories of the body; histories of emotions; histories of subjectivity. The relationship of history to memory and all the associated social and cultural practices has drawn a huge amount of interest, as have the possibilities of everyday life and microhistory. All of these areas required intensive borrowings and cooperation with the relevant other disciplines. We are aware of all these areas and honor them, but dealing with them directly would outgrow the scope of our more modest purposes here.

In this chapter, we have tried to take stock of a key aspect of the so-

called culture wars in the discipline, which consumed so much of our collective time and energy from the end of the 1980s. The postmodernist
critique of historiography took shape around that time as one leading
edge of the rise of the "new cultural history" that proved so unsettling for
the given practice of social history and its core reliance on the category of
class. For while the cultural turn was decisive in allowing many social historians to escape from what they had come to regard as the impasse of a
materialist epistemology, the consequences carried many of them
beyond the old materialist frameworks altogether. Others, including a
major contingent working in labor history and the social history of the
working class, chose to reject the culturalist challenge, instead digging
themselves in behind the established materialist paradigm. As should be
clear by now, our own view is definitely that as a result of all the intervening critique this former ground of the social history of the 1970s has
ceased to be available. Indeed, if we want to understand the challenges
now facing any further use of the class concept, whether for social history
purposes or for politics, the damage inflicted by the last two decades of
poststructuralist critique needs to be honestly admitted.[39]

The urgency of this argument becomes all the greater given the vigor
with which the Thompsonian approach to a class-based social history has
been defended.[40] There is no need yet again to explicate the extensive literatures of response and counterresponse that the relevant debates accumulated, as the participants can now be left perfectly well to speak for
themselves. In Marc Steinberg's apt characterization, the approach associated with Thompson involved "a modernist grand narrative of class that
provided the foundation for the new social history." Each of the elements
diagnosed by the postmodernist critique discussed here can then be readily found: "Falsely predicated on a unified view of the social, agency and
identity were directly imputed from an overarching social structure,
which itself contained a teleological motor for social change, i.e., class
conflict founded in relations of production."[41] In effect, Thompson's
influence comprised the "modernist" history that the postmodernist critique logically presumed.

Such a modernism seemed to insist that the world is knowable, providing the historian proceeded by reasoning, by "listening" to the
sources, and by accumulating all the appropriate evidence.[42] True
knowledge emerges from rational reflection and meticulous research.

Epistemologically speaking, Thompson seemed to base this claim to knowability on an inductive natural-science model of research proudly deriving from an Enlightenment tradition, one emphasizing apprenticeship, empirical accumulation, verification, orderly reflectiveness, and paradigm. If true to the historian's disciplinary calling in this sense, or the historian's "craft," to use Marc Bloch's preferred term, Marxists and non-Marxists would be doing history in exactly the same way, Thompson believed. The historian's scholarly procedures were thus fixed and permanent, more or less transcending historical time, requiring an obligatory and painstaking attention to the rules. There was but one road to true knowledge, which led through the archive. Thompson's reflex of destructive polemics had precisely this source: Perry Anderson was wrong, Richard Johnson was wrong, Louis Althusser was wrong, but not so much because of this or that particular error of fact and interpretation, rather because their fundamental points of departure were illegitimate and misconceived. This, then, was the modernism behind Thompson's work: with appropriate training, appropriate empirical materials, and the right epistemological mind-set, the important histories could be truthfully told.

The postmodernist critics discussed in this chapter successfully problematized that model of the production of knowledge, and for us their critique now measures out the difficulties with the Thompsonian approach: history cannot be done on that earlier basis any more. But to banish with the epistemology all the conceptual elements composing the analysis—meaning, in the broad tradition influenced by Thompson, class, class formation, class relations, class conflict, even class struggle—does not follow at all. Simply to dispose in this fashion of the outcome of a method because we no longer endorse the epistemological grounds of its production as knowledge would be to proceed in the most essentializing of ways. To do so would be to say: only that knowledge provided by methods of which we approve can be brought into the canon of the acceptable.[43]

Yet the legitimate and fruitful use of concepts does not require the observance of this sort of strict philosophical foundationalism. Rather than having to swallow the whole package of method, assumptions, and findings in a particular case, we ought to be able to pick and choose. With due attention to critical historiography, we can take what we want and leave the rest—not randomly or whimsically, nor as an uncontrolled relativism, but in ways that might serve our contemporary methodological and substantive needs, as well as keeping open the dialectical conversation with previous historical writing. We can still talk about class without embracing the entirety of the Thompsonian universe. Merely by talking about class, we are not committing ourselves to Marx's account of how class arises in history, still less to any expectations that the working class will be always and everywhere the bearer of a better and freer world.

Here we follow the argument of Judith Butler in a number of recent writings, which specifically uphold the importance of continuing to use conceptual terms strategically or pragmatically, notwithstanding the lack of "a full and grounded philosophical account" of what they might mean for all applicable purposes. As she says, "terms do not need to be foundational in order to be used": a category like "the social," while contested and in many respects in recession since the 1980s in this larger philosophical sense, remains useful "precisely because it carries a historical resonance and because it opens up a certain notion of transformation and change," and (we might add) because it remains completely embedded in the public and everyday languages of politics.[44] Historiographically it also remains unavoidable. We may withdraw from the older conception of society as a fully integrated totality, that is, whether in its Marxist or other sociological versions, without vacating analysis of the social altogether.

Thus to engage the social in that spirit is not to succumb to the myopia of materialism. The pursuit of social history does not in itself restore the social and the economic to priority in a structural sense. Nor does an older and no longer workable model of unified social totality have to be reinstated. It may well be, as Nikolas Rose suggests, that "society" in its older sense of entities that were "discrete, bounded, and territorialized (usually by the nation-state) . . . with their own kind of relatively uniform culture, mores, family forms, patterns of socialization, and so forth," no longer exists.[45] "Society" and a "social vocabulary" may no longer be the best way of describing "all the forces and processes that bind human beings together beyond their individuality and their family relations."[46] But that does not prevent us, in carefully historicized ways, from specifying the distinct fields of ideas, relations, and practices through which "the social" can acquire presence or become imagined, instated, and performed. As we shall see, the same also goes for "class."

So where does this leave us? The postmodernist critique of history's guiding assumptions we have described loses none of its indispensable importance. But in many ways, we feel, by the time historians started borrowing its slogans, postmodernism per se had turned into a gigantic red herring. As a disorderly portmanteau concept, it now conflated and confused too many different motifs together. For one thing, the field of antinomies postulated with modernism and modernity was certainly falsely or incompletely historicized, as many of postmodernism's much-vaunted aesthetic, philosophical, and cultural innovations were patently anticipated in the supposedly superseded moment of modernism between the earlier fin de siècle and the 1920s. In another direction, moreover, many of the claims made for a postmodernist history belong more properly to poststructuralism, especially the attention to language and the problematizing of the relationship between knowledge and power, but also the questioning of agency and the general challenge to meaning posed by deconstruction. In these ways, advocates like Patrick Joyce did their own program a disservice by adopting a term that in their opponents' usage was already question-begging and diversionary, crudely occluding the needed specifics of meaning.[47] Otherwise, by the mid-1990s the high-water mark of postmodernism as a general move-ment of social and cultural theory had long since past.

However, this has not stopped a small number of maximalists from continuing to radicalize their claims. For the most self-conscious "post-modernist historians" like Keith Jenkins, the relationship of epistemology to history has become curiously oppositional. Applied really rigorously, they argue, epistemological critique disallows most of what the working historian takes for granted. It dissolves the foundations that conventional historians need in order to do what they do. Indeed, in their view history in its given disciplinary forms, summarized here as a "modernism," *has* no epistemological grounds. History, no less than God, is dead. Jenkins holds that history's claims to larger meaning are vitiated by the collapse of "the flawed experiment of modernity" and the associated foundational thinking of the Enlightenment; that history's claims and procedures are wholly equivalent to those of a literary genre; and that history is there-fore entirely reducible to historiography.[48]

History, in this view, becomes a purely "self-referencing concept" or a "name given to the things historians make, i.e., historiography." Likewise, the academic discipline of history is "merely the mythologizing way of legitimating a particular approach to the past *as if* it were the way that the past itself prefers to be read." Yet, ironically enough, this understanding proceeds from a foundationalist axiom of Jenkins's own—"that we live, and have always lived, amidst social formations that have no legitimating ontological, epistemological, methodological, or ethical grounds for our beliefs or actions beyond the status of an ultimately self-referencing, rhetorical conversation."[49] In fact, Jenkins claims, apparently predicating his case on an argument about the explanatory determinations exercised by the actually existing world, the postmodernist standpoint is simply "given" by our inescapable conditions of being in the world.

> Today we live within the general condition of *postmodernity*. We do not have a choice about this. For postmodernity is not an "ideology" or a position we can choose to subscribe to or not; postmodernity is precisely our condition: it is our fate.[50]

There is no space here for a fully developed discussion, but in general it is hard not to be troubled by such prescriptiveness and its tonalities. We reject both the sovereignty of epistemology that this maximalist standpoint seems to imply and the particular narrowing of possible epistemologies that in practice it seems willing to undertake. For, as postmodernists like Jenkins also have to acknowledge, in the practicing world of historians history can actually be attached to a range of possible epistemologies. Furthermore, each of these will continue generating knowledge adequate to the procedures used and the questions asked. Even if we accept the absolute demarcation between various "modernist" epistemologies on the one hand and "postmodernist" ones on the other, there seems no basis beyond the oddly normative assertion of the inescapability of the "postmodern condition" to constitute the latter's superiority.[51] So far, moreover, postmodernist history's actual practitioners are still confined to a small self-styled avant-garde of authors who produce highly abstract, extremely esoteric, and increasingly repetitive meditations on the historical works of others. For those of us wishing to ask other kinds of questions, this is not yet very helpful.

Freed of its realist and objectivist ballast, according to Jenkins, history is now available to do the historian's bidding. As representation of the past, it can fulfill or perform whatever sophisticated purposes we choose to demand of it. Both Jenkins and Munslow are admirably clear and forthright about the ethics entailed by this process and the opportunities it delivers to the historian. Yet there is also a certain aggrandizement and presumption in this stance. Bringing ethical questions to one's historical writing does not require a postmodernist perspective. Ethics can shape and guide a variety of historiographies. An ethics of acting consciously and responsibly in the world, guided by a pedagogy and a seriousness of purpose, with the aims of "making a difference," is not the prerogative of a postmodernist sensibility or understanding, contrary to what Jenkins and Munslow often seem to imply. Marxisms of various kinds, other kinds of socialism, humanisms, feminisms, and so forth, all of which retain some footing of various kinds on the ground now dismissed as "modernism," also approach historical work with an ethical purpose, as of course do many liberalisms and conservatisms.

It may well be that in the end there is no history, and that instead there are only historians trying to do the best they can. But that "best" is still an important endeavor, one that produces knowledge founded upon collectively agreed-upon protocols and procedures, one that is organized around the fashioning of meaningful questions, and one that has definite effects in the world. This last point is especially pertinent. For the knowledge produced by historians resonates and articulates with other knowledges, some of which exercise more power than others, and some of which are hegemonic. Unless we participate in the process of shaping that wider field of knowledges, we irresponsibly vacate the space to those who want to control it. Deciding not to participate is certainly one's right. It is even very good there are some like Jenkins who want to opt out and question the very basis of the process itself. But for our own part we would like to continue finding the ways modestly to make a difference.

# IV.  MATERIALISM & DISAVOWAL
## From the Social to the Cultural?

We first began writing about class in the early 1990s, after a long period of debate among social historians, sociologists, and scholars in many other fields, through which the concept's usefulness had fallen seriously into question. In the heyday of social history's self-confidence between the 1960s and 1980s, of course, class had been an indispensable term of analysis, part of the generalized common sense of the field, a master category even. During that period its explanatory purchase had acquired two vital dimensions, each founded in the sovereign materialism anchoring the social historian's basic sensibility. On the one hand, social historians perceived and pursued those logics of social coalescence accompanying processes of capitalist industrialization, which brought the working class into being as a distinctive social formation. Then on the other hand, they ascribed to working-class formation a further logic of cultural solidarity, which allowed popular political affiliations to be predicted and explained. Beginning in the early 1980s, however, and for all the complex reasons discussed in our first two chapters—growing partly from the cumulative logic of intellectual inquiry among social historians themselves, but also through intense interactions with wider theoretical debates and the surrounding political developments—both these uses of the class concept encountered problems of growing severity.

In any of the attempts to make sense of this intellectual history, including our own first two chapters, Edward Thompson's influence has invariably been at the center. This is clearly because Thompson's work—certainly *The Making of the English Working Class,* but also the remarkable eighteenth-century essays, and his charismatic intellectual presence in so many of the key moments of social history's heroic days—proved so inspiring for those who identified themselves with social history's promises and hopes. As a polemicist and rhetorician of compelling power, Thompson also contributed personally to the earlier phases of the divisiveness in the discipline, devoting great energy between the mid-sixties and late seventies to the forming of camps and drawing of lines. In setting the scene for this chapter's discussion of the unfolding assault on the use of the class concept during the 1980s and 1990s, therefore, it makes sense briefly to recapitulate what Thompson stood for in this respect.

First, as we suggested in the previous chapter, Thompson practiced a type of "modernism" historiographically speaking. His early critics on the left during the 1970s had originally focused on the undertheorized weaknesses of his Marxism, insisting that it was not structuralist enough. But the later ones—Joan Scott, Gareth Stedman Jones, Patrick Joyce, and others—criticized the materialism per se, emphasizing rather the foundationalist assumptions organizing Thompson's modernist approach to knowledge. For these critics of the 1980s, the flaws in Thompson's work emanated from his particular epistemological standpoint: the belief that the world could be made knowable through a process of rational reflection grounded in the evidence.

Second, while formally rejecting "base and superstructure" models of causation, Thompson nevertheless thought inside a field of sovereign determinations that he conceived as *social,* whose effects eventuated through *experience.* If outcomes could be explained on the basis of rationally retrieved and reconstructed real experiences, then the primary ground for grasping the dynamics of working-class formation and the growth of class consciousness became the experience of shared exploitation, which itself was always structured by political relations of domination emanating from the state and a variety of other local and supralocal influences. If consciousness of belonging to a class was grounded in the interpreting of collective experience, moreover, for Thompson this meant that class formation could only be grasped in action, as a process.

> Class eventuates as men and women *live* their productive relations, and as they *experience* their determinate situations, within "the *ensemble* of the social relations," with their inherited culture and

expectations, and as they handle these experiences in cultural ways. So that, in the end, no model can give us what ought to be the "true" class formation for a certain "stage" of process. No actual class formation in history is any truer or more real than any other, and class defines itself as, in fact, it eventuates.[1]

Third, for Thompson's procedure the authority of the archive lay unquestioned. He was certainly aware of the partialities in historical collections or archives and keenly alive to the complexities entailed in interpreting them. But the suggestion that histories might be based on only delimited categories of materials or grounded in the reading of only a small number of texts, often published ones, offended him. The idea of composing histories like those of Foucault, which rely only incompletely on archival investigation in the conventionally understood sense, was particularly suspect. History to be taken seriously required sustained immersion in the sources across a period of many years. That was essential to the historian's apprenticeship.

Though pugnaciously and unapologetically a Marxist, finally, Thompson systematically anathematized other Marxist theorizations not his own, especially those associated with the influence of Louis Althusser, which he perceived in sectarian terms as Stalinized. He instinctively refused any efforts he thought were aimed at constituting Marxism's apartness as a self-closed or self-sufficient system, preferring instead to identify a Marxist approach with certain broad concepts and their allied methodological assumptions, which here we have been calling materialist. These can be summarized as the precedence exercised—ontologically, epistemologically, analytically—by those intricate patterns of economic and social relationships ("mode of production" and "mode of life"), crystallizing around work and property yet always imbricated in wider fields of social and cultural organization and meaning, and further structured by law, politics, and government, through which ordinary people experienced and handled their lives. On this basis, he developed his dynamic and relational understanding of how classes could only ever be recognized and encountered: namely, through collective motion, contestation, and struggle. This understanding of Thompson's was always avowedly flexible: it could be realized only via archival labor and rational thought, what he liked to call Marxism in the empirical mode. In this sense, Thompson's materialism had closer affinities with allied non-Marxist historiography appropriately practiced than with theoretical Marxisms insufficiently attentive to the remit of research.

Our point here is that the version of Marxism guiding Thompson's view of class was extremely flexible and open-ended, amounting to not much more than a model of social determination proceeding upward from material life, combined with a theory of social change based on the motor of class struggles and their effects. The energy in Thompson's histories came less from any explicit Marxist theorizing, which he dismissed rather contemptuously as a wrangle over "scriptural authority," than from the subtlety of his detailed analyses, the density of their evidentiary groundedness, and the grandness of his interpretive ambitions.[2] The appeal of The Making, confirmed by his famous 1965 riposte to Tom Nairn and Perry Anderson, "The Peculiarities of the English," no less than by the eighteenth-century writings that followed, was its broadening of the class-analytical vision to take in the entire range of experience of the emergent working class, or what Raymond Williams called its "whole way of life." He located the potentials for political radicalism not just in the institutional world of the organized party and trade union formations, but in cultural forms and practices, in collective community organizations, in associational life, and of course in the workplace.

From any one of these bases a complex historiography might be imagined, and in fact a huge volume of scholarly activity proceeded to unfold during the next two decades after the appearance of Thompson's book. Taken overall, the scale, ramifications, and reach of the resulting literatures were prodigious. Of course, in quality the scholarship varied a lot. Some of it might be narrow, methodologically flawed, thinly researched, naive, tendentious, pedestrian, or question-begging. It might fall short of the ambitious grand-scale arguments Thompson's own writings always pursued. But much of it was also imposing in its achievements. It could measure up to those highest standards of disciplinary best practice that transcend the differences among historiographical schools and traditions and exist independently of the epistemological distinctions discussed in the previous chapter. It could be self-conscious and sophisticated in its use of theory quite beyond the terms of Thompson's own idiosyncrasies. And it could sustain a wide variety of analytical perspectives and particu-

lar lines of interpretation inside the broad church of materialist historiography as we have been describing it.

It is worth pursuing this point about the diversity of analysis compati-
ble with social history's underlying materialism a bit further. For one
thing, Thompson's preference for seeing class as a relationship in
motion—as only graspable through the experiential dynamics of conflict
and negotiation linking mutually hostile social forces together—was
always driven by his own polemical purposes. By any sober criteria, his
advocacy of "class struggle without class" was at best question-begging, at
worst illogical and incoherent. Despite all his inveighing against the sociologist's drive for "classification" and the impassioned desire to free class
from its "static" or functionalist definitions, in fact, Thompson could no
more dispense with a form of structural understanding than anyone else.
At some level of one's thinking within a materialist paradigm, it is impossible not to accept that class needs to be conceptualized structurally as an
isolable collectivity. And in many places, as Huw Beynon points out,
Thompson did indeed write about classes in that way—for example, as "a
very loosely defined body of people who share the same congeries of
interests, social experiences, traditions, and value system, who have a
disposition to behave as a class."[3] Given the centrality of "experience" to
Thompson's thinking, however, this made class more a matter of ontol-
ogy than of the economy or social structure in a more precise theoretical
sense.

On the basis of such broad working assumptions, social historians
inspired by Thompson might tackle questions of working-class formation
in a wide variety of ways. They might focus on the workplace and particular categories of workers; they might prefer a residential community
study; they might focus on particular aspects of popular culture like
recreation, religion, crime, drinking, or song; or they might choose a
particular event like an uprising, a political agitation, or a strike. The
breadth of the resulting repertoire might be measured, for example, by
the distance separating Asa Briggs's classic collection *Chartist Studies,*
published on the cusp of social history's arrival in 1959, from *The Chartist
Experience,* a showcase of new research edited by James Epstein and
Dorothy Thompson two decades later: where the one presented a mosaic
of regional political narratives supplemented by commentaries on Char-

tism's national arena, the other offered a far more nuanced and varie-gated vision of the movement's character, sometimes biographically focused, sometimes thematically driven, and at other times using partic-ular localities, but now on a far more richly contextualized basis than before.[4] For this one setting alone—the emergent forms of popular pol-itics in industrializing Britain in the first half of the nineteenth century—an imposing bibliography either published or conceived during the 1970s can easily be assembled. This would range from local and regional accounts of working-class community to studies of particular groups of artisans or wage earners, from biographically centered portraits of work-ing-class politics to studies of particular agitations or strikes, from the new forms of working-class associationism to longitudinal studies of class formation.[5] Such illustrations can be easily replicated for other periods and national cases.

What these studies shared in common was a desire to use their inten-sively investigated specificities of context—which exemplified precisely the strategies valued by the social historian—in order to ground a more general argument about political trajectories of development or the forms of cohesion in society at large. Such studies did not always move explicitly or ambitiously enough from the local to the general. They might also slot themselves too comfortably into received frameworks of interpretation. But in aggregate and at its best, such scholarship delivered an invaluable cumulative resource—painstakingly and creatively assem-bled evidence, densely empirical analysis, carefully grounded interpreta-tion, and usable middle-range theory—which remained available for continuing use. We take the view that this work ought to be considered recuperable—substantively, pedagogically, interpretively—irrespective of the epistemological standpoint it holds or the particular interpreta-tions it develops.

## FOUR EMBLEMATIC WORKS

We want to illustrate this by means of a few emblematic works from the 1970s, two of them taken from French social history, two from British. The range of possible examples for this purpose—monographs of high quality seeking to ground a general thesis about the course of political development or the sources of societal crisis and stability by means of a carefully delimited case study about class formation—would obviously be extremely wide. Thus in the German context we might well have gone to David Crew's study of Bochum and Mary Nolan's of Düsseldorf in order to make the argument, in the Italian context to the work of Donald Bell and Louise Tilly, or in the Russian context to the work of Reginald Zelnik and Ronald Grigor Suny.[6] Moreover, our particular choice of nineteenth-century monographs—William Sewell's study of Marseille, *Structure and Mobility,* and Joan Scott's *The Glassworkers of Carmaux,* plus the work of Patrick Joyce on Lancashire factory culture and that of Gareth Stedman Jones on the restructuring of the London labor market—is definitely not innocent.[7] As already indicated toward the end of our first chapter, each of these authors was to emerge during the 1980s in the forefront of the "culturalist" critique of social history's foundational materialism. From this point of view, to consider their earlier works brings a certain added poignancy to our argument.

Scott's study of the glassworkers was as adept and accomplished an exercise in the new social history as one could want. Wrenching the history of the French labor movement away from the studies of leaders, ideas, and organizations where it was mainly to be found, she re-placed it in a setting of workplace relations and occupational community. In a paradigmatic account of the breaking of a skilled craft and its élan through a process of mechanization in the 1880s, she showed how under the pressure of deskilling, the previously exclusive glassworkers became radicalized into class consciousness. Having traditionally marked their difference from Carmaux's other working-class population, the coalminers, the glassworkers now began learning from them, turning to unionization, militancy, and socialist politics.

Chapter by chapter, Scott laid down the familiar elements in a post-Thompsonian social history of U.S. incarnation: a concise vignette of industrially driven urban growth, with Carmaux's population growing during 1856 to 1896 from 3,743 to 9,993; a quantitative portrait of the impact of industrialization on a specific artisanal trade; a comparative analysis of different occupational communities (glassworkers versus miners); the disruptive effects of mechanization; the forging of working-class political community via socialism; the eventful denouement of the failed 1895 strike. The book declared its dual indebtedness to British Marxist historiography and U.S. social science history, invoking the inspiration of

Thompson's *Making* and Stephen Thernstrom's *Poverty and Progress: Social Mobility in Newburyport,* as well as the "master's tutelage" of Charles Tilly. It hinged on the couplet of proletarianization and class consciousness. It found the possibilities for political action in a workplace-centered analysis of class.

With Sewell's study of Marseille, we find the same influences assembled into more substantial and systematic form. Trained like Scott in the distinctive intellectual culture of U.S. social-science history (and indeed directly attached to Tilly on an SSRC Training Fellowship), Sewell anchored his Thompsonian vision of the making of the working class in an elaborate social-structural account of urban industrialization between the 1820s and 1860s, which used sophisticated quantitative methods to emphasize changing occupational hierarchies, patterns of migration, and prospects of social mobility. As in Scott's book, the strategic concept was again a Marxist-influenced model of "proletarianization," redeployed via Tilly's readings of capitalist development. This located the impetus toward a radicalized political consciousness in the surrounding demographic transformation and restructuring of the Marseille labor market (the city's population tripled from 111,000 to 313,000 during the first two-thirds of the nineteenth century), which repositioned the older artisanal trades and divested their conservatism of its previous political centrality.[8]

As Sewell himself remarks, the argumentative logic of his Marseille study—its sequence of discussions, its chain of causality running from demography and social structure to politics and ideology, and the overall direction of its narrative—was characteristic for an entire literature of social history shaped by the late 1960s and early 1970s. Here it was not just that "the new, sociologically aware, histories of labor" had extended the repertoire of the field's topics, pushing past the older institutional histories of parties and unions and the accounts of socialist ideology to study the measurable facts of ordinary social life—"urbanization, political mobilization, demography, occupational recruitment, voting behavior, social mobility, family structure, migration, kinship, residential patterns, the fine structure of work experience, and so on." For there was also a larger ambition. Such work wished to locate "the emergence and development of working-class consciousness" precisely in a structural account of those underlying processes, whose consequences were taken to be determinative. In that sense it was very much true to social history's guiding materialist purpose—namely, to develop "much firmer and more complex connections between political or ideological events and social and economic processes."[9] At the same time, we would argue, only *certain kinds* of political questions tended to be posed by these new social histories rather than others.

The typical form taken by the social history of the working class in the United States—the local community study—often made it hard to give a full or rounded account of political changes whose impetus came from elsewhere, whether they issued from the national center or circulated via some larger regional or transnational domain.[10] Local studies became hardly less well established among historians of the working class in Britain, given the same practical pressures toward manageability of scale. But perhaps owing to Thompson's inspiration or that of the broader Marxist historiographical presence, historians working in Britain seemed more willing to carry their arguments onto a larger canvas, whether in relation to national politics and the state, or by generalizing them to an entire industry, type of employment, or region. At all events, general connections to the character of the polity, its stabilities and instabilities, seem to have been more often made.

In Patrick Joyce's study of factory towns in the textile districts of Lancashire and Yorkshire in the later nineteenth century, it was precisely this level of political explanation that was engaged. With larger debates over the bases of the mid-Victorian stability and the consequences of the defeat of Chartism very much in mind, Joyce built in this book an important argument about the rooting of popular conservatism "in the soil of the means of production" accompanying mechanized factory production. Under these modern conditions of the Lancashire cotton industry, he argued, wide sections of the northern working class acquired the disposition to accommodate to the economic inequalities and power disparities organizing the emergent social order of industrial capitalism. A distinctive social formation now crystallized around the factory regime of mechanized production, its distinctive authority relations, and the associated patterns of quotidian life, in other words, which could act as the medium for the securing of working-class consent and subordination. To use the Gramscian terms Joyce himself implicitly refused, the resulting factory milieus became the "cellular" basis for the regional form of an emergent capitalist hegemony.

Joyce centered his thesis on the cultural reciprocities of paternalism and deference that a definite type of factory environment permitted, one where the conflicts over craft control, mechanization, and workplace authority agitating the social peace earlier in the century had now largely been settled. Once the militancy and radicalism of the Chartist period ebbed during the 1850s, Joyce argued, the cotton industry's prosperity, the concomitant successes of a moderate trade unionism, and the reestablishing of family work units in the factories among many of the cotton operatives could all enable the new authority relations to stabilize. As a movement geared mainly to the defensive circumstances of a threatened artisanate, the earlier radicalism of the 1830s and 1840s now had far less appeal to this newly formed factory labor force, whose independence and ability to control the labor process had already been lost. In any case, Chartist critiques of capitalism had little to say to the modern industrial order of factories and machine production. As Joyce said, those earlier critiques still had an earlier model of the economy in mind.

> The goal of a non-capitalist economy of free producers [characteristic of the thinking of the Chartists] did not encompass the changed social relations modern industry was ushering in. The employer's rights of direction in industry were not attacked, merely his role as a middleman. Industrial capitalism was equated with a politically based system of unequal exchange . . . the causes of poverty were political and not economic.[11]

Their loss of independence in the workplace left Lancashire cotton workers less available for radicalism while exposing them to the influence of the employers. The social precedence of the millowners, their power over local government, and their dominance of associational life combined with their authority as employers to sustain an interlocking machinery of paternalism. A dense system of rituals, cultural practices, philanthropy, and organized social provision bound their workers into deferential patterns of allegiance, embracing everything from Sunday schools, libraries, brass bands, and sports clubs to coming-of-age ceremonies and similar rites of passage, festive railway outings, and ceremonial works dinners. This striving for a hierarchically secured ideal of social solidarity translated successfully across spheres, producing popular electoral loyalties for Liberal or Tory millowners as well as acquiescence in the social inequalities of the class system. The stabilizing consequences of the new paternalism had vital gendered dimensions too: the reconstituting of the family economy inside the factory walls helped imbricate work and home on the basis of the workingman's familial authority, while the millowner's casting as the father of the community helped further naturalize the dominance of the pervasive patriarchal model. In both respects, work and family pulled powerfully together.

These efforts of Joyce to move out from the locality onto a much broader regional plane of discussion had some costs. They produced an argument that became typological rather than grounded in more finely textured analysis of any particular place. While drawing careful distinctions between Lancashire and Yorkshire, across different industrial settings, and among different types of towns, with some recurring attention to Ashton, Stalybridge, and Blackburn, Joyce opted in the end for assembling a composite picture by drawing materials from all over the region. Partly for that reason, the interconnectedness of the various elements in the employers' paternalism—such as the relationship between the factory milieu and the support for millowners in elections—was established more via correlations and suggestiveness than by detailed demonstration. In emphasizing the conservatism of factory communities, moreover, Joyce consistently downplayed the spaces for continuing opposition and dissent, associating these with fairly small minorities of radicals *outside* the factory workplace rather than exploring the tensions and contradictions within.

Thus while both Scott and Sewell stressed the radicalizing consequences of proletarianization, Joyce gave that process a very different reading, seeing rather its deradicalizing effects. For Scott and Sewell, the possibilities for a broad class-conscious form of workers' militancy arose from the collapse of an older craft-centered culture of work under the pressure of mechanization. Through industrial change and urban growth, the exclusivity, corporate pride, and privileged labor markets enjoyed by traditional artisans gave way to the growing preponderance of differently skilled and unskilled industrial workers lacking those more segmented collective capacities, thereby assembling the conditions for class coales-

cence and its attendant forms of consciousness on the wider scale. But for
Joyce, in contrast, those cultures of early working-class radicalism celebrated by Thompson, which later became characteristic of Chartism, had
been precisely *sustained* by the persistence of workshop production and
craft control; assailed by mechanization and the factory form, not only
the old forms of production but also the earlier traditions of radicalism
became undercut. The rise of the factory system, at its most modern in
south Lancashire textile districts, may have fashioned the common experience of a new industrial working class, but it did so by delivering the
means of its subordination. For Joyce, it was *this* architecture of class
domination that became paradigmatic for the emergent forms of society
crystallizing around industrial capitalism, *not* the more optimistic projections of working-class formation detected by Scott and Sewell.[12]

But despite this substantive divergence, the underlying analytical procedure remained the same: namely, that of tracing the particular forms of
working-class political consciousness and local political organization
accompanying industrialization back to the changing forms of the economy defined by workplace relations of production. Among these three
emblematic accounts, Scott's was the most closely focused on the workplace per se. Studying a major city rather than an extremely small town,
Sewell then offered a more exhaustive sociology of its changing social
structure and the associated forms of mobility, while in his composite
regional portrait Joyce analyzed the wider and more intricate worlds of
sociability and political loyalty elaborated around the factory core. In
each case, an argument about class—one centered on the changing relations of production, but complemented and reinforced by the other
material factors of industrial living, especially housing and family, residential community, and all the forms of collective social life—became
generative for the understanding of politics. That is, the potentials for
political action were best to be grasped by carefully analyzing the work
relations that resided "at the center of people's lives."[13] If in the one set
of cases (Scott and Sewell), class consciousness was the result, in the
other case (Joyce) it was rather the *absence* of class consciousness that
emerged. Either way, political history became the effect of a sociology of
the changing composition of the working class.

There are clear points of equivalence between Joyce's approach and
that of Gareth Stedman Jones in *Outcast London*. For one thing, the struc-

turalist argument about the origins of political change was built up by Stedman Jones even more explicitly from its foundation in the analysis of transformed class relationships. With his citywide analysis of the structure of the London labor market, the collapse of industry in the central districts, and the resulting crises of the casualization of labor and disastrously overcrowded housing, Stedman Jones used the first two parts of his book to establish the actual circumstances of the London poor against which the political anxieties of the middle and upper classes could later be set. Further grounded in relation to the city's growing importance as an imperial metropolis and the disproportionate influence exercised over its politics by the "older professions," the book's final part then approached the crisis of liberalism during the last quarter of the nineteenth century as a complex set of responses to what was perceived as a new and unmanageable scale of poverty and resulting urban degeneration.

As in Joyce's Lancashire cotton districts, central London's craft-based industries underwent dispersal and decline during the century's middle decades, while from the 1860s shipbuilding and the smaller-scale manufacturing industries of the East End and south of the river also migrated elsewhere. In the process, one historic sociocultural formation of the London working class, based on the central artisanal trades and the radical political culture of the earlier nineteenth century, collapsed. It was replaced by the deskilled and disorganized labor market of the casual poor and the sweated trades, whose shapelessness was exacerbated after the 1870s by a major spatial restructuring of London's housing geography. Lacking the smaller-scale community infrastructure upon which the factory-based paternalism of the Lancashire millowners could be constructed, the London middle classes confronted the casualized masses of the London poor through a shifting repertoire of charitable, coercive, and moralizing interventions. If in London "a certain form of proletarianization took place," accordingly, it did so either "within the shell of small-scale workshop production," or else in the massified form of increasingly rampant casualization.

Nineteenth-century London was a city of clerks and shopkeepers, of small masters and skilled artisans, of a growing number of semi-skilled and sweated outworkers, of soldiers and servants, of casual laborers, street sellers, and beggars. But, with the exception of some isolated communities on its periphery, it was a city virtually without a factory proletariat.[14]

*Outcast London* was more akin to Sewell's study of Marseille in the scale of its chosen context and the resulting methodological entailments, although of course London was incomparably larger again, growing from over two million to some five million inhabitants during the second half of the nineteenth century. Whereas Joyce made an argument about the politics of one strategic region of the country, moreover, Stedman Jones now addressed the politics of the nation per se, assisted of course by London's special status as the capital city. Yet while seeking to explore the key shifts in national politics, especially pertaining to the emergence of the New Liberalism, he was ultimately more concerned with explaining the sources of working-class conservatism. And here the argument repeated once more the basic materialist question posed by the new social history: what forms of political consciousness were permitted by this or that pattern of working-class formation?

The answer given by Stedman Jones was clear: London's distinctive social structure—in particular, the absence of a sizable industrial labor force organized into factories, combined with the preponderance of the casually employed poor—militated against any potential appeal of social-ism. The various radicalisms that persisted in the interstices of London's political culture after the 1860s, including the Marxist Social Democratic Federation (SDF) and the other sects produced by the socialist revival of the 1880s, always stopped well short of graduating into the full-fledged working-class movement whose possibility Stedman Jones—no less than Scott or Sewell—sought to abstract from the logic of capitalist industri-alization. Lacking the strong backbone of a militant and organized factory proletariat, he implied, this London activity should not strictly be con-sidered a labor movement at all. The London SDF and other socialist groups were still recruiting their activists to a striking degree from among artisans, skilled craftsmen, and other self-improving minorities, but *not* from the mass of the laboring poor.

In the crucial years before 1914 the weakness of mass trade union-ism, the sharp almost hermetic division between skilled and unskilled, and the sparseness of the factory proletariat had remained insuperable [obstacles] to the formation of a mass party. The particular configuration of social strata in London had produced sects rather than parties.[15]

Instances of successful popular organizing before 1914 in London can certainly be found—including movements of the unemployed, trade unionizing of the semiskilled and unskilled, progressivist electoral coalitions in the more industrialized districts, and so forth—which laid down some of the bases for what later became the Labour Party's future metropolitan support.[16] But these were decidedly *not* the realized manifestations of the type of class consciousness implied by the works of Scott and Sewell or explicated earlier by Thompson. Once again, "proletarianization" was implicitly the organizing concept here, albeit freed from the technical context of mechanization (and the distinction between "formal" and "real" control of labor) per se and redesigned for the London economy's threefold peculiarities: as the country's major port, its "largest single consumer market," and the center of government, London experienced the consequences of industrialization fundamentally differently from the industrial cities and districts of the Midlands and North, leading to the restructuring of the citywide labor market in the ways indicated earlier.[17] Just as in Joyce's Lancashire, therefore, proletarianization in the capital city provided not a basis for radicalization or for the kind of class consciousness commonly ascribed by Marxists, but on the contrary for a new culture of working-class conservatism. In a subsequent generalizing of this argument, Stedman Jones called this a "remaking" of the working class, through which London's working population fashioned a defensive and depoliticized "culture of consolation" best captured via the new commercialized entertainment forms like music hall.[18]

By the early 1980s Stedman Jones had markedly disavowed *Outcast London*'s commitment to the social analysis of politics, which at the time had seemed so axiomatic:

> I did not possess a clear conception of the limits of social explanation, i.e., in what senses the political could not be inferred from the social. My ambition at the time was to show how much political history could be explained in social terms and my attitude was, "on s'engage et puis on voit."[19]

Yet we should be careful to understand precisely what kind of reduction to social explanation politics had undergone. In a manner quite typical of the self-confident materialist analyses of the time, *Outcast London* had offered a structural account of an urban labor market in process of transformation, against which a reading of political developments could then be counterposed. The links and mediations between these two levels were very subtly and richly explored, in an argument that moved back and forth with great suggestiveness and nuance. But the relationship was patently hierarchical: the politics was held to have been determined, however complexly and indirectly, by the social history preceding it. We were asked to read the meanings of the political discourse in terms of the structural account presented earlier in the book.

But the respective parts of this analysis were not commensurate: if the social history was macrostructural in form, the political history remained conventionally textual-discursive. If the one rested securely on top of the other, it did so more by logical fit than by tightly integrated analysis. How exactly the social "facts" of the casualized labor market may have translated into the agency of particular categories of workers, for example, by both constraining and enabling their possible choices and forms of action, remained undiscussed. The more concrete consequences for local political action of the various public discourses surrounding the social question were also not explored, whether through the fashioning of specific policies and practices, via the reshaping of the social imaginary, or by any of the other routes that brought politics down to the ground. Thus Stedman Jones may have begun with his carefully mounted structural argument about the reshaping of the London labor market, the spatial reorganizing of the city's residential geography, and the remaking of the London working class, but he ended with an argument about the changing bases of national politics, which was offered only at the level of the most general discursive and ideological change. Once we reached that very interesting argument about political discourse, the working class was no longer present as the main ground of analysis in social historical terms, but only as an ideological referent, an object of the politics being formulated elsewhere. Its place in that project became intelligible only via the discourse about it.[20]

In his introduction to *Languages of Class* a decade later, Stedman Jones developed a compelling critique of his own earlier treatment of politics.

This took two main directions. On the one hand, he admitted, he had neglected "the importance of the national political dimension," more specifically the ways in which "the temporality of periods of heightened *political* conflict and *political* mobilization" required "in the *first* instance" a political explanation, as opposed to an economic or a cultural one. To be endowed with meanings as a basis for action, particular events like a strike or a riot, or the public recognition of the existence of a social problem, presumed the existence of political agencies with the capacity for addressing and shaping them. While in these reflections Stedman Jones identified such fields of political intervention unnecessarily with a *state-centered* model of politics—with "the activity of all those institutions of government and political order, both legislative and executive, central and local, which in short we call the state"—he nonetheless rightly upheld the necessity of political analysis per se.[21]

On the other hand, he also developed the more challenging argument about the contingent and conjunctural work of discursive negotiation needed before any political intervention that hoped to be concerted or coherent—whether by government, party, or any other organized group or current aspiring to efficacy—could occur. This was especially important for understanding precisely how "social and structural changes" might have acquired an impact on political life. In Stedman Jones's revised view, "what matters" in this respect was not "these changes in themselves," but "which of [them] are articulated and how, within the successive and various discourses which have coexisted within [a particular political party], or which have impinged upon it or threatened it from the outside." Given the pivotal importance of this recognition for our coming discussion of the relationship between the political and the social, it is worth quoting what follows in full.

The place of the social would have to be, in this context, resituated within discursive relations. Messages are sent to addressees. They are amended or recomposed, according to whom they are sent. Speakers address audiences, whom they conceive (or project) to be composed of a specific type of social being. Political discourses are addressed to particular constituencies, indeed at certain formative turning points are able to constitute or reconstitute such constituencies. There is an intimate connection between what is said and to whom. Yet it cannot be said that such a connection can be conceived in terms of a recognition of the pre-existence of the common social properties of the addressees. It should rather be thought of as the construction, successful or unsuccessful, of a possible representation of what such common properties might be. Of course, the almost definitional claim of political discourse is to be a response to a pre-existing need or demand. But in fact the primary motivation is to create and then orchestrate such a demand, to change the self-identification and behavior of those addressed. The attempted relationship is prefigurative, not reflective.[22]

In retrospect, we can see this as one of the early attempts to break out of the impasse that by the start of the 1980s some social historians thought their chosen materialism to have now reached. In the final sections of our first chapter, we briefly outlined the course that those efforts took, culminating during the 1980s in the range of new departures that came to be summarized as "the linguistic turn" or "the cultural turn." Interestingly, a number of social history's leading generational practitioners, who came of age during the phase of ambitious and expansive growth when "social explanation" seemed to carry everything before it, now also took the lead in breaking away. Before Stedman Jones published *Languages of Class,* Sewell's *Work and Revolution in France* had already appeared, and during the next few years Scott's influential articles on gender then followed. Joyce's *Visions of the People* came in 1991 at the end of this process, soon to be accompanied by a variety of polemical articles pushing the debate still further along.

In what follows, we want to begin the process of taking stock. Our preceding chapters have outlined some of the main features of the discussions among historians and others, theoretically and epistemologically, through which the cultural turn came to be effected, indicating in the process what seem to us to have become the lasting gains. Rather than rehearsing once again the detailed course of the various cycles of controversy and critique, we will now take much of this to be understood, refocusing our attention on the unresolved and persisting difficulties that the largely successful critiques of social history have left in their wake. The rest of this chapter will try to exemplify those problems by an extensive discussion of the more recent contributions of Joan Scott and Gareth

Stedman Jones, while our next chapter will develop more positive proposals for how the relationship between politics and social history, or
"the political" and "the social," might now be approached.

For these purposes, we take the position expounded by Stedman Jones
in 1983 to be a very good place to begin. After all, his advocacy of a "linguistic" or "discursive" approach nowhere took the work of the social historian to have been nullified or rendered nugatory. He did not take social
history to be disqualified *tout court*. On the contrary, the importance of
properly and carefully acknowledging the course of "social and structural
changes in twentieth-century England" (or in other places and times) was
specifically upheld, if any sensible discussion of politics was to be
achieved. The point was rather to grasp the complexities in the nature
and import of the relationship, to see "that between the changing character of social life and the order of politics there is no simple, synchronous,
or directly transitive line of connection, either in one direction or the
other." To begin with the analysis of politics by taking a "discursive"
approach to the social "does not obliterate the significance of the work of
the social historian, but locates its significance in a different perspective."[23]

## HISTORIES OF LANGUAGE, HISTORIES OF CLASS

Taking full note of these difficulties encountered by the social explanation of politics, the force of whose implications we certainly accept, we
want to push carefully back against some of the solutions that came to be
offered. If the assumptions and promises of a self-confidently materialist
social history had achieved striking dominance within the discipline during the 1970s, then by the next decade its persuasiveness and prestige had
sustained serious damage. During the 1990s, under the severity of the
"postmodernist" challenge to the historian's established practices, the
damage increased. In light of all the resulting turmoil in the discipline,
we wish to probe the terms of the resulting critiques. We want to ask
what follows once the turn toward discourse or linguistic analysis is
embraced. That is, what consequences do poststructuralist and deconstructive approaches have for the shaping and contents of the earlier
social historian's agenda? How do they affect the agenda of historians for
whom "the social" had been such a powerfully motivating category?

In the case of Patrick Joyce, his self-described postmodernist "history of identity" (of "the self and the social") increasingly departed the ground of social history as usually understood in favor of a particular type of Foucauldian vantage point, from which the dispersals and patternings of power and knowledge could be read. In his *Voices of the People* (1991), which thoughtfully marked the difference from the earlier social-history problematic, the rich culture of the Lancashire laboring poor provided the moorings for an original and challenging analysis of popular discourse. In contrast, *Democratic Subjects* (1994) confined itself to a detailed reading of two individual biographies: where an interest in working people ("class" in a collective sociological sense) had previously described the context for an argument about populist identifications that creatively destabilized "the question of class," Joyce's subtle and complex narratives of political selfhood in the later book now circulated freely through the nineteenth century as a whole, with no groundedness in the densely contextualized studies of working-class life that social historians had usually required. By the publication of his most recent book, *The Rule of Freedom* (2003), he had returned to an impressive density of analytical groundedness, but now wholly from the avowedly Foucauldian standpoint of governmentality (as the "business of governing"), which approached the social entirely in terms of its "knowability" and "mappability," as material available for governance: the former domain of the social historian was now reimagined as everyday life or "the ordinary," but a terrain apparently depopulated of its former working-class subjects.[24]

In Joyce's trajectory, in other words, there seems to have developed a definite pull toward what can only be described as a redeployed intellectual history based on restricted readings of the printed word, rather than the ramified and creatively defined cultural archive still grounding his earlier *Voices of the People*. This predilection for intellectual history has characterized the more recent careers of other leading advocates of linguistic analysis, from Gareth Stedman Jones to Joan Scott, or for that matter William Sewell.[25] But here we do not want to be misread. There is nothing wrong with intellectual history or close readings of published sources per se; on the contrary, we would strongly uphold the empowering impetus of works like *Work and Revolution in France, Languages of Class,* or *Gender and the Politics of History* during the past two decades. But for some practitioners at least, opting for types of linguistic analysis now seems to have entailed an exclusive choice. When measured against histories acknowledging the primacy of language, the legitimacy of social analysis seems to have become disputed as such, as something distinct and problematic, or flawed by epistemological error. But why should attention to language require disparagement of social history in this way?

The most cogent objections to Stedman Jones's essay on Chartism—which originally set the linguistic cat among the social history pigeons—were not leveled against the importance of studying language as such, either as research strategy or theoretical program. Rather, they were raised against the attenuated quality of Stedman Jones's particular version of linguistic analysis, which moved from his quite radical initial proposals to what turned into a straightforward exegetical account of the Chartists' public rhetoric. Aside from the substantive case Stedman Jones made there about the nature of Chartist radicalism, which remains largely persuasive, this clearly exchanged the archive of social history and its sites, contexts, and sources for an intellectual history very specifically based on published texts, a move that in the meantime seems only to have been heightened. Rather than elaborating his argument about Chartism per se, Stedman Jones has withdrawn still further into the history of formal intellectual traditions, from those of utopian socialism and the early Marx through political economy to legacies of the Enlightenment.[26] The complexities of Chartist language—its ordering around multiple and incommensurate discursive fields, where incompleteness and instabilities of meaning mattered as much as the unities of its outward appeal—were too rapidly passed over. Rightly castigating the unproblematized materialism of social explanation that was commonly assumed by social historians, Stedman Jones advanced an oversynthesized conception of public political language in its stead. But as Robbie Gray observed at the time, language is "multi-layered, complex, fractured, composed of incoherences and silences, as well as the smooth flow of would-be authoritative public discourses," and therefore must be read for its exclusions as well as its unifying appeals.[27]

In her essays of the mid-1980s, Joan Scott helped define the space where social historians might begin to conduct such readings. Prising open Stedman Jones's exegesis, and breaking its silences over gender, she shifted the focus from Chartism's "particular politics" to "the processes by which social relationships were conceived and constructed."

As she argued: "A theory of meaning that assumes a multiplicity of references, a resonance beyond literal utterances, a play across topics and
spheres makes it possible to grasp how connections and interactions
work"; and if the potential for contestation ("reinterpretation, restatement, and negation") is held to be inscribed in the production of meaning
as such, the problem of change can also be grasped.[28] This is partly an
issue of sources. As we have seen, an extended notion of textuality has
become one of the liberating gains attending the advent of the new cultural history. Even where restricted to "politics" (as opposed to social history), the potential archive has become immeasurably richer than before.
For example, in studying nineteenth-century popular politics, James
Vernon eschewed the normal ground of political history, which he
defined by "the organizations, personnel, or policies of the national institutions of politics." And he searched out instead the "neglected traces like
ballads, banners, cartoons, handbills, statues, architecture, the uses of
time and space, and the rich vein of ceremonial and iconographic forms,"
as well as creative rereadings of standard sources "like newspapers and
poll books," in order to expand our understanding of how politics
worked, or "the ways in which politics defined and imagined people"
during the first two-thirds of the nineteenth century.[29]

But whereas Stedman Jones's impact seems to have encouraged a new
focus on politics as *distinct* from social history, Scott's challenge has also
enriched social history itself. Cultural meanings have become constitutive for social relations, the economy, and other aspects of material life in
the work of many recent historians. On this evidence, contrary to what
Joyce and Stedman Jones seemed to imply, there is no reason why "the
social" should be held graspable as the effect of linguistic analysis alone.
In their different ways, Michael Sonenscher, Richard Biernacki, and Robbie Gray have all shown the necessity of cultural analysis if the meanings
of labor are to be grasped, for example, while at the same time staying
intensely focused on the social historian's classic terrain.[30] The linguistic
turn was certainly not the only impulse in the 1980s toward innovation
in that kind of fashion. Studies of gender and work were well under way
before Scott published her essays, as were the gendered critiques of the
welfare state, and neither area was especially informed by poststructuralist theory per se.[31] But what all this work did have in common was
the impact of feminist historians working with gender. If there was an

"acute sense of 'epistemological crisis' that accompanied the feminist interrogation of established categories, narratives, and chronologies," then the study of class has benefited powerfully from the intervening feminist revisions.[32] Those critiques decisively destabilized approaches to working-class history based on productivist or social-structural theories of labor, life chances, and social inequality. If Stedman Jones had successfully exposed the fallacies of explaining the politics of movements by their sociologies—of deriving Chartism from class relations and social changes in the economy—it has fallen to others to show how class analysis, or at least analyses making use of the category of class, might become more viable again.

In exploring the constitutive importance of gender in the politics, cultural work, and social binding of working-class formation, Kathleen Canning's work has brilliantly accomplished this task—that is, of disengaging class from the previously assumed sovereignty of "objective" economic and social interests *without* turning it into an artifact of language or a figment of the collective imagination.[33] Grounded in imaginative and meticulous studies of labor markets, workplace organization, job cultures, family and household dynamics, industrial relations, and so on, her analysis nonetheless opened class formation to a wider process of cultural and political definition. Here at least, social history of the classical kind and readings of language and political history were the opposite of incompatible. They worked creatively and persuasively together. The meanings of class became historicized via the kind of discursive analysis Scott had proposed.

In Canning's work, the pre-1914 German working class appeared as a partial, historically situated, and contingent formation, whose institutions and subcultures, its solidarities and divisions, offered powerful but exclusionary ways of organizing the social world—some of the most crucial of which were structured around gender. But however powerful the logics of workplace and other experiences, in the local and everyday processes of working-class living, these could only ever be shaped by wider forces. Sometimes these came from the outside, emanating from the state, churches, parties, charitable agencies, and the circulation of commercial goods and entertainments. Sometimes they operated in and through working-class communities themselves. But all of those languages need to be disentangled and understood. Furthermore, however exactly languages of working-class identity came to be ordered, they remained only one of "several possible ways of describing, ordering, organizing, and making sense of the often diverse and contradictory realities of workers' everyday lives and experiences" under capitalism. Working-class formation was a never-finished and unstable ensemble of possible histories in that sense. As David Crew has said:

> In Germany, between 1890 and 1933, class languages had to compete with many other social and political languages—Catholicism, nationalism, liberalism, Nazism—which ordered the same social facts in quite different ways and gave them other meanings and significance.[34]

## JOAN SCOTT: FROM EXPERIENCE TO SUBJECTIVITY

In several essays of the 1980s, including the critique of Stedman Jones alluded to here and Scott's justly renowned "Gender: A Useful Category of Historical Analysis," Joan Scott did as much as anyone to unlock the opportunities we are exploring in this book. Amid enormous controversy, she opened a path for historians to a body of theory—the thought of Foucault, Derrida, and other poststructuralists—which during the next decade passed into a kind of common currency, acquiring influence far beyond what might have been predicted, given the vociferousness of the initial objections. Scott's lucid advocacy vitally eased this intellectual change.

But in some other ways her conclusions actually occlude certain possibilities of understanding. Her commitment to treating the primacy of language as the site of analysis of first recourse has a variety of entailments. For one thing, it seems to translate into a kind of microperspectival privileging of the particular text under consideration and the forms of subjectivity deemed to be described or contained therein. Here, her insistence that a properly historicized analysis of subjectivities and their construction positively requires finding new ways of reading has been extremely persuasive. And for that purpose, we may well need to abandon some well-tried categories that for much of social history Scott rightly sees as foundational. In an important 1991 essay she especially singled out the category of "experience," which she found inimical to a historical practice focused on the construction of subjects and their positioning. Yet we also worry that a properly historicized account of the construction of subjectivities and their relations may not exhaust the historian's task in quite the exclusive way she implies.

What according to Scott is wrong with "experience"? For Thompson, she claimed, experience served as a bridge over which to escape the narrowing consequences of a mechanical Marxism, meaning in his case the model of materialist determination to be derived from the relation of being to consciousness in *The German Ideology*. For Thompson, experience nevertheless operated foundationally in the sense of providing a ground through which forms of social being can be "handled" by the people who experience them to produce, through consciousness, agency. As she said, quite rightly:

> In Thompson's account, class is finally an identity rooted in structural relations that pre-exist politics. What this obscures is the contradictory and contested process by which class itself was conceptualized and by which diverse kinds of subject-positions were assigned, felt, contested, or embraced. As a result, Thompson's brilliant history of the English working class, which set out to historicize the category of class, ends up essentializing it. The ground may seem to be displaced from structure to agency by insisting on the subjectively felt nature of experience, but the problem Thompson sought to address is not really solved. Working-class "experience" is now the ontological foundation of working-class identity, politics, and history.[35]

Scott then subjected feminist history to the same kind of reasoning, arguing that its rhetorical focus on experience has worked to universalize the identity of women and

> to ground claims for the legitimacy of women's history in the shared experience of historians of women and those women whose stories they tell. In addition, it literally equates the personal with the political, for the lived experience of women is seen as leading directly to resistance, to oppression, to feminism. Indeed, the possibility of politics is said to rest on, to follow from, a pre-existing women's experience.

But invoking the authenticity of an immediately, sensuously, and viscerally encountered "experience" effectively removes that concept and its claims from critical interrogation. It protects declared experiences from uncomfortable questions. It short-circuits the process of deconstructive critique. That "kind of argument for a women's history (and for a feminist politics) . . . closes down inquiry into the ways in which female subjectivity is produced, the ways in which agency is made possible, the ways in which race and sexuality intersect with gender, and the ways in which politics organize and interpret experience—in sum, the ways in which identity is a contested terrain and the site of multiple and conflicting claims."[36]

Within the terms of Scott's own focus, this was a brilliantly succinct account of her position. It disposed of the category of experience in both Thompson's and some feminist history as a device that gives the permission to connect the "handling" of experience by collectivities, through a consciousness of shared oppressions, too easily to a politics. As Scott's critique characterized them, such uses of the concept of experience are governed by some unspoken and problematic assumptions. On the one hand, experience is made into the primary machinery by which the world's realities become sutured to social movements, whether working-class or feminist or whatever. On the other hand, experience is postulated as the privileged empirical sphere from and by which analysis can proceed to uncover the ontologies of social and political agency and to discover their mobilizing forms of consciousness.

On the basis of this critique, Scott was able to free her own concerns with the construction of subjectivities and the historical positioning of subjects from those categories that she described as being foundational for important genres of social and feminist history. She was able to uncover her principal lines of disagreement with Thompson in particular and, if in a less well focused way, with feminist historians too. She laid out a series of anxieties about these historiographical forms: their commitment to practices at least congenial to an empiricist orthodoxy, given their studied valorizing of the absence of the observer ("historians as men, women, white, black, straight, or gay") at the moment of the observation;[37] the absolute authority of data and their accumulation via the archive as a repository whose biases, incompleteness, and skewed realities can be exposed and ultimately accommodated; the expectation that a "true" account of experience by these means can inherently explain collective political outcomes in the past; and, at the same time, the belief that exposure of these truths can lend intensity to collective politics, such as versions of feminism, in our times.

According to Scott, Thompsonian history (however brilliant) and certain versions of feminist history ground themselves in illegitimate foundations that tend not to historicize, but to essentialize their objects of study. To this extent, Scott's wish to study the constructions, valencies, and positionings of subjectivities cannot be realized under the rubric of these available histories, but on the contrary needs to declare their difference. If in the particular essay this declaration of difference was effectively discharged without the heat and dust commonly associated with such declaratory moments, its valency also shifts as soon as we refer it to the surrounding "culture wars" of the time. From the postmodernist perspective then being enunciated, after all, the accusation of foundationalism was always and everywhere a severe one. Such a charge functioned not just as a distancing statement, but as a naturally destructive one. This was a problem not exclusive to Scott's interventions, but became a wider effect of the tonalities, not to say purposes, of the debates of the early 1990s.

What we want to question is the degree to which Scott's not unsympathetic but nevertheless firm shutting-out of Thompsonian and types of feminist history narrows the range of possible focus for legitimate historical work, indeed narrows it to precisely those topics that Scott herself now wishes to valorize—namely, those embracing what she has defined as the production of subjectivities and histories of difference. In her very firmly stated opinion, the project of understanding "the inner workings or logics" of any particular dominant structure of meanings, including both the associated patterns of normativity or dissidence and the strengths or limitations of all the repressive and enabling mechanisms involved, is actively impeded by the social historian's passion for reconstruction and retrieval, whether it be Thompson's desire to "rescue" the marginalized working-class subjects of the early nineteenth century "from the enormous condescension of posterity," or feminist strivings to restore agency to women "hidden from history."[38] As Scott said in no uncertain terms: "The project of making experience visible *precludes* analysis of the workings of this system and of its historicity. Instead, it reproduces its terms."[39] For all her article's coolness and generosity, therefore, it was nevertheless an act of closure, especially against forms of historical work that may lie beyond the approved discursive terms of focus.

If our goal is to explore how subjectivities are constructed and how subjects are multiply positioned by powers acting through discourse, then we can have little quarrel with Scott's proposals for deconstructing foundationalisms and finding new ways of "reading." On the other hand, it remains far less clear how successfully those proposed methods might account for the centering of extensive *social* movements around issues of "class" or "the interests of women," let alone for how those movements achieved continuity over time, how they secured and reproduced the allegiance of measurable collectivities of actors and social populations, or how they achieved efficacy within a particular society and its complex of institutions. It is also unclear, parenthetically, how new movements seeking the kind of efficacy sometimes demonstrated in the past by, for example, socialist movements might be built under the changed circumstances of the present. We remain unclear, after Scott's incisive critique of existing historiographies and their claims for the complicated convergence of social histories to politics, just how she would argue that large-scale movements construct themselves around programmatic political centers. This remains, surely, an important question for historians, for feminists, and for citizens. How does this happen?

On the question of class, we can agree that Thompson was wrong both in his foundational assumptions and in his belief that lived and felt experience leads directly and expressively to politics. But once we have acknowledged that class is a site of multiply constituted cultural construction rather than either an objective or an ontological ground, then the existence of large-scale movements, sharing a common stock of ideas, trespassing across national frontiers, occasionally moving toward radical or even revolutionary goals, can still not be denied. Such movements will still need analysis as such and perhaps of a different order than Scott's prescriptions imply.

Citing Gayatri Spivak, Scott drew clear distinctions between literary and historical work, both methodologically and politically, on the grounds that the two procedurally "interrupt" each other.[40] If we extend this argument to embrace social and cultural anthropologies as well, critically juxtaposing *those* procedures to the procedures of history, this may illuminate some of our reservations about Scott's argument. Versions of anthropology concern themselves with an intense focus on fairly specific empirical fields and problematics. Thompsonian history, while validating precisely those specificities of research, also demands a wider field of view. Thompson's desire to move between a microworld of individual experience and a macroworld of class formation and action was not impeded by his commitment to anthropological and cognate culturalist approaches but plainly rested on them. It is striking how Scott's principal critique of Thompson brilliantly disrupted his intellectual maneuver from individual experience through cultural handling to political agency. It does not follow, however, that all future attempts to bring into focus large-scale social and political movements will necessarily break on the same rock. In fact, there may well be important spheres of human endeavor that still require an approach that is hard to conceive under the rubric Scott places on offer. We can certainly accept Scott's critique of Thompson. But there is no reason to accept that *all* large-scale ("societal," "structural") analysis has to be dissolved or refused on the basis of Scott's characterization of subjectivity and difference.

Scott's recent writings seem predicated on a self-denying abstention from certain kinds of larger-scale analysis—indeed, from precisely those questions she seemed so passionately committed to addressing earlier in her career, as well as from the types of theory appropriate for addressing them. This abstention requires a certain separation of spheres, actually a kind of territorializing—whose implications extend not just into the theoretical and epistemological hard work needed to attain the positions occupied in intellectual and historical analysis, but into the everyday practice of the nonacademic lifeworld too. We are sure, for example, that Scott holds many ideas and coherent beliefs that serve as a basis for venturing opinions and exercising decisions in numerous parts of her professional, personal, and public lives. In exercising her agency at those different sites, we imagine she marshals a range of knowledges and procedures, which employ a variety of registers, with varying self-reflexiveness, and drawing on more than one epistemology. Those knowledges and procedures will also have a variety of pragmatic, ethical, and political applications.

We assume that Scott does not approach every decision in each and all of these spheres in exactly the same spirit of deconstructive indeterminacy and caution all of the time but rather brings to them a variety of already formed judgments and larger-scale understandings as well. The latter are likely particularly to inform her behavior as a citizen, which may often require the kind of spontaneity and decisiveness that presuppose not only continuities of already formed social, political, and ethical judgment, but also a set of structured understandings about an actually existing social world. In acting as a citizen, Scott's opinions would probably embrace the economy, the state, and the operation of large economic forces in the wider world, whether considered as globalization or in some other way. We are sure she exercises her citizenship on the basis precisely of these larger concerns. Why must they be bracketed from the intellectual agenda of Scott the historian?

However much Scott may argue that Scott the citizen is a subjectivity differently constructed from Scott the historian or Scott the woman, citizenship nevertheless represents a particular domain of difference in a number of important ways: in the knowledges that inhabit this subjectivity significantly; in the means by which those knowledges are obtained; in the effects that modify aspects of social and political behavior; and in the willingness to come to political judgment sometimes shared with others. All these, and much else besides, entail an openness to larger questions of society, of politics, and of economic process than Scott seems to make available in her specifically historiographical critique. Scott the historian, on the contrary, confines her focus with forcefulness and consistency to the process of the construction of subjectivities per se. In itself this is neither negligible nor in any way a bad thing. But for the engaging of some important questions of historical analysis it can be confining. It can lead to a perception of Scott's argument as essentializing, as claiming that these processes of subject formation trump everything else on the historian's possible agenda.

Scott claimed in her article that Thompson essentializes class rather than historicizing it because he neglects, actively effaces in fact, the complex indeterminacies of difference and contestation intruding themselves between the putative "facts" of class positionality and the processes of performance and recognition through which class will only ever be manifest and actualized. In other words, Thompson assumes that class makes itself by processing ideologically its experiences of exploitation and pain in the delivery of a working-class movement. Against this, Scott seemed to be claiming that what matters most is how the subjectivities of class position come to be constructed linguistically and culturally. We do not wish to dispute the significance of that claim in itself, but rather to suggest that it too can become essentializing in subtle and unexpected ways—namely, by confining its frame of reference to the important question of subjectivity alone, and in the process refusing all others. Scott declines an account of *collective* political practice more or less altogether, failing to see that her critique of class and feminist history, though effective, still leaves untouched in historical time the huge and complex history of the organized and larger-scale contexts through which class and gender-based politics have sometimes achieved efficacy.

Scott's more recent book on French feminism, *Only Paradoxes to Offer,* is an illuminating attempt to employ these insights for the purposes of writing an actual history.[41] In that case, what sort of history is it that she writes? The book is focused around the gendering of citizenship in France between the Revolution and 1944. It considers the shifting relationship between two notions, variations of whose construction become pivotal for an argument about the longer-run trajectories of French feminist politics, and by implication for the structure of French political history overall: the first is difference in its sexual notation, and the second is equality as the basis for extending citizenship rights, in this case to women. The complex and varying interplay between these two points of orientation or sites of discursive return is closely read through the ways in which French feminists identified contradiction inside the dominant exclusionary "orthodoxies" of national political life, whose exact terms likewise fluctuated across periods. From the perspective of the dominant political culture itself, of course, despite any feminist working of the contradictions, a recurring logic of privileging and marginalization persisted over time: "the production of 'sexual difference' was a way of achieving the otherwise inconsistent exclusion of women from the categories of individual and citizen."[42]

Throughout, Scott is careful to distance herself from versions of the older celebratory histories of retrieval. She does "not think of these women as exemplary heroines," but rather "as sites—historical locations or markers—where crucial political and cultural contests are enacted and can be examined in some detail." Although we might doubt whether all pre-Scottian treatments of such early feminist struggles with the "paradoxes" of political claim-making were really as inattentive to complexity as Scott now implies, this careful unpacking is obviously to be welcomed.[43] To adopt this approach is to honor feminist agency rather than to deny it: "To figure a person—in this case, a woman—as a place or location is not to deny her humanity; it is rather to recognize the many factors that constitute her agency, the complex and multiple ways in which she is constructed as a historical actor." But yet again, Scott's particular deconstructive method, in the medium of this kind of textually based intellectual history, is not the *only* way of getting to this important destination. Scott is hardly the first to argue "that feminist agency has a history." Allowing for the particular poststructuralist inflection, her substantive thesis might have been generated by a variety of more eclectic and less purist critical readings. ·

> [Feminist agency] is neither a fixed set of behaviors nor an essential attribute of women; rather it is an effect of ambiguities, inconsistencies, contradictions within particular epistemologies. In order to make these arguments, I must write the history of feminism by reading for the historically specific paradoxes that feminist subjects embody, enact, and expose.[44]

In *Only Paradoxes to Offer* Scott confirms the main direction of thought we found in the programmatic essay on "experience." She is interested in writing a history of the ways in which political subjects are produced: "I want to understand feminism in terms of the discursive processes—the epistemologies, institutions, and practices—that produce political subjects, that make agency (in this case the agency of feminists) possible even when it is forbidden and denied."[45] And of course, this was *exactly* the deficit that she ascribed to Thompson in her earlier 1983 critique and again in the essay on "experience"—and correctly so. By this procedure she hopes to explicate the ways in which agency is composed and to elucidate its inner world of involuntary contradiction. Her principal method is that of close reading for contradiction, a contradiction internal to feminism itself, in particular a feminism constituted by liberal individualism in the demand for equal rights but at the same time constantly undermining this in terms of the continuing expressions of difference.

This is a valuable technically deconstructive reading, but of course it cannot exhaust all possible readings, nor exclude the employment of other methods. There is a way of reading Scott's trajectory from the

1983 article contra Thompson, through her other theoretical interventions, to this history of French feminism as all of a piece, as consistent. *Only Paradoxes* is in the clearest possible ways the outcome of Scott's theoretical perspective developed partly in polemics for example against Thompson and partly in substantive interventions, as in the essay on "experience." And some of her polemical claims bear exclusivist meanings. She says in effect: social historians cannot do it that way any more, their reliance on preexisting structures for historical explanation, such as the economy or class, is now in a final sense delegitimated.

But we have the strong sense that Scott would be reluctant to apply these rhetorics of exclusion of alternatives to her own substantive analysis in *Only Paradoxes,* mainly because of the conventional form this new book employs and all the consequent space it leaves—indeed, *requires*—for further and complementary kinds of analysis. In other words, something slips between the 1983 critique of Thompson and its line-drawing polemics and the empirically focused trajectory of this book. In response, we want to pose the question What do Scott's prescriptions make possible or allow in terms of history writing, and what do they seem to be less capable of addressing and enabling? As far as this new book goes, we would argue, the answer seems to be that they license an interesting but narrowly circumscribed commentary on central political debates of the nineteenth and twentieth centuries, using the well-tried repertoire of critical intellectual history. And here there are two comments to be made.

On the one hand, the book's argument is extremely limited in both its contextualizing and the kind of sources it uses, offering basically a history of ideas focused around the careers of a small number of symptomatically selected prominent French feminists. Scott's discussion in these terms is highly intelligent and illuminating, to be sure, but it is hard to see where it diverges methodologically from the best practice of a non-deconstructive European history of ideas of the past several decades. Scott's *particular* route to this book has certainly led through a sustained and intellectually rigorous encounter with the thought of Derrida, Foucault, and other French poststructuralists. It presupposed an impressive process of personal self-refashioning in that sense. But it is difficult to find what is *distinctively* deconstructionist in this particular book, in other than the loosest (and perfectly appropriate) of ways. It seems indistinguishable, in fact, from highly intelligent forms of intellectual history that could be far more eclectically and pragmatically founded. In terms of its procedures, its sources, and its general modalities of analysis, the new book simply does not *need* the epistemological program Scott so fervently put forward.

On the other hand, we would argue, *Only Paradoxes* does not follow through on the more ambitious version of the program Scott's epistemologically founded strictures about the now-permissible forms of historical writing seemed to suggest. We learn how political subjects are produced only at the most familiar level of discursive generality, at which a few notable individuals are made to do the work of exemplary representation, just as the classic works of intellectual history before the advent of social history had always assumed they should. Yet that challenge of social history had always resided not just in its particular totalizing wish, or in its structurally oriented model of materialist determination, or in the related centrality of the old master category of class. Social historians had also urged a particular density of contextualizing, a microhistorical pursuit of bounded concreteness, and the validation of the needs, interests, and hopes (their subjectivities) of previously disregarded, belittled, and marginalized social categories of people.

It is this double-sided commitment that in Scott's work now seems to have receded. Her critical appraisal of the thought and careers of several prominent French feminists is done excellently well. But it does not tell us very much about the relevant wider social contexts where the production of political subjects occurred. It hardly delivers the promised access to "the epistemologies, institutions, and practices" involved in the more diffused and localized operation of those "discursive processes . . . that produce political subjects." The political subjectivities of the female counterparts of the miners and glassworkers of Carmaux seem to have dropped out of the picture.

Scott's dissent from Thompson's methods, her diagnosis of their deficits, and her insistence on the neglected significance of the historical processes by which symbolic meanings and political subjects are produced, all serve to underpin her latest book. Her previous polemics, however, tended to suggest that these new methods should utterly supersede the old, whose now identified deficits are held to vitiate them. What she seems not to offer in this respect, though, is a way of continuing to address either the microhistorical and localized contexts of social history we have just mentioned or social history's equally important challenge to consider the bigger picture—that is, those questions concerning capitalism, the state, the place of violence and coercion in political life, the structured reproduction of widening forms of social and economic inequality, the differing capacities of particular populations for collective action, and so forth. For these were also part of the social history agenda and have not exactly ceased to matter.

Of course, we now understand much better, thanks in large part to Scott's own careful and lucid advocacy, that such phenomena at the level of capitalism or the state are vitally constituted precisely by factors like the dominance over representation, the contest over meanings, and the discursive powers that produce subjectivities. These are among the conditions of the enablement of the larger-scale problems and are crucial to understand. But at the level of the history of ideas such analysis will take us only to some of the discursive *effects* of the grand-scale problems as they are felt and observed in certain kinds of commentary on the incidence of abject poverty, material deprivations, disease, and death, which in our own time can increasingly be grasped on a scale of colossal global inequality. As a basis for either critique or action, this hardly seems enough. And only if we also try to return critically to the types of contextualizing social historians sought to explore, we would argue, will our grasp be deepened. Knowing how capitalism's symbolic meanings and congenial subjectivities are produced in relatively local spheres will help us understand its operations all the more effectively, on the one hand, including the terms ("paradoxes," as Scott calls them) under which oppositions might be mobilized. This element of the "locally discursive" at least falls within the potential reach of Scott's theoretical program. But on the other hand, the equally pertinent larger-scale levels of the structural circumstances of society, capitalism, and the state seem rather to have disappeared.

In other words, what we called Scott's territorializing, her choice of a textually demarcated analysis of subjectivities as the main priority of historical writing, seems to have displaced certain other kinds of questions from the agenda altogether. It seems to have effaced the importance of considering those questions, whether through lack of interest, neglect, or even evasiveness. In saying this, we are not leveling an accusation, but rather probing some of the consequences of Scott's chosen direction of thought. Like all forthright intellectual programs, her poststructuralist advocacy for historians involves the foregrounding of some questions over others. That remains both unavoidable and perfectly legitimate. We are glad she has been making these arguments, whose positive effects we definitely uphold. But at the same time we want to ask: what has been gained and what has been lost? Which questions can Scott's program enable us to address, and which not?

Scott might reasonably claim, with unimpeachable justification, that under present circumstances some questions have grown politically *so* important—and in the past were so egregiously neglected—as now to demand definite pride of place. But that need not be true for all historians—or all citizens—all of the time. Other kinds of discussion have no need to cease entirely. We take the view that, in the right spirit of collaboration and generosity, divisions of labor and distributions of priority might be arrived at which allow different registers of analysis to be employed and a diverse range of questions to be addressed. In particular, the according of full and due priority to questions of sexuality, the discursive formation of gender practices and relations, and the complex production of political subjectivities do not require the suspension of other kinds of work. Indeed, to address the new questions most successfully we positively *need* those other discussions to continue—discussions, that is, of systemic capitalism, of the structural operations of the state, of the exercise of violence and the coercive forms of power, of the relations among states and other large-scale agencies, of the actual existence of large-scale political movements, of *class* in all its structured and systemic dimensions.

We can illustrate this very pointedly from a not unrelated source. Pressed during one of his final interviews to explain an apparent unwillingness to "open your discourse clearly onto the level of the political," Michel Foucault reacted allergically to this criticism. His interlocutor, Duccio Trombadori, had challenged Foucault's reluctance to connect his immediate micropolitical concerns with any "wider action or program that at the same time is linked to certain historico-political conditions"— that is, to a politics conceived in national or societywide terms, linked to parties and social movements, and with some aspiration toward change at the level of government or the state. It was no diminishment of the brilliance of Foucault's distinctive contributions, Trombadori suggested, to raise this as a problem: "One of the observations that could be made of the way in which you confront the theme of power is this: the extreme fragmentation or 'localization' of the questions ends up impeding the transition . . . to a vision of the totality within which the particular problem is inserted."[46]

In response, Foucault insisted that the "localizing" of problems had furnished what was actually a different and indispensable route to the general: "The generality that I try to make apparent is not of the same type as others." Referring it to the conventional binarism of the local and the general "usually discussed by historians, sociologists, economists, etc." would only be to confuse matters.[47] For their own part, Foucault's critics had always neglected, ignored, or actively suppressed the particular approach to "general problems" he advocated, which made those "localized" manifestations into the priority of his thought.

> If you prefer, I will pose the question in another way. Why haven't the great theoretico-political apparatuses that organize our society and that define the criteria of consensus ever reacted to the truly general problems that I have sought so hard to illuminate? When I raised the problem of madness, which is a general problem in every society and very important in the history of ours, why in the world was the first reaction one of silence and at times of ideological condemnation? . . . That's why I say, how can one accuse me of not posing general problems, with not ever taking a position with respect to the larger questions posed by the political parties? In fact, when I pose general problems I am anathem[at]ized; then, when it is noticed that the anathema hasn't stuck, or when a certain importance to the problems being raised is recognized, I am blamed for not being capable of developing an entire series of questions in, yes, "general" terms. But I reject that type of "generality" which above all, as it is construed, has as its first effect that of condemning me in my way of posing problems. . . . I am the one who poses the problem for others: why do they reject the general problems as *I* pose them?[48]

In effect, Foucault was being challenged on two counts. The first concerned the means by which his methods and concrete histories as well as his philosophical work might be seen to converge to a politics of program and action. Here Trombadori pressed him on the forms of productive and efficacious action capable of making a difference in political processes at the level of the nation or the state ("a vision of the totality within which the particular problem is inserted," as he called it). Trombadori's second query then concerned the possible relationship between Foucault's particular way of conceptualizing the general-in-the-local and the conventional forms of generalizing and systemic analysis usually pursued by historians, sociologists, and economists.

It was here that Foucault's self-defense seemed evasive. Each of his particular ripostes was entirely apposite. He established a distance from the PCF (French Communist Party) and the other established voices of the Left; he rested the case for his own version of localized studies on an implied incommensurability of his purposes with those of more conventional social science; he complained that these disciplines had declined to recognize the general meanings his localized methods were meant to deliver; and he described how his own concrete work with respect to prisons had always been vilified. Yet those questions of state-related action, national-political (and now increasingly transnational or nonnational regional) intervention, and the more structural or systemic critiques of capitalism and class remained stubbornly on the table. No one expected Foucault suddenly to stop what he had always been doing and turn to those other kinds of analysis instead. But acknowledging their validity and importance was surely possible. Developing collaborations and forming alliances across epistemological differences, for both intellectual and political purposes, might even have been a desirable goal.

This describes very well the questions we have about Scott's work. As the source of necessary critique, her essays were brilliantly enabling. They may have done more than any other single intervention to help bring the importance of feminist ideas from the barely tolerated sidelines of women's history into the central territories of the discipline and profession of history in the United States. With admirable lucidity, they made difficult and unsettling forms of theory available for discussion among historians. They helped decisively in freeing many from the impasse that social history had reached by the start of the 1980s. They opened a space of debate and creative departure where various radicalisms were able to convene, historiographically, intellectually, and politically. Her subsequent interventions of the early 1990s, exemplified by the essay on "experience" focused on here, remained comparably challenging and empowering. Yet, in some important respects, the resulting agenda seems both limiting and incomplete. Scott's work neither follows through on the most exciting methodological and empirical possibilities it enunciates nor engages with a vitally important domain of larger-scale questions. In both these connections, we would argue, the category of "the social" ought still to remain key.

## GARETH STEDMAN JONES: FIXING DETERMINISM

After publishing *Languages of Class* in 1983, Gareth Stedman Jones was for some years largely silent in print, except for occasional short pieces in *History Workshop Journal*. From the pages of *New Left Review*, for example, which had carried his notably influential articles between the mid-1960s and mid-1970s, he now disappeared entirely. Consistent with the logic of the long essay on "Rethinking Chartism" and reflecting a longer-standing interest in the history of Marxism, he was known to be working on aspects of the history of social and political thought in Europe after the French Revolution, focusing especially on the ideas of the utopian socialists. Then an edition of Charles Fourier's *The Theory of the Four Movements* appeared in 1996, followed more recently by a book-length introduction to a new edition of *The Communist Manifesto* and a short book on nineteenth-century debates over poverty. For our purposes here, we are interested in an article provocatively titled "The Determinist Fix," which was the shortened version of an essay published in full in Germany the following year.[49]

In this essay, Stedman Jones offered a well-focused reflection on the debates associated with the cultural turn. It began in a manner not dissimilar from our own procedure in this book, with a potted account of the influence of the "Anglo-Marxist" group of historians between the 1950s and 1970s, the diffusion of their particular understanding of the Marxist tradition (as "the determination of consciousness by social being"), and the consequences of their difficult encounter with the ideas of Althusser and other European Marxists.[50] The essay then recapitulated the changes in Stedman Jones's own thinking between his earlier Marxism and the reconsiderations in *Languages of Class,* before turning to an extended discussion of the "linguistic" or "discursive" approach to history, the influence of Foucault, and the current attractions of approaches taken from intellectual history.

> It was . . . as part of a rising tide of criticism, both political and historiographical, directed at the Marxist paradigm, that I brought out a collection of essays, entitled *Languages of Class*. This book—or at least the later essays in the collection—challenged the Anglo-Marxist approach directly since class was no longer treated as a foundational reality, but as an artifact of discourse. Language, the book argued, was a self-contained system of signs whose meanings are determined by their relationship to each other—the so-called non-referential theory of language—rather than to some primordial or transcendental extra-linguistic terrain. What particularly provoked controversy was the application of this approach to the interpretation of Chartism. For it challenged a long-standing consensus deriving both from a Marxist historiographic tradition beginning with Engels and from a local labor history tradition descending from the Webbs, that Chartism was the first "working-class movement."[51]

The new essay had three moments. The first was the now-familiar story of the crystallizing of Anglo-Marxism from the Communist Party Historians' Group in the late 1940s and 1950s, dividing in 1956 and thereafter. In this telling, Anglo-Marxist history developed in an environment unchallenged by the epistemological tensions of European Marxist debate, but preferred to align itself instead with the empirical and sometimes antitheoretical traditions of characteristically English practice going back to Locke.[52] The essay's second element proceeded through a critique of Althusser to a demolition of the epistemological coherence of Marxism. Its third element charted the decline of Marxism in Britain from the early 1980s to what Stedman Jones regarded as its interment as a result of the fall of the Berlin Wall in 1989. Here, Stedman Jones also rejected Foucauldian concerns with discourse and language as the viable source of an alternative, for by substituting relations of power for relations of production, he argued, Foucault succeeded only in replicating Marxism's flaws. For this reason, historical practice grounded in nonreferential theories of language could find no future in following a Foucauldian path.

Throughout this exposition, Stedman Jones tacitly equated social history in its mature 1970s realization with the diffusion of the influence of the Anglo-Marxist historiographical tradition. The latter's loose and flexible understanding of social determination had even become tantamount to a "part of the common sense of the profession."[53] This equation was important for a key step in his argument: if social history was conflated with Marxism, both could be disposed of in the same breath. For Stedman Jones, the independence of social history, even its primacy, presumed the very Marxist theories that the intellectual and political developments of the 1980s, culminating in the fall of the Berlin Wall and the collapse of the Soviet Union, brought to an end. If one fell, so too must the other. The social was tied *essentially* to Marxism in that sense. That is, the essence of social analysis was understood to be intimately connected with reductive and no longer acceptable versions of Marxist analysis. Thereby essentialized as Marxist (or "Anglo-Marxist"), the social as an explanatory form could be cast out.

What remained for historical analysis, according to Stedman Jones, once the social was excluded? First and foremost came intellectual history, privileged we must suppose by its basis in text and language. Second, Stedman Jones sought to restore the central position of political history, including the need "to recast the preoccupations of the social historian as a set of concerns encompassed within it."[54] Third, he raised to central significance something rather mysteriously called "commercial society"—not markets, not capitalism, not exchange, but commercial society: "The fall of communism in 1989 confirmed what had been increasingly apparent in the preceding twenty years: that there was no self-sustaining form of economy beyond commercial society, only centralised and authoritarian regimes in which bureaucratic direction substituted for the processes of commercial exchange."[55] For the "triumph of capitalism over the communist world" was no mere consequence of "a technical flaw in Marx's argument." Nor could "the Marxist conception of class" be salvaged simply by adding some equivalent attention to gender and race. On the contrary, the collapse of Communism and the preceding crisis of Marxism proclaimed the latter's utter analytical failure.

It therefore needs to be repeated that the near total failure of both the Marxian "critique of political economy" and of its theory of history requires something more drastic than a minor readjustment of former assessments of the theory. In effect, it requires the demotion of its status from that of *explanans* to that of *explanandum*.[56]

Once again, therefore, a critique of accepted modes of doing social history, broadly characterized as Marxist, has compellingly identified a genuine and severe difficulty. The linguistic critique leveled by Stedman Jones against established uses of the class concept decisively shifted the ground for any subsequent viability of the latter, in ways that the various loyalist reiterations "in defence of class" have never been able to gainsay.[57] For example, it seems clear that previously class *had* provided social historians with a kind of working and consensual description for societies in general, operating as an unchallenged assumption about the nature of all past societies. "Class" acted as the analytical category promising best intellectual access to the structure of those societies and how they worked. It allowed us to disaggregate the conflicting interests we encountered there: all societies were organized into classes, which in some primary sense became the bearers of those societies' most fundamental interests. Beneath one of the most famous of the classical Marxist rubrics—all history is the history of class struggles—narratives could then be composed that centered around the relations linking those various interests together, whether through mechanisms of solidarity, fields of divisiveness, or complex and varying repertoires of negotiation.[58]

The older consensual assumption of the social historian, that the language of class delivered the best access to a society's past and present realities, describing both the basic building blocks of the social formation and the epistemological principle of its coherence, has now definitely dissolved, as we have been broadly arguing in this book. The universalizing, transferable valency of the class concept, its standing as the social historian's metacategory, has gone. A series of other positions, which would have tacitly marked out the ground for the social historian's discussions thirty or forty years before, have also gone into recession where not entirely abandoned. These include all those arguments about class as the organized social and cultural expression or conditioning of economically distributed interests; about the economic determinants of class formation in relation to work, labor markets, and incomes; about the gendered reproduction of class affiliations within families and other living arrangements; about the spatial organization of class-defined residential communities; about class and the forms of collective political agency. That repertoire of class-analytical assumptions, along with the questions associated with them, has increasingly been pushed to the margin and often thrown out altogether.

As should be clear, these arguments taking their cue from Stedman Jones had important affinities with the thinking of Joan Scott, although any straightforward convergence of the two authors was certainly mutually refused.[59] In consequence of Stedman Jones's critique, no less than of Scott's, the foundational ground of Thompsonian social histories of the working class can never be reclaimed or reoccupied in the same way again. Yet, as too in the case of Scott, certain reservations can still be entered. The maximalist program of the linguistic or discursive approach offered by Stedman Jones seems to us gratuitously restrictive in the kinds of legitimate histories it seems able to envisage. Conversely, existing social histories may not be quite as completely vitiated in their usefulness as Stedman Jones and other advocates of that program appear to think.

Stedman Jones would have us believe that everything takes place within discourse, that politics is tied to discursive formations with no point of reference beyond the available terms of their discursivity. Beneath this dispensation, it remains possible to use concepts of class, to be sure, but only in a strictly nonstructural or nonobjectivist way—in which case, these would refer really to the *languages* of class and the *symbolic iconographies* of class, while refusing other than linguistic or discursive connections between class and, say, the patterns of economic interest and distribution. On this basis, for example, historiographies of class might be imagined that account for those historical moments when class has been discursively configured as one of the elements in a process of political, constitutional, and intellectual conflict. In Stedman Jones's reading, Chartism seems to have represented one such powerful moment of that kind: not a form of class politics with a referent outside itself, but a way of discursively convening an oppositional politics whose political content was far less centered and more diffuse than a more classical argument from class politics would have supposed.

That kind of reasoning would make class only one of the possible discursive formations of the political process. And at this level the argument seems persuasive: it draws highly focused attention to the languages of "real" historical actors, and it restores voice and agency to political movements in terms of their own discursive formations and linguistic practices. What it does *not* do is to connect class discursively understood with class as a component of the structural relations of, let us say, England in the 1840s. Indeed, in the terms Stedman Jones has provided, the discursive take on class must refuse every conceivable Marxian understanding of class as an element of a social formation existing beyond or before discursive interpellation. And in any Marxism or cognate sociology we can, conceive, class *has* to be considered as structurally inscribed in human societies, more or less permanently or at least continuously, whether or not it gets called into the domain of public politics by discursive and linguistic address.

If we are to keep a place for structural understandings of class, on the other hand, what weight might these receive? One orthodox Marxist answer to that question, now so persuasively discredited by the critiques of Scott, Stedman Jones, and others, was to have made class into *the* master category, around which everything else—other forms of social practice and social relationship, of exploitation and domination, of pain and pleasure, of manifold human activity—could then be arranged. Yet if we want to continue using the class concept in a structural sense, is that the only intellectual strategy available? Class itself might perfectly well be considered polyvalent. There are in any case other lines of conflict in society and other ways of understanding them than those of social class, obvious ones being race, ethnicity, gender, sexuality, religion, and so forth. Why should these be considered mutually exclusive categories? Class analysis, we can certainly agree, has frequently, maybe even usually, neglected or subsumed important historical forms of subordination and exploitation. That is, class analysis turned out to be far less inclusive or sufficient than some of its more extravagant supporters had claimed. But, recognizing this, why is it necessary to draw the conclusion that in failing to embrace every aspect of human pain, subordination, and conflict, class analysis thereby becomes completely vitiated, fit only for the scrap heap? Why should the possible fruitfulness of class analysis be tested only against its most extreme and extravagant claims?

Of what work might a post-Marxist version of class analysis be capable? Is it possible, in full acknowledgment of the force of poststructuralist critique, to argue that beyond discourse there exist structures of importance for understanding our own society as well as past ones? For example, can it be argued that the unequal distribution of the economic product operates with such regularities as to allow us to postulate—and then study—at least partially distinguishable nondiscursive sources? The perpetuating of inequality in a society is discursively secured, reproduced, and defended in all sorts of ways, we can agree. But are we convinced or satisfied by an argument that inequality is discursively *enacted* or *produced* in some wholly sufficient way? While making all careful, knowing, and due allowance for the necessary and inescapable mediations of language, or for the postmodernist precepts about constructedness discussed in our previous chapter, accordingly, is there no place we wish to hold for continuities and regularities of a "structural" or systemic kind? Does worrying about that question make us into hapless intellectual conservatives—into structural*ists*—who are not capable of leaving flawed and superseded shibboleths behind?

Let us pause for a moment on the matter of the "economic." What do the scare quotes around this category mean? First, they convey the axiomatically culturalist recognition: the economic is constituted, like any other domain, by fields of meanings that are discursively constructed, and so become accessible only through language. Next, of course, the quotes perform symbolic labor: they serve to distance the writer from any allegation of economic determinism. Yet, the boundaries of the economic may be more copious than either of these two explanations allow. While only comprehensible in discursive terms, the structural regularities of the economic are not themselves entirely the constructions of discourse. Defining something as "discursive" *because* it can only be accessed discursively does not logically follow. If we wish to talk about the movement of the earth around the sun, in the broadest sense we have to employ the language sets and concepts available to us for the purpose; we proceed discursively in that sense. But it would be folly to assume that these languages and those discourses actually *are* the movement of the earth around the sun. If the earth was ever to be dislodged from its orbit, moreover, new languages would urgently be generated to address both the resulting physical results as well as the experiential trauma involved.

It all depends on the kinds of questions we want to ask. So long as the operative field of vision remains structured around questions of identity, the production of subjectivities, and individualized understandings of the social and other collectivities, or so long as we continue talking about variations on the theme of the social imaginary, the dynamics of recognition, and the contingencies of public voice, then the conflation of discourse as object of analysis with discourse as method of analysis remains feasible. But once we begin talking about the movement of the earth around the sun, or about the demonstrable regularities through which capitalism creates rich and poor, on the other hand, then the conflation becomes harder to maintain. These latter contexts raise acutely the question we continue to worry about. While always recognizing that our possible access can only ever be linguistically and discursively managed or understood, we need to ask again the question: is there a nondiscursive or extradiscursive field?[60]

On this score in his recent essay Stedman Jones seemed unequivocal, hardening the stance taken earlier in *Languages of Class*. In his current view, a discursive approach not only affords the appropriate epistemological legitimacy and coherence, given everything learned in the course of the cultural turn, but also provides the sole guarantee of nonreductiveness and complexity of explanation, of respect for rights, and even of the historian's ethical probity. Inscribed in the terms of Stedman Jones's advocacy of the "discursive approach," accordingly, there is also a politics: "Only by acknowledging that politics occurs wholly within discourse and by refusing to counterpose discourse to an extra-discursive reality," he asserted, "is it possible to arrive at a historically grounded sense of the significance of the place of law, authority, and legitimacy in historical development." Indeed, the biggest indictment of Marxist and equivalent forms of social history arising from the 1960s was precisely their inability to give these autonomies their due. This was not a contingent failure, he suggested, but one epistemologically embedded in the very commitment of the social historian to the prioritizing of social determinations.

Systems of thought, like those of Marxism and perhaps of the later Foucault, which juxtapose discursive practices to extra-discursive domains and accord a primary reality to the extra-discursive, tend also to reduce law to ritualized violence, and authority, legitimacy, and justice to post hoc forms of ideological justification. What is lacking in such accounts is an explanation of the way in which such norms are historically formed and the means by which they are sustained, or indeed how they came to connect through forms of internalisation with basic forms of human emotion.[61]

For Stedman Jones there seems to be no space any longer between the full-blown discursive approach expounded here and the most reductionist version of economistic Marxism, into which he now seems to have entirely subsumed the possibilities for doing social history. There seems no intermediate ground, no room for the kind of agnosticism that continues to grapple with the enduring conundrum of finding an epistemological vantage point from which the materiality of the world might be theorized beyond the now established languages of constructionism and discursivity. But of course this is a false polarity. Between the maximalist or purist version of the discursive approach Stedman Jones wishes to occupy and the particular description of social historical analysis he offers there exist many other opportunities. For his characterization of social history is actually a doubly caricatured and essentialized redescription: equating Marxism exclusively with its economistic versions massively simplifies the intellectual history of the Marxist tradition, not least during the last four decades; while dismissing social history as always already disqualified by the same associations summarily banishes the diversity of the work social historians have actually done. In fact, there exist many practical cases of analysis in which historians show very creatively how Stedman Jones's dichotomy can be escaped, whether they be "social" historians in the conventional sense, "cultural" historians as we now know them, or historians of some other stripe.

Confusion commonly arises here from allowing the distinction between the "discursive" and the "extradiscursive" to become fallaciously mapped onto that of the "material" versus the "nonmaterial." In fact, one of the earliest antireductionist gains in the broadly Marxist and feminist theoretical discussions of the 1970s had been precisely to have established the material qualities in the conditions of existence of "ideology" and "the cultural," or the "discursive" as we would now say. Surely, "materiality" in this context is less about studying the "social" or the "economic" in contradistinction to "ideas" and "language" in the narrower formal sense than it is about the degree of concreteness and density of contextualizing with which any particular work of history can be pursued. The distinction between "discursive" and "extradiscursive" becomes in that sense something of a red herring, giving some advocates of the linguistic approach permission to withdraw from the more arduous types of what used to be called social history, while allowing dyed-in-the-wool older-style social historians to continue ignoring or setting themselves against the challenge of the cultural turn.

To take Stedman Jones's own example quoted earlier, for instance, it could be perfectly possible and legitimate to confine one's study of the law to legal treatises, judicial proceedings, statutes and judgments, court cases, and other legal documents, thereby meeting the standards of one orthodox model of intellectual or legal history. But such a study could also be pushed in the direction of the sources and methods characteristic of the now-established social history of criminality and the practice of the law, just as it might be further extended into the post-Foucauldian historiographies of punishment and social discipline. Likewise, while "the rise of commercial society" can certainly be studied by the classic methods of intellectual history, as Stedman Jones seems to wish, it might equally be approached via the richly developed social and economic historiographies of the eighteenth and early nineteenth centuries accumulating since the 1970s. But in either case, surely, some notion of the structural coordinates of the economy would need to be included as an important element of the project.[62]

If we are reading Stedman Jones correctly, however, even to postulate the existence of a separable social or economic domain seems now to have become suspect, necessarily inscribed with its essentialized and relentless logic of reductionism. Yet we cannot see how such an implication could be embraced. Unless accounts of what Stedman Jones is calling the "rise of commercial society" are to remain wholly within the history of ideas, they can no more avoid dealing with the structural and systemic aspects of the development of the economy or the social structure than could the earlier accounts of the most recalcitrant of Marxists and older-style social historians. We are not dealing here with an issue of the "discursive" versus the "extradiscursive" at all, in fact, but rather with the depth or density of the proposed analysis, the "levels" or domains of the social formation we are mainly concerned with, the most appropriate archive for studying them, and the kinds of theory best fitted for the purpose. So while we are personally entirely sympathetic to the "discursive approach," we are not convinced that much good purpose is served by seeking to establish this as the sole operative standard for the discipline's best practice, if only because large bodies of excellent scholarship continue taking the existence of an extradiscursive realm to be understood. Purely on the basis of this continuing diversity in the historiographical landscape that historians are actually fashioning, it seems hard to deny that a great deal of useful knowledge can still result, even if not everyone chooses to follow or learn the ruthless logic of linguistic maximalism.

At first blush, Stedman Jones's argument is wholly persuasive. We agree that the process of politics cannot properly be derived from the nondiscursive field of determinations identified with the economic, pre-existing classes, and the associated underlying structures of "interests." We agree that the project of analyzing the forms of stability and cohesion, conflict, and contestation within the systems of power and representation of a society has to be disengaged from the practice of referring them to the structural facts and "realities" of the social world in an old-style Marxist or "materialist" way. But whoever was it that made this maneuver anyway and claimed a privileged understanding of political process based exclusively on a referral to "extradiscursive" factors? For example, when Marx himself wrote history, the resulting analysis is widely acknowledged to have been far more complex and subtle, messier in fact, than such caricatures allow.[63] It might certainly be possible to draw up a modest list of strategic instances of reductive social histories from the past few decades in which the argument is organized around these simple materialist precepts—for example, in treating the political process as a superstructural reflex of the economic base. But that has not actually been a very common practice. Quite conventional histories inspired by Marx have paid very close attention to questions of difference—both in different places and times and in different countries, in the sense of having to bring to the explanation of differing outcomes all the appropriate intelligence and subtlety. In that case, how many social historians have actually taken the "determinist fix" described by Stedman Jones?

We suspect we are being offered false opposites here, in which the wholly discursive is being counterposed against the wholly extradiscursive. Approaching politics entirely via its own discourses, language sets, and repertoires of representation is certainly one possible way to proceed. But alternative strategies of analysis are equally clearly available that fall short of the reductive and deterministic lumpen-Marxism that Stedman Jones rightly wishes to refuse. Many of those choosing a Marxist affiliation during the last few decades, including Stedman Jones himself, had certainly never swallowed such an unappealing version of what the Marxist tradition was able to offer. Stedman Jones ended his essay by saying he wants to put Marx back into history. But after taking the force of this forgivable rhetorical flourish, we also need to say equally rhetorically that—by intention, and with varying success no doubt—there were some who never took him out of it.

Ironically enough, Stedman Jones himself could not avoid imagining, incidentally and almost as an afterthought, the possible grounds for an extradiscursive standpoint. That is, he also postulated realms of actuality that precede articulation in discourse, although rather than residing, for example, in concretely and practically manifest and structurally encountered forms of economic inequality, these are now to be found in "basic forms of human emotion" and "a range of powerful and repeatedly encountered human emotions." While ourselves definitely accepting the importance of addressing the realm of emotions, we confess here to some puzzlement. We cannot understand how the one ground for extradiscursive analysis can be admitted and the other not. Listing half a dozen forms of discursive appearance of these "basic human emotions," Stedman Jones uses a footnote in order to validate the basicness of these emotions by the regularity of their occurrence. He also allows them to underlie if not determine "forms of political and religious discourse."[64] In other words, Stedman Jones *did* after all seem to keep a place for a nondiscursive sphere whose importance rests upon knowledge of its regularities. Yet if the one is to be admitted into the historian's range of vision, then why not practical manifestions of economics and social inequality as well?

There seems something evasive in suggesting that the only way of contributing to the clarification of the place of Marxism in historical research is to go back to the eighteenth century to study the Enlightenment. We obviously would not oppose any reconsideration of post-Enlightenment forms of social science, of pre-Marxian socialisms, of the historical formation of possessive individualism, and other aspects of the intellectual settings for the "rise of commercial society." These are patently important areas of historical study. But historians of liberalism already address them fairly frequently in one form or another. If the project is to historicize Marx within the modernity that such things composed, certainly, this becomes a proper but surely not exclusive project. But in this declaration of priorities there are clearly ulterior purposes also at work. Stedman Jones's own interest in the complex genealogies of liberalism in the late eighteenth and early nineteenth centuries is related to a deeply felt and carefully conducted reconsideration of political choices and affiliations, which extends well beyond those more specific questions concerning the genealogies of political economy and other aspects of Enlightenment thought.

As should be clear from the contexts of debate through which the relevant arguments have been advanced since the 1980s, that process of revision advocated by Stedman Jones has a relationship to contemporary postsocialist politics, to the choices facing supporters of the Left in Britain, and to the ethical and philosophical dimensions of all the changes entailed, as well as to the more specifically historiographical issues we have been discussing and the associated epistemological dilemmas. Further, in the wider body of work in nineteenth- and twentieth-century British history that Stedman Jones has helped to inspire during the past two decades, there has also developed a powerful reinterpretation of the character of the Labour Party, its relationship to other and earlier forms of radicalism, and its affiliations in particular with forms of popular liberalism in the era of Gladstone and since.[65]

All these political implications deserve to be openly and clearly faced. Central to them is Stedman Jones's unproblematized idea of "commercial society," which in his article was counterposed against "centralized and authoritarian regimes in which bureaucratic direction substituted for the processes of commercial exchange."[66] But this again proposed a false polarity. It occludes entire histories of democratic socialism in Europe, including everything descending from the democratizations of 1918 and 1945, from the formation of welfare states, from the pursuit of redistributive social justice via taxation and other means, from the regulation of labor markets, from the addressing of economic priorities through the public sector, and from a huge amount else besides, including of course the general capacity to postulate collective social and cultural goods as desirable and legitimate goals for a society. Where do these desiderata reside in the stark polarity permitted by Stedman Jones's binarism of market liberalism ("commercial society") and Stalinism ("centralized and authoritarian regimes")? Even from a vantage point in the 1990s, when the residual forms of post-1945 social democracy had come to seem so ineffectual and threadbare, there were surely intermediate projects of reform admissible into the possible trajectories of European history between the Enlightenment and Tony Blair. Not to acknowledge this more complex range of political choice amounts to an important reductionism of its own, as if there is nothing beyond the ground of market freedoms and liberal constitutions that a Left could ever now imagine trying to demand.[67]

Indeed, Stedman Jones does seem to have settled for a limited liberal conception of rights as the one reliable ground of politics. In rejecting "the reductionist character of Foucault's vision of 'governmentality,'" he advanced a strong but poorly specified idea of justice (as "notions of right"), whose generative contradictions he argued are essential for grasping the actual complexities within civil society from which the possibilities of contestation and change can grow. Without such "notions of right," he insisted, we have no means of distinguishing "the formation of competing and conflicting claims within civil society from the putatively pure struggles of power which characterize Foucault's picture of power and government." In particular, the unidirectional logic of Foucault's approach to the exercise of power in a society "renders it incapable of distinguishing between states which abide by norms of legality and those that do not." In the absence of a theory of contestation, accordingly, Foucault was prevented "from accepting that changing norms of right may—in favorable circumstances and conjunctures—provide the principal means by which the weak are occasionally enabled to combine together and defeat the strong." To escape this reductionist logic, we need some "account of how in modern constitutional states legal and ethical norms are produced through participation in the institutions of civil society," a process for which Stedman Jones offered his own reading of Chartism's contestatory "language of constitutionalism" as an illustration.[68]

Whether or not this is a fair and accurate reading of Foucault, the claim that "notions of right are indispensable to the task of historical explanation" necessarily takes on board a generation's worth of contentions within liberal philosophy in Britain and the United States. Quite aside from the tasks of negotiating *those* complexities, though, there also arises the classic social historian's objection, which remains quite as subversive as it ever did: by what processes were such notions of right produced, circulated, diffused, imposed, contested, embedded, disregarded, assimilated, or transformed through the everydayness of ordinary people's practices and attitudes? What were the connections between the formal discourse of rights at the level of political philosophy and the operative contexts of popular culture and social exchange where such ideas got taken up? What were the media of those processes, and who were the agents? In his essay on Chartism, Stedman Jones offered a fine example of how to begin answering those questions, but in all truth he never pushed much beyond another level of the formal circulation of ideas through a different category of the intellectual historian's written sources. Going further in the meantime, to explore the broader popular contexts where the meanings and efficacies of those ideas came to be negotiated, has mainly been the accomplishment of precisely those social historians whose collective epistemological misguidedness has been so commonly bemoaned.[69] So we need to ask once again: how do we get back to the formation of these notions of right *before* they become employed in the more formal processes of political action and political thought that Stedman Jones now concentrates on studying? Or is there no longer any "back" to get to?

Invoking his own analysis of Chartism would certainly be one perfectly reasonable response here for Stedman Jones. Yet "notions of right" seem to be doing double service in his argument. On the one hand, they provide a stick with which to beat Foucault and other ultraleft versions of the disregard for liberal freedoms. But on the other hand, they are also deemed essential for explanations based on the linguistic approach to history, and much of the detailed argumentation for this deeper standpoint remains opaque. While it may possess unimpeachable justification within a certain contemporary discourse of Anglo-American liberal political philosophy, why should we accept the argument that politics is ultimately and overridingly about conceptions of rights in that very specific sense? Such a claim neither exhausts the wider repertoire of available political theory, even within the sector of pluralist thinking about democracy, nor precludes the possibility that nondiscursive elements may also be considered in play. We assume that Stedman Jones would acknowledge the pertinence of at least some of these comments. But our larger point is that a huge area of clarification is left by the formulations he so far provides. He seems to be taking his stand on the ground of a modest liberalism protecting the primary values of the market, but this seems so radically at variance with most of the other statements he has been making over the years that we hesitate to draw such a conclusion. What is the more elaborate politics disclosed by these arguments?

What, more specifically, *are* the "norms of legality" invoked against Foucault and presumably other left critics of the liberal democratic state, who have continued to criticize any primary reliance on constitutionalism and liberal conceptions of rights as the self-sufficient objects of political desire?[70] In his conclusion Stedman Jones takes recourse to a set of concerns surprisingly characteristic of a moderate contemporary liberalism in the English-speaking world—notably, "constitutionalism," "basic human emotions" (habits of the heart and individualism), "commercial society" (possessive individualism and markets), an unclear maneuver around "rights" (discursively constructed or not?), and finally that entirely unqualified use of "norms of legality." One common anxiety accompanying the post-Marxist advocacy of new forms of radical democracy amid the iconoclastic and antireductionist explorations of "New Times" in the 1980s had concerned precisely this limiting proximity to a kind of repluralized liberalism, from which anything smacking of socialism or the critique of capitalism would then be excluded. Now the space of any democratic socialist critique of capitalism and its forms of social inequality and exploitation does indeed seem to have been abolished, identified instead with only the most antidemocratic, authoritarian, and economically inefficient forms of statist bureaucracy. The variant forms of the development of capitalism during the nineteenth and twentieth centuries are subsumed within a single and wholly unspecified category of "commercial society." The operative value offered by either the "Marxian 'critique of political economy'" or "its theory of history" has shrunk to virtually nothing.[71]

## BACKING AWAY FROM THE SOCIAL

So in the end, we have serious doubts about the maximalist conclusions Stedman Jones wishes to draw from his advocacy of the "discursive approach." Much of the substance of his critique of social history remains extremely compelling. The promises and excitements associated with the forms of materialist or Marxist-inclined social history prevalent in the 1970s certainly encouraged an overambitious investment in the power of social explanation and social determinations. What Stedman Jones calls the "determinist fix" betrayed us into misunderstanding the relations between the material world and the possibilities of politics. It rendered sovereign the working class as the agent of worthwhile change. It compressed the particular differences of working-class formations in different times and different national configurations. It suppressed important differences within the working class and extending beyond it, notably those associated with gender, sexuality, ethnicity, race, religion, and so forth. In general, it provided, within a sophisticated analytical language, a highly simplified account of the social terrain on which a progressive politics had to be founded. In all of these terms the analytical cast of mind entailed precisely a determinist fix of the kind Stedman Jones attacks.

In opening a discussion of these problems, Stedman Jones's earlier essay on the language of class in Chartism was absolutely crucial. There he argued convincingly that the wish to recuperate a "real" working class by studying political movements like Chartism erected on forms of class-collective understanding and assumption was a chimera. Until this intervention, the broadly consensual view, not exclusively Marxist by any means but consonant with Marxist logics of inquiry, had been that the languages of Chartism, its rhetorics, its local political forms, its petitions, its newspapers, the whole panoply of its activity and leadership, brought into being *not* the working class per se, but the working class as a *political agent*. That is, it brought to consciousness and political voice an already assembled class collectivity.

But what Stedman Jones argued, in contrast, was that the languages of Chartism became constitutive for the ontologies of the class itself. The coarse Marxist position argued that the working class was heaved into being by inexorable capitalist processes: the economically defined process of working-class formation came first; politics came after. Not so, Stedman Jones argued, for it was the politics and the rhetorics of Chartism focused around linguistic conceptions of class that first enabled Chartist political agency and by extension summoned the class presence into being. Class was not the actually existing terrain rendering possible a progressive or revolutionary politics. On the contrary, class was the linguistic heuristic rhetoric that convened highly disparate social elements around the principal centers of Chartist politics in the 1840s and thereby allowed a working class to be imagined.

But we are not convinced by the polarity inherent in these distinctions. In the first place, what may have worked as an orthodox understanding of the relationship of class to politics in the sectarian worlds of the Leninist parties never held sway in any but a handful of scholarly social histories of class formation and agency. Even the work of John Foster, which Stedman Jones himself brilliantly criticized in an earlier essay, did not conflate with the axioms of his avowedly Leninist politics. For other social historians of the same generation, in the main, the authors' political affiliations were even less obviously readable in their scholarly work. Robbie Gray, more or less an exact contemporary of Foster and fellow member of the CPGB, could not remotely be accused of drawing sectarian purpose into scholarly perception, and so it was for most left social historians of the 1970s working within a broadly Marxist social historical problematic. In that sense Stedman Jones's characterization of the earlier work, against which his own approach was counterposed, came close to parody. What he *was* correct in seeing was the basic analytical orientation, reflecting a Thompsonian belief in the relationship of being and consciousness. Few challenged the ontologies of class as a basic ground of their work in that sense: class existed. But the social history of the 1970s was exceptional in the range and diversity of the studies of class it generated within this broadly consensual framing, emphasizing at different times cultural, political, economic, communitarian, and other aspects of the lives of those thought to be members of the class concerned. Stedman Jones's conflation of this diverse and complex region of social history with coarse Marxist readings of an orthodox and sectarian kind had no adequate foundation.

In fact, since the 1960s the social history of class has always been a contested field, never a consensual one. Its copious and complex historiography has been marked by recurrent argument and polemical conflict over the better part of forty years. More recently, as this book has extensively explored, voices like Stedman Jones's have been proposing an examination still more fundamental, one that challenges the utility of the concept of class itself rather than merely problematizing some of its particular uses. It was always clear, moreover, that such challenges were highly politically charged. Just as the ambitions of the great turning to social history during the 1960s and 1970s reflected palpable political optimisms, linking class analysis in the past to a set of radical hopes in the present, so did this new bout of revision bespeak a more pessimistic prognosis of change. For large numbers, maybe even a majority, of practitioners, social history and politics usually marched together. "In recent years," writes Patrick Joyce, "the concept of class has come under increasing scrutiny as a means of explaining both the present and the past. The reasons for this lie in the profound economic, political, and economic changes marking our time. Class is seen by some to be unequal to the task of explaining our present reality. And this view has been of great effect among historians too: if class fails to interpret the present, perhaps it has not given an adequate account of our past either?"[72]

For leading participants in the debates we have been describing like Joan Scott and Gareth Stedman Jones, and also for ourselves, this interconnectedness of politics and historiography has been fundamental. The valency of the kind of history one prefers, whether in relation to the underlying issues of epistemology or the particular debates about class, is profoundly affected by one's attitude toward the political choices of the past two decades, whether we consider these in relation to the politics of subjectivity in personal and everyday life, in relation to questions of identity, or in relation to the transformed bases of progressive electoral and social movement politics in national and transnational arenas. In one way or another, those political choices either speak clearly and directly through contemporary historiographical debates or else shadow them with varying degrees of immediacy. It remains, therefore, for us to return explicitly to this question: from what grounds might we address the politics of class formation today?

# V. WHAT IS THE VALENCY
## OF CLASS NOW?

When we published our earlier article, "Why Does Social History Ignore Politics?" (1980), we were trying to engage the complex field of interconnections between the social histories of labor and the organized practices of politics as they presented themselves to historians of a particular generation. Most left-inclined historians in Britain and the English-speaking world more generally who came of age in the 1960s, we believed at the time, took Marxist and allied approaches to social analysis to provide the essential grounding of their political commitment.[1] From that earlier vantage point, it was precisely the enriched understandings of social history, in conjunction with contemporaneous redefinitions and expansions of the category of the political, that incited our critique—not because we were opposed to either of those things (quite the contrary), but because we were worrying about their existing logics of merger. To explain the direction of our current argument—to explore how discussions of class and discussions of politics might be working together *now*—some revisiting of this earlier intellectual-political history makes sense.[2]

As social history began taking off, let us say from the mid-1960s to mid-1970s, its practitioners tended to define themselves against the narrowness of political history as it was then practiced and understood. But as the political turmoil of the time began invading the seminar rooms, it seemed not enough simply to counterpose social history to political history as a separate specialism and a necessary source of contextualizing for developments in the political sphere. The positive case for doing social history became not only the power of social determinations in explaining how politics took place at the top, fundamental though this was. It also

139

resided in an argument for changing our understanding of politics per se, for expanding the meanings of politics in society at large. A decisive effect of the social history upswing was thus a radical *expansion* of politics—that is, an enlarged perception of the presence and effects of "the political" in the ordinary parts of social life. This made it possible to claim previously "nonpolitical" locations for politics in a new way, and sometimes for the first time: the workplace, the neighborhood, the subculture, the family, the home. These places were already present as the *objects of policy,* through law, welfare, social administration. But they were now claimed as sites of political identification and contestation too, as places where power was organized and embodied, and where accordingly resistance might also be expected to occur.

This was a decisive perspectival shift. It moved politics away from the conventional institutional arenas where the imagination, established political practices, and disciplinary conventions all confined them—including the state, parliaments, the parties, public organizations in the narrower sense—into a much broader and less manageable societal domain. It took politics "out of doors." It allowed the biggest questions of political life—the potentials for stability and cohesion in the social order, the possibilities for conformity and opposition, the circumstances under which dominant interests and values might be challenged, restored, or even overcome—to be very differently posed than before. "The personal is political" was one dramatic naming of this opening up, one that proved extraordinarily resonant and successful in the course of the 1970s. The radicalism of the time proved ever more inventive in finding new political sites across a potentially limitless terrain of previously private and unclaimed everyday transactions.

In this period, social history produced two distinct and countervailing logics. If in one sense the turning to social history encouraged a definition of "society" as separate and distinct from politics, as the distinct jurisdiction where social historians would practice their craft, then in another sense it discovered political potentials precisely within the "social" itself. If one possible consequence was the depoliticizing of the social into a discrete and manageable object for study, then another was to invest it precisely with political meanings. The tension of these two logics supplied both the excitement and the frustration, the shared identity and the divisiveness, in social history. When some social historians argued for explicitly reconnecting social-historical work *back* to the political sphere, in the second half of the 1970s, at a time of wider theoretical debate among Marxists and others over the specificity of the political and its autonomies, that divisiveness grew. In the course of the 1980s, via combinations of new empirical fields, radical politics, and extensive theorizing, many social historians brought themselves to an understanding of what politics *includes* that markedly differed from the assumptions with which they had originally begun, when social history had been viewed as a contextually determining and conceptually superior alternative to a narrowly institutional model of political life. In this new situation, getting back to politics—that is, trying to reconceptualize the relationship between "the social" and "the political," once the older and limiting boundaries had been breached—seemed an increasingly urgent task. But bringing "society" and "politics" back together again has been an immensely complicated thing.

Simplifying enormously, during the later 1970s and early 1980s there seem to have been two main routes. One of these came through state theory. The enlarged understanding of politics just described brought an expanded but deinstitutionalized appreciation of the state's involvement in society, outgrowing the boundaries of government in the narrower sense to embrace arenas of social administration, public health, the law, schooling, religious practice and belief, the organization of private life in families, sexuality, gender divisions, work for wages and in the home, and the shifting distinctions between the private and the public. Along all of these dimensions, especially under the impact of feminism, public power has been tracked through its main thoroughfares and alleyways, into the protected spaces and hidden crevices of social life. The state's presence now became sought in less visible and more indirect ways than before. Beyond the conventional business of governing, the state was seen to consist in wider systems of regulation and intervention, involving the larger process of social reproduction, of constructing and reconstructing social relations on the broadest of fronts. In its early days, social history often implied a mechanical distinction between "society" on the one hand and "state," "ideology," and "politics" on the other. But so far from belonging on one side of that dichotomy, social history now increasingly positioned itself inside the complex force field between the two. Moreover, though we now commonly see this deinstitutionalizing of our perceptions of how the state operates in social life as a distinctively "Foucauldian" insight, it actually owed far more to the unfolding of the politicized logic of social historical inquiry per se.[3]

The second route has been through various kinds of what might be called culturalism, providing we separate that term from its place in an earlier set of polemics.[4] Among the plethora of major influences, running from Thompson and Geertz through Bourdieu, cultural studies, feminism, literary theory, and various poststructuralisms, this is where Foucault's reception can deservedly be singled out. Above all other key encounters of the 1970s and 1980s, the protracted wrestling with Foucault's ideas helped shift our perceptions of politics still further, confirming the movement away from the state's core institutions in the national-centralized sense toward their "micro-physics," what Foucault called the emergence of new individualizing strategies, functioning "outside, below, and alongside the State Apparatuses, on a much more minute and everyday level."[5] Power in this Foucauldian sense becomes more widely and insidiously diffused through society than the older antinomies between social and political history, or society and the state, allowed us to think. Power—and hence political meaning—is organized in and by all types of social institutions, cultural practices, and informal transactions, as well as through the formal contexts of national and local politics, or through the more visible and obvious locations of public decision making. Power and thus the chances for political action are structured into both the most basic and usually unspoken assumptions through which we perceive our relationship to the social world and the practices of the everyday. Consequently, power is no longer just the property of the state—whether we see this as coercion and repressive interventions, as a machinery of ideological apparatuses, or more broadly as the ensemble of public institutions—but may be sought in the smallest and most intimate of human relationships too.

If "power," or at least our understanding of how power is ordered and where it can be found, has been "moving around the social space" in that way, then "culture" (as the production, interpretation, and contest of meaning) becomes vital to how its definition needs to be approached.[6] This has required a certain blurring of categories while recognizing their mutual permeability—an antireductionist recognition that politics, law, culture, beliefs are not external to the economy and its social relations or to each other, but are always-already imbricated together in complex unities of structure and action, indissolubly and constitutively interconnected whenever we encounter them in concrete practices, specific events, and individual lives. Such a recognition encourages an interest in microhistory, in the hidden histories of the local and the everyday, because it is there that the dynamics of such relationships, their profane interconnectedness, might be realistically and manageably approached. Further, if power is to be found in social as well as in formally political arrangements, and culture can be both an effect and a medium of domination, then all the mundane relations of everyday life fall beneath power's sway. People in their multiform identities, thinking and acting across the different dimensions of their lives, all produce and are produced by relations of power—relations, that is, through which the participants are continuously negotiating and renegotiating aspects of inequality, authority, and the varying capacity to define the meanings of the world.

Here it is the element of *negotiation* that becomes key. If power secures the silencing of certain voices by ordering the experienced world into definite regimes of truth and intelligibility, allowing some things to be spoken easily or legitimately, while other things go normally unsaid, we certainly are not able to leave it at that. For in so doing, power also puts itself at risk, by producing positions from which subjects can try to speak. This is an absolutely vital caveat, frequently neglected when "power" and "domination" are under discussion beneath this post-Foucauldian dispensation: power relations are never simply vectors of domination or "social control" but are simultaneously media of possible contestation, even sometimes of emancipation too. As Foucault himself repeatedly reminded us, where there is power, there is always resistance. If this point is to be grasped, if the politically incapacitating temptations of an overtotalized conception of power as domination can be overcome, then "resistance" as well as "power" needs to be thought. In effect, perhaps, Gramsci has to be added to Foucault.

## WHAT HAPPENS WHEN GRAMSCI MEETS FOUCAULT?

As labor historians broadened their vision into the new social history of the working class during the 1970s, some of their most fruitful work focused on the reproduction of class relations under historical conditions of noncoercive rule—under conditions, that is, where the defense of socioeconomic inequalities was accomplished without resorting to any obvious use of violence, or at least where the latency of such violence, the implied use of force rather than its physical exercise, was enough. Under the influence of the reception of the ideas of Antonio Gramsci, much attention was paid to this question of how the "consent" of the subaltern classes in civil society came to be secured. The state and its apparatuses receded from the centerground of discussion, if indeed they had ever been particularly salient. Detailed social histories of the police or the military or the bureaucracy had never exactly been very common, after all. The classic text for these newly "Gramscian" discussions has been quoted many times.

> In Russia civil society was primordial and gelatinous; in the West there was a proper relation between State and civil society, and when the State trembled a sturdy structure of civil society was at once revealed. The State was only an outer ditch, behind which there stood a powerful system of fortresses and earthworks, more or less numerous from one state to the next, it goes without saying—but this precisely necessitated an accurate reconnaissance of each individual country.[7]

This direction of thought has given us some of the most fruitful accounts of the history of class relations in specific societies and at specific times. It freed analysis from seeking an infrastructural cause for each and every political event. Departing the less cautious instincts of an earlier Marxist historiography, it recognized the historical particularities of single, national societies, together with the need for their detailed empirical mapping and historical recuperation. At the same time, it insisted that the relations of power were imbricated in the practices of daily life, not simply at those points where individuals or groups encountered the state in the more obvious institutional sense. And it suggested, accordingly, that the life of a subaltern class encompassed something fuller, richer, and more complex than simply the reflexes of its subordination. Gramsci's concepts of "consent," of "civil society," and of cultural rather than merely political "hegemony" fertilized social history in this manner, aiding its escape from any narrowly determinist problematic. The particular studies flowing from the resulting insights assembled a rich catalog of the varied sites of struggle, significant points of the exercise of class power, and possible forms of resistance.

Nonetheless, the underlying theorization of power remained broadly familiar. The presumption that the political institutions of a class-structured society should be interpreted functionally, precisely by referring them back to the relations between classes, as a set of necessary, logical, and determined entailments, stayed basically intact. The Gramscian contribution failed to transform that understanding of class power per se, or indeed to query its absolute centrality, but rather transferred the analysis of the exercise of that power to new sites. If it shifted focus toward the spheres of culture and civil society in particular, moving away from the repressive apparatuses of government, then the essential alignment of those institutional forms of rule with the inequalities and inequities of class remained a primary axiom of understanding. In that sense, Gramsci's notation of power and Foucault's were fundamentally discontinuous.

Facing the tenacity of capitalism's hold on society, Gramsci recognized that much of its capacity for reproduction and self-renewal lay beyond the state's ability to mobilize force through police, law, and explicit regulation, residing rather in cultural practices and civil society's wider associational field too. His resulting account of the relationship between state and civil society fluctuated considerably, as Perry Anderson and others have shown, sometimes claiming an autonomy for civil society, sometimes placing it inside the state's field of relations itself.[8] Yet whichever precise definition Gramsci deployed, and however rich his conception of the cultures and practices inscribed within civil society, he preserved his understanding of the latter as a site of class-derived relations of power. It was an arena in which the contradictory relationships and power play of classes under capitalism were enacted. However far from recognizable economic reductionism Gramsci's thinking carried us, accordingly, the fundamental object of analysis remained nonetheless the derivation of power *from* class.

Despite all his insights, in other words, Gramsci sought the unitary and dominant source of power in society in the classic foundationalist manner on the familiar terrain of unequal class relations. He gave us a refined view of the particular historical enactments of class domination and subjugation in Italian and other capitalist societies. He exposed a subtle tissue of power relations not simply at the level of the state, but across and through the daily life of a whole society. Yet however they occurred, however silently they moved, and however subtly they mobilized the subaltern consciousness, the pivotal relations of power in society remained those anchored in the structural inequalities of class. Their principal purpose was to secure the social and other conditions required by capitalism for its self-reproduction—not just social stabilities or freedom from class war, but also the biological reproduction of labor power and its cultural conditioning. The fields of contestation surrounding the relations of class, and the balance of forces within them, determined for Gramsci the chances of stability or change and conditioned the possibilities for revolution. Class was simply a given. Its centrality for Gramsci's understanding of power was essential and absolute. Class was the conceptual headquarters from which proceeded all repressions, all hegemonies, all bids for consent. Power and its purposes were at root class power and class purposes.

These comments are meant only to state the obvious: namely, that Gramsci, for all his subtleties and innovations, remained embedded in a Marxist tradition for which the contradictions between the forces and relations of production remained the axiomatic starting point for judging the mainsprings of historical change. Those contradictions, famously described in Marx's 1859 Preface, defined the limits of significant conflict, if not its precise historical form.[9] In the latter was to be found Gramsci's distinctive and principal insight: to have illuminated some of the peaceful mechanisms through which capitalism reproduces itself, and to have called all those associated questions onto the agenda. He addressed the problem of power as something more than merely the repression and coercion of one class by another. His notion of "consent" at least started to suggest that the structure of consciousness of the subaltern classes was more complex than the brute conditions of their subjugation had led many of his fellow Marxists to suggest. And his belief in the construction of counterhegemonies proposed forms of class resistance different from any full frontal assault on the power of the ruling-class state.

Of course, Gramsci's analysis of the workings of capitalism was also designed to deliver the levers of its future revolutionary transformation.

That analysis was meant precisely to converge to the conditions of an effective revolutionary politics, to a political strategy adequate for the broadest based popular democratic mobilization. The degree to which the Italian Communist Party (PCI) under Palmiro Togliatti and his successors was able to employ the resultant strategy between Gramsci's death in 1937 and the 1970s remains open to argument. But the partial relocation of revolutionary struggle to the institutions and practices of civil society was plainly a key part of that story. So profoundly unlike Foucault's thinking about power, Gramsci's analyses were specifically intended to convene practical forms of revolutionary opposition, exactly to create a new political strategy appropriate to the socially complex conditions of capitalist modernity in the West. In that respect, his methods, his purposes, and his procedures were those of Marx himself. First, an intense reflection on the world as object, as "outside," and as difficult to penetrate, but as nevertheless open to the intellectual's independent and critical mind. Second, the discovery, through such reflection, of the mainsprings of power in a capitalist society, together with the levers by which it might be resisted or overturned, its laws of motion reversed. Third, the careful fashioning of a working-class political strategy consistent with the sophisticated analysis of bourgeois class power thereby provided. The structure of class, the centrality of state power, and a Marxist understanding of contradiction were at the very crux, a set of "absolute presuppositions" apparently valorized by a scientific procedure.

Foucault, in contrast, radically disengaged from these concepts, methods, and assumptions. In principle, like Gramsci, he certainly did not deny the existence of the state as a locus of power, but he had still less interest in making it the main or even a significant object of his attentions. The sovereignty of the state, class domination where it exists, the subtle subjugation of the subaltern, were all, by his account, the productive *effects* of the workings of power, the shifting terminus of its processes, the indistinct and endlessly remapped destination. "Social hegemonies" were the consequences of the endless play of power, not its source, its center, or its cause. In this way, Foucault reversed the essential flow of the argument about the nature of power. Measured by Gramsci's affiliation with the Marxist tradition, what is most striking here is the discontinuity.

By power, I do not mean "Power" as a group of institutions and mechanisms that ensure the subservience of the citizens of a given state. By power, I do not mean, either, a mode of subjugation which, in contrast to violence, has the form of the rule. Finally, I do not have in mind a general system of domination exerted by one group over another, a system whose effects, through successive derivations, pervade the entire social body. The analysis, made in terms of power, must not assume that the sovereignty of the state, the form of the law, or the overall unity of a domination are given at the outset; rather these are only the terminal form power takes.[10]

Foucault did not entirely refuse a conception of social hegemony turning around social divisions of class. He did not rule out, in the manner of some poststructuralists, the analytical pertinence of the social formation—what he referred to as the "entire social body." Rather, what he argued was this: that far from being the centralized, unitary source of power, "society" was the result of power's circulation through other, more localized domains. All these amounted to a whole field of *prior* power relations. In this account, for example, the state did not control, manipulate, or inaugurate by acting as the Committee of Public Safety of the ruling class. On the contrary, the ability of dominant classes to act through the institutional avenues and modalities of a state rested upon the "complex, strategical situation" of the power relations of a particular society extending into its most localized and mundane places. And this was not a given. It was not a prime cause. It did not represent a pervasive or inexhaustible sump of class power exercised through mechanisms of repression by violence or those of winning the grudging and forcibly exacted acquiescence of the subordinated, although in specific instances those coercive means might of course apply. What Foucault wanted to avoid was the easy recourse either to an image of an "essentially repressive" state—"the army as a power of death, police and justice as punitive instances, etc."—or to that of an authoritative "society," each of which preempted the harder tasks of understanding the other ways in which power was able to work.

I don't want to say that the state isn't important; what I want to say is that relations of power, and hence the analysis that must be made of them, necessarily extend beyond the limits of the state. In two senses: first of all because the state, for all the omnipotence of its apparatuses, is far from being able to occupy the whole field of actual power relations, and further because the state can only operate on the basis of other, already existing power relations. The state is superstructural in relation to a whole series of power networks that invest the body, sexuality, the family, kinship, knowledge, technology, and so forth. True, these networks stand in a conditioning-conditioned relationship to a kind of "metapower" which is structured essentially around a certain number of great prohibitive functions; but this metapower with its prohibitions can only take hold and secure its footing in a whole series of multiple and indefinite power relations that supply the basis for the great negative forms of power.[11]

Thus Foucault was not asserting that the multiple networks of actual power relations were simply the building blocks of a "metapower" at the level of the state or of social hegemony. They were not the fragments of localized practices that accumulate spontaneously to form the great, unitary forms of state power, or indeed any other generalized presentations of social authority. On the contrary, only the multiple, local, micropolitical relations of power create the conditions of that overarching possibility: "the state consists of a whole number of power relations which render its functioning possible," he argued.[12] But this occurred through complex and subtle processes of codification, not through absorption or subsumption, or even through annexation. Nor did the state represent a field of centralized intentionality and rationality openly reflected in the practices of power as Foucault saw them. The state was not the condensation of these practices into a transcendent form of metapower. To the contrary, he frequently expressed doubts about the clarity of the relationship between the local or sectoral forms of the exercise of power and the alleged general purposes of class domination or capitalism. Doubts of that kind were constitutive, one might argue, for the understanding of power he wished to pursue.

In short, Foucault disengaged from the broad raft of assumptions—those "absolute presuppositions"—that inhabit Marxist analysis, whether reductionist or not. The significance of that disengagement was crucial.

It did not amount to a finalized delegitimation, to an essentialized rejection or falsification. Indeed, it should not be assumed that the critique of these assumptions lay at the center of Foucault's project; he certainly did not start from them. His disengagement was a consequence and not a starting point of his work: a result of his own readings of power, not a polemical point of departure. But it did give him a startling exit from the labyrinths of Marxist debate, with relevance not least to the development of modern social historiography as it emerged from the excitements of the 1970s. It opened a space for the consideration of questions much harder to deal with before.

## THE LOCAL AND THE CENTER

Thus for Foucault, the practices of power were not given within the coordinates of any general theory of capitalism. Their consequences could not be read off from the assumptions and assertions of such a general theory, however rich and sophisticated the supporting empirical analyses might be. In Foucauldian terms, analytical distinctions drawn between what, for economy's sake, we have been calling reductionism or culturalism have little meaning. For both proceed from a shared tissue of assumptions about the underlying nature of capitalism and its characteristic structures of class, even while the enactment of their political consequences gets ascribed to different sites, different procedures, and different levels of sophistication. Furthermore, Foucault asked, what if the categories given within the general theory were themselves also constructions, deriving from intellectual or scientific practices themselves inscribed in the actual power relations of historical and contemporary societies? What if the procedures by which the givens were provided and the knowledges created were themselves part of the discursive practices of power? So far from being the results of rational reflection on an objective world outside and beyond, what if those knowledges lay *inside* the networks and practices of power and serve to constitute them, to "authorize" them within certain mutualities of power and knowledge? In that case the exquisite distinctions of Marxist debate collapse, each forming instead the support for a contingent "regime of truth," a discourse of power or a fragment of one.

This line of reasoning will be familiar enough from a reading of Foucault. He insisted, for example, that his concern was not with truth, but with "truth-effects"; not with scrupulously neutral knowledge of an objective world, but with the power and truth-effects of the "knowledge" per se. "I believe that the problem does not consist in drawing the line between that in a discourse which falls under the category of scientificity or truth, and that which comes under some other category," he patiently pointed out, "but in seeing historically how effects of truth are produced within discourses which in themselves are neither true nor false."[13] He was interested in a quite distinctive object of analysis. This was neither the attempt to recuperate an "objective" world in thought, nor even to discriminate between the competing "truths" of any such recuperation. His focus was rather upon the knowledges themselves and their truth-effects, on the ways in which power inflects the production of knowledge itself and knowledge contributes to the exercise of power.

Here, then, we are back to several of the discussions running through earlier chapters of our book. This lengthy reflection on Foucault's dissentient and distinctive theorizing of power and its operations brings us back to the impact of postmodernism and the consequences of its critique of the accustomed practices of historiography, which we wrestled with in chapter 3. Foucault's oeuvre bespoke the salient features of the late twentieth-century critiques of foundationalist thinking we have been considering under the rubrics of "culturalism" or the "linguistic turn," both working these through in the course of his major studies and turning himself into a prime instigator of the broader intellectual changes across the academic disciplines that ensued. Here is Foucault's own commentary on this encompassing intellectual context.

[W]hat has emerged in the last ten or fifteen years is a sense of the increasing vulnerability to criticism of things, institutions, practices, discourses. A certain fragility has been discovered in the very bedrock of existence—even, and perhaps above all, in those aspects of it that are most familiar, most solid, and most intimately related to our bodies and our everyday behavior. But together with this instability . . . one . . . also discovers something that . . . was not initially foreseen, something one might describe as the inhibiting effect of global, [totalizing] theories. It is not that these global theories have not provided nor continue to provide in a fairly con-

sistent fashion useful tools for local research: Marxism and psychoanalysis are proofs of this. But I believe that these tools have only
been [deployed] on condition that the theoretical unity of these discourses was in some sense put in abeyance, or at least curtailed,
divided, overthrown, caricatured, theatricalized, or what you will.
In each case, the attempt to think in terms of a totality [would otherwise have] proved a hindrance to research.[14]

Of course, as will be apparent from this quotation, Foucault also takes
us down to the microhistorical contexts and sites of the production of
subjectivities that we discussed extensively in chapter 4. In advocating
this "*local* character of criticism" as the predominant feature of his work,
moreover, he took pains to argue its importance as a different approach
to the hard work of abstraction rather than any refusal of the "general" or
the "large scale" per se, an approach just as conducive to the distinguishing of general problems as Marxism and other totalizing theoretical systems had been. By vacating the Olympian analytical vantage point of
state-centralized institutional power, from which authority and political
relations are most commonly taken to be organized, he wanted to claim
a different standpoint from which to theorize the inscriptions of power
relations inside the social behavior, cultural practices, and everyday
transactions or ordinary life: "I believe that what this essentially local
character of criticism indicates in reality is an autonomous, non-central-
ized kind of theoretical production, one . . . whose validity is not dependent on the approval of the established regimes of thought."[15]

The territories of Foucault's own work in this respect are by now
familiar: the asylum, the clinic, the prison, the body, and sexuality. This
list is not exhaustive, let alone any completed oeuvre inviting us to abandon our own grounds of research. The point is not that Foucault
retrieved from obscurity some neglected empirical terrains, or filled gaps
in the historical account of the development of modern societies, but
rather that he sought to identify and expose in these social and institutional spaces the actual workings of power. Crucially, he did not deny,
indeed forcefully asserted, the ways in which power invested all discourses and discursive practices: "relations of power are not in a position
of exteriority with respect to other types of relationship (economic

processes, knowledge relationship, sexual relations), but are immanent in the latter."

> Power relations are both intentional and nonsubjective. If in fact they are intelligible, this is not because they are the effect of another instance that "explains" them, but rather because they are imbued, through and through, with calculation: there is no power that is exercised without a series of aims and objectives. But this does not mean that it results from the choice or decision of an individual subject; let us not look for the headquarters that presides over its rationality; neither the caste which governs, nor the groups which control the state apparatus, nor those who make the most important economic decisions direct the entire network of power that functions in a society (and makes it function).[16]

Power is everywhere. Exercised from innumerable points and places, in Foucault's account, it is immanent in the interplay of mobile relations. The binary oppositions of rulers and ruled neither lie at its root, nor serve as a key to its explanation. It has no headquarters. There is no Central Committee of Public Safety. Likewise, "there is no single locus of great Refusal, no soul of revolt, source of all rebellions, or pure law of the revolutionary."[17] Though an analyst of power, Foucault could not be at the same time a revolutionary strategist. Like ourselves, he was located *inside* the networks and discourses of power, not just repressed by them but *created* as a subject by them too. There is no "outside," no place where objective knowledges are gathered by minds independent of all "authorizations" of truth, free of all discourses and the power of their truth-effects. There can be no "science" of revolution or change based upon contemplation of the "objective" world and its laws of motion, precisely because such a science would necessarily share, in its very methods, the terrain of power and knowledge of the system it seeks to oppose. To make his point, Foucault imagined a revolution, plainly a socialist one, that claimed to dispossess the dominant classes and supplant the rulers, while entirely failing to modify the existing relations of power in the more extensive and insidiously durable sense, leaving in place all their actual processes.

Thus in Foucault's thinking, power, resistance, and their understanding may not be found in "objective," scientific macroaccounts of society, politics, or history. Such totalizations are abstract and limiting, their grand concepts necessarily restrictive, if not downright illusory. Local research, in Foucault's contrary account, approaches politics from behind and cuts across societies on the diagonal. It makes no claim to a reflective understanding of an objective world existing beyond the knowledge-producing procedures; it belongs to no immune and superordinate regime of truth. It sets aside the question of whether such knowledges reflect a true reality. It focuses rather on the knowledges themselves, their truth-effects and authorities, their place and function in the generating of concrete and ever-changing networks of power.

In this way, Foucault insisted, local research permits consideration of actual mechanisms of power and the discursive contents of the relations of power, without any ascription of motives, ideologies, false consciousness, or other explanations favored by conventional forms of social and political analysis. The latter focus less on the question of why people behave as they do, and more on people's failure to behave as they should by the lights of some higher intellectual or theoretical "truth." Why would the proletariat in the West not behave as a proper proletariat, take hold of its manifest destiny, and become organized for revolution? Why do I accept as true some knowledges, while discarding others? From where does the "authority" of the acceptable come? Does it simply make a junction with subjective identities, with a series of "recognitions" through a process Althusser called "interpellation"? How is "authority" produced? Where does the "authority" of science, of intellectual procedures designed to provide objective knowledge, reside? Are those forms of knowledge categorically different from the "authorities" and truth-effects inscribed in nonintellectual discourses? The propensity to consume is not the same thing as the "objective" laws of the market, for example, but the power of its discourses to exact and enact truth-effects in our own practices seems at least as great. In Foucauldian terms, truth is not at issue. Authority is.

If Foucault's work focused in this way on the discursive authorizing of subjectivities, how might its insights be joined to those deriving from the thought of Gramsci? As we argued, a Gramscian approach suggests a nonreductive Marxism concerned precisely with the ways in which class power is enacted nonviolently in peaceful and local spheres. While

Gramsci remained committed to class and class relations as a master category in the explanation of conflicts arising inevitably in capitalist societies, he did not at the same time reduce all social and political practices to a single source in structuring the consequences of capitalism in that way. He detected multiple centers of resistance forming around local issues and sometimes cultural questions, which did not directly confront class domination or the power of the associated state. Local government would be one such area; schooling and education another; folk beliefs and practices a third; the power of religious culture a fourth. Such a perspective gave permission for acts of resistance that were not necessarily in the simplest ways grounded in class affiliation or centered directly around the confronting of ruling-class power and its institutions. If he remained firmly on Marxist ground in upholding the essential centrality of class struggle and the strategic potential of the working class for the ultimate overthrow of capitalism, Gramsci's thinking was yet able to encompass forms of cultural politics available to those beyond the basic Marxian affiliations.

While sticking with Marx's rationalist epistemology and programmatic hopes for revolution, Gramsci nevertheless foregrounded the significance of what he called "wars of position." At least in the short term, the objectives of these fell well short of strategic or revolutionary change, the displacement of the ruling class, or the overthrow of the state. If there is a voice from inside the Marxist tradition emphasizing the significance of short-range, multiple forms of cultural politics, in other words, then it has to be that of Gramsci. To that extent he remains useful in envisaging a notion of political centering far more complex and contingent than the approaches to politics proposed by Marxists who preceded him. He showed a willingness to transfer the negotiation of class relations onto territories that were often less than openly political. If we return to our discussion of social history's expansion of politics, of the taking of politics out of doors, then an appreciation of that process certainly belonged to a reading of Gramsci's *Prison Notebooks*. But for Gramsci himself the analysis remained in general terms strictly under the rubrics of Marx's own social analyses. It remained locked inside the given classical terms of class-analytical understanding we find in the Marxist tradition, while providing a more pluralized grasp of the complex distribution of power relations under conditions of advanced capitalist societies.

Yet nonetheless, here is one Marxist who patently *cannot* be disposed of by calling upon the all-purpose magic of a poststructuralist critique of Thompsonian versions of Marxism, whose thinking about possible working-class agency remained ontologically founded on the central idea of experience. Moreover, pace Foucault and his localized and microhistorical understanding of the operations of power, we persist in believing that carefully deployed forms of macrohistorical analysis focusing on the state, the public sphere, and the institutional order of the political system will continue to be needed too. As we argued in chapter 4 with respect to the work of Joan Scott and Gareth Stedman Jones, for anyone interested in questions of social justice, social inequality, and the associated forms of politics—however carefully grounded these must remain in all the insights accumulating from the discursive analysis of the production of subjectivities—the more "global" or generalized issues of state and society are in dire need of revival. In other words, for us there *does* remain a viable structuralist register.

Such a register admits the possibility of organization, of institution, and of agency, all operating behind people's backs. For example, the World Bank, the World Trade Organization, and the International Monetary Fund of course operate through and within modalities of complex discursive justification. But what they *do,* often, is to inflict neoliberal coordinates upon the economic relations of parts of the world that are less than ready and less than willing to absorb them. There consequently arise questions of power of a more classical sort, invariably backed by force. We cannot see how this area of analysis can be ruled out. But where are the poststructuralist accounts of how such systems of economic, legal, and military power operate on the world? To imply by silence that they work only in discursive ways seems an evasion.[18] At the same time, we want to suggest, one type of analysis can hardly be expected to explain each and every aspect of a problem. As we argued in our response to Scott and Stedman Jones (chapter 4), intervening effectively on different questions involves drawing upon the research strategies, forms of knowledge, and epistemologies appropriate for addressing them. We may speak in one voice for some purposes and in another voice for others, without having to unify them. Yet why can there not be traffic across these different registers of analysis too?

Finding ways to move between a more Foucauldian register and the more structuralist registers of analysis of politics, we believe, has become an urgent task of historiography. And Gramsci's conception of hegemony, with its stress on consent as opposed to domination, and on the processes of moral persuasion needed before popular acquiescence or participation in a particular ordering of the world can be secured, is an excellent place to begin. It accepts the pervasiveness of power in society, and certainly presumes the inscription of political meanings in both social relations and the practices of the everyday, in the ways alluded to earlier. It also avowedly conceptualizes power as a space of contestation, a terrain of struggle, rather than a one-way street. Yet, while historicizing power, and stressing the contingencies and conjunctures on which power regimes depend, hegemony also postulates the structured inequalities predisposing certain sets of outcomes as opposed to others, the stacked deck of concentrated ownership, access, and control, which ensures that any sustained and effective process of contestation will be a tiringly uphill struggle, requiring more than simply individualized and local resources in order to work.

In other words, Gramsci reminds us, or allows us not to forget, that as well as being insidiously dispersed, power is also organized, accumulated, engrossed, stockpiled, put aside for a rainy day, configured into institutions, concentrated into forms of agency, normalized and systematized into a public sphere, naturalized, made opaque. Of course, these large-scale or societal modalities are no less susceptible to contestation. But there is a sense, for example, in which a post-Foucauldian stress on power's dispersal can back us unnecessarily away from power in the state-centralized form, so that when power in that more conventional sense speaks—through armies, emergency decrees, policing, and repression—we are left protesting ineffectually from the sidelines. Focusing on power's microphysics can also obscure the regularities and normativities, the logics of social structuration, which the concept of class was always so useful in helping to reveal. This should perhaps be obvious. For why should the vital recognition that power has no single center ever be taken to mean that centralized locations cannot be found? How did an understanding of power's dispersals somehow give us permission to ignore the state? Why should it deceive us into thinking that class differences and class inequalities have no generalizable potential for societywide order in the political sense? The Gramscian idea of hegemony gives us a way of seeing precisely how *different* sources and locations of power can be organized into working together.

Finally, if the discussions set into motion by the reception of the ideas of Foucault and Gramsci can be made complementary for rethinking the politics-and-society relationship—the one making power a dimension of all social relations, the other returning us to the specificities of politics as a process of hegemonic construction—we should also not forget a third key influence: namely, the past three decades of feminist theory. On the one hand, feminist critique has been key to expanding the category of the political in the ways we have been suggesting—that is, *away* from politics in the old institutional and state-centered sense, and *toward* the other sites and situations where contestation occurs. Family, health, sexuality, food, reproduction, and the general subject of the body—all these entered political discourse in new ways thanks to feminism, with profound effects on how social and other historians came to approach their work. On the other hand, such critiques have problematized older assumptions about the individual as a rationally acting subject, whether as the author of political initiatives or their intended object. The poststructuralist insight that power itself *produces* forms of subjectivity, rather than operating on already constituted autonomous individuals, has been taken up extensively by feminists, with unsettling effects for how questions of agency, experience, and consciousness can now be broached. The theorizing of gender as the mobile construction of sexual difference, the recognition that gendered assumptions of masculinity and femininity are inscribed in the basic languages of social identity, and the radical claim that everything is gendered, that nothing can be innocent of gender's codings and asymmetries, are now inescapable dimensions of the discussion we are seeking to provide.

### GETTING BACK TO CLASS

Our earlier essay had worried that the given logics and established routines of social history, particularly in its "culturalist" versions, were encouraging labor historians to subsume the specificities of political history into overgeneralized or overabstracted arguments about "hegemony" and "social control." That is, such arguments were based on a simplified usage of the Gramscian term, which demoted all the process of negotiation we have just described into a *given*. They made hegemony into a very *un*permeable boundary, along which political and ideological domination was certainly exercised, but behind which popular cultures and working-class experiences could then also disclose their forms of resistance. Moreover, there was a growing presumption, we thought, certainly in the preponderance of the impressive amounts of historiography being generated around the social history of the working class, that the concerns of the social historian belonged with the latter, with resistance as opposed to domination. There were many exceptions, of course, but by preference and general sensibility it was where "hegemony" encountered its limits that social historians sought to begin.

Using the example of the German Social Democratic Party (SPD), one of the largest and most prestigious of Europe's pre-1914 labor movements, we argued that labor's institutional histories—the studies of parties and unions—should be treated as one of the key sites for the production of working-class *consent*. They provided the contexts, that is, where logics and potentials of conformity, opposition, acquiescence, independence, assimilation, resistance, indifference, anger, gratitude, deference, and straightforward bloody-minded refusal could be translated from the everydayness of working-class experience into workable political agency, whether for local or national ends. In arguing this, we were definitely not rejecting social history in any way, let alone reverting to the earlier organizational approaches, but pleading for new ways of keeping social and political history together. In fact, we saw some of the new trends, like *Alltagsgeschichte* in Germany (the history of everyday life), as very conducive to this goal, making it easier to avoid some earlier pitfalls.[19] Yet at the same time, we thought, a curious recession of interest in the SPD—or more accurately, a growing skepticism among social historians about the degree to which that party had managed to embed itself in ordinary working-class lives—was effectively removing from this picture a central element of working-class political culture.

By the 1970s, social historians were tending to sidestep the SPD's importance: either they viewed it as an increasingly bureaucratized political formation, practically removed from ordinary working-class life (the more left-wing critique); or else its Marxist affiliations and socialist rhetorics were treated as formulaic and ritualized posturings likewise disconnected from authentic working-class culture (the more "realistic" reading of the SPD's formal revolutionism). Indeed, this system of distinctions severing the SPD from the working class per se had become a standard trope of the historiography. Yet if we are to understand the capacities for conformity and opposition in German working-class culture before 1914, the formal institutions of the labor movement must surely be part of the investigation. The history of the SPD should not be evacuated. On the contrary, rather than doubting the latter's relevance to ordinary working-class experience, we should be exploring just how complexly it was, and was not, successfully rooted there.

In other words, we were trying to create a space for political analysis in the expanded sense given to "politics" by the politics of knowledge of 1968. We were worried by the collapse of politics into culture via simplified versions of the ideas of Gramsci, which made "hegemony" into a name for the closing down of cultural contestation in a totalized societal sense. That is, we thought that the stability of capitalism and its relations of domination was being conceptualized too easily through an overgeneralized model of societywide consensus, implying an all-encompassing dominant culture, for which "Gramscian" vocabularies of hegemony then offered themselves as the master key. Since we originally published our article, the accumulating social histories of the working class have delivered a range of new work across national historiographies, whose richness and subtleties form the best sort of rejoinder to our 1980 complaint.[20] Yet the institutional world of politics—in which state apparatuses, civil agencies, parties, clubs, and all manner of organizations play their part—still remains relatively neglected, we would suggest.

What is the answer? In an important article of 1994, Ira Katznelson urged social historians to return precisely to political history, that is, to the institutional study of government, parties, and law. Invoking our own 1980 article, he argued:

> The fracture dividing social from political history not only made analyses of the domain between state and civil society impossible but impaired our understanding of the mutual constitution of institutions and culture, organization and ideology.[21]

So far, so good. But amid the general intelligence of Katznelson's discussion, we have some basic disagreements. We endorse his desire to avoid binarisms of epistemologically based choice—that is, between "hard-to-soft *Marxisant* versions of linear causality flowing from the material base to secondary superstructural constructs, and, on the other hand, the full elimination of the dualism of structure and agency." We also like the idea of holding these two approaches in creative tension, in order to explore how the "plasticity of identity" and the institutional forms of politics combine together.[22] But by making the institutional categorically separable as an object of research, and then seeking to correct its neglect by means of freestanding studies of the institutional realm, Katznelson addressed this problem only at the expense of a new severance. Moreover, his positive recommendations confirm our skepticism, for neither of his preferred examples, Henry Pelling's works and the collection edited by Eugenio Biagini and Alastair Reid, grounded their political histories in the densities of social history we have in mind.[23]

As Katznelson said, Pelling's work reflected "the quest to understand how the labor movement in Britain, in all its aspects, has forged institutional ties of representation, influence, and negotiation with the state within a broadly liberal framework of rights and citizenship."[24] But Pelling's work bore little relationship to the vast historiography of working-class formation generated during the past few decades in Britain, with its intensive mapping of trade and occupational cultures, industrial geography, and community studies.[25] More to the point, Pelling made no effort to relate Labour's rise to either the uneven histories of class formation or the unstable and fluctuating constructions of social identity, let alone the dynamic interrelations of the two. His work remained utterly innocent of anything resembling gender analysis, and that alone, given the centrality of gender relations to our understanding of the "ties of representation, influence, and negotiation with the state" Katnelson described, decisively compromises Pelling's corpus as a model.

Likewise, the Biagini-Reid volume assembled an excellent array of work on the architecture of post-Chartist parliamentary politics, grounding its claims about liberal public culture in a series of case studies, some of which reached far down into particular issues, careers, and localities for their analyses of popular political discourse. But that work was also a polemic *against* social history of the established kind, insisting that public language provided the best key to working-class political allegiances and behavior, as opposed to the kinds of materialist grounding of popular politics social historians have preferred. "Ideas matter," Biagini asserted, because "people's behavior is deeply influenced by what they think, and especially by what they believe firmly." Thus the crucial binding force of political movements (in Biagini's case, Gladstonian liberalism) was "the values shared by activists, electors, and supporters in general," and *not* "the material interests of the social groups to which they belonged."

> Politics then did not have the function of providing favorable legislative changes for class-conscious groups: rather it supplied a collective identity to groups whose social and material interests did not in themselves lead to a politically relevant class consciousness.[26]

In its freeing of the political question from the determinist causalities of social explanation, this statement repeated the basic antireductionist move of the past two decades, whose origins in the British case go back to the earliest post-Marxist debates associated with Ernesto Laclau and Chantal Mouffe, and then with the essays of Stedman Jones.[27] This basic commitment is one we also share. But there are some distinctions here that still need to be drawn. First, the Biagini-Reid approach framed an argument about broad continuities of British radicalism from the early nineteenth century to the twentieth-century Labour Party, which remains enormously contentious and problematic. Second, it presumed an overall reading of Victorian politics "as based on status and culture, rather than class," which went unexplicated, while the structural "facts" of class and status in the patterning of social life (in residential communities, in production, in access to social goods, in the general distribution of social inequalities, and so forth) merely backshadowed the analysis rather than entering directly into its terms.[28] Third, an entire historiography—tagged as Marxist, but subsuming both the latter's diversities and other social histories of a non-Marxist kind—was dismissed per se as "reductionist" in a polemical positioning that inevitably foreclosed debate. Fourth, it was wholly unclear why making the case for political history's autonomies—in this case in relation to public political language—should require the total bracketing of social analysis, and even in the most extreme versions the banning of social explanation altogether.[29]

We want to break this logic of disavowal. To our minds, the goal of thinking nonreductively—from questioning the sovereignty of the social and acknowledging the "discursive character of all practices" to seeing the autonomies of politics and their effects—does *not* require abandoning the attempt to do social history in the ambitious ways given to us since the 1960s.[30] Similarly, if we "acknowledg[e] that politics occurs wholly within discourse," and "refus[e] to counterpose discourse to an extra-discursive reality," as a fundamental axiom of understanding, with all the attendant methodological effects, that does not require us to abstain from social history in the accepted usages of that term—as practiced in the work, for example, of Anna Clark, or Lizabeth Cohen, or Robin Kelly, or Stephen Kotkin, or Kathleen Canning—although the advocates of a discursive approach sometimes seem to be saying we should.[31] Moreover, we want to uphold the value of the work still being produced by social historians, some of whom we have been citing, who provide far more sophisticated approaches to the analysis of politics than critics such as Joyce, Stedman Jones, or Biagini and Reid are willing to allow. As Robbie Gray said in a response to the Biagini-Reid volume:

> The best work on class has been informed by a strong sense of the complex, sometimes tense relations between diverse and uneven class situations, and the fragile and contingent construction of broader class interests and identities.[32]

### WRITING WORKING-CLASS HISTORY *NOW*

In this discussion, we are trying to escape from the polemics interrupting and disfiguring the conversation among historians interested in the working class during the past two decades.[33] We have been excited by the opening of new theoretical perspectives, particularly those that complicate the older understandings—which remained stable and obdurately resistant to critique for many years—of the relationship between "the social" and "the political," in all the ways referred to earlier. We have been inspired by the linguistic turn, through which the manifold antireductionisms of Marxists, feminists, and the pioneers of cultural studies in the 1970s became so powerfully radicalized. We are challenged by the condition of postmodernity and accept many of the arguments about contemporary transformations of capitalism articulated around globalization, transnationalism, and the post-Fordist transition.

We accept that the reconfiguring of identities and the shifting terms of political affiliation, which have been delaminating citizens from accustomed and previously secure social locations, are the inescapable starting point for thinking about politics at the start of the twenty-first century— particularly in the traditions of the Left, with their stress on the collective agency of social movements, the concerted pursuit of socially organized measures of democracy, the struggles for more equitable distributions of the social product, and the practical imagining of modalities of societywide change. Amid all of this, we welcome the critiques of social explanation, and the necessity of all the debates mobilized by Joyce, Stedman Jones, Scott, and others, which came to render the sovereignty of the social so rightly problematic.

Without making exaggerated claims for the influence of Marxism as such, we would agree that some classical *materialist* assumptions, sometimes Marxist in derivation, but perhaps as often not, provided the commonly accepted grounding for the new social histories of the 1960s and 1970s. These included robust conceptions of social causality, social determination, and social totality; the analytical priority of social context if the forms of politics and ideology in a society were to be understood; and the foundational valency of social explanation for ideas of historical stability and change. In this intellectual history, "class" did tend to serve as a generally accepted master category. Its power for labor history in particular was its totalizing utility. It not only provided an effective means of organizing the analysis of the social world, it also contained an inscription of political meaning and agency. It provided an extraordinarily flexible analytic in that respect.

When labor history broadened its charge after the 1960s, it encouraged three types of engagement with politics. It explored institutional processes and their conjunctural forms, and eventually extended this from parties and the state to the forms of power operating behind people's backs, in ways that had not been accessible to studies of experience, agency, or consciousness in a Thompsonian mode.[34] It encouraged the linking of historical work to the wider project of making the world into a better place—for example, by recuperating incidents and moments of class struggles that emphasized continuities of past with present, making social and cultural histories a bridge to contemporary transformations. And it urged the unearthing of narratives "hidden from history," as a means of both enriching historical analysis and providing self-consciously generative accounts designed to inspire a politics precisely by attacking the exclusionary narratives of conventional historiography. But if we consider each of these three forms of labor history's relationship to politics from a vantage point several decades later—the institutional domains of politics and the public sphere, the betterment of the contemporary world, the production of counternarratives within the valorizing of subaltern identities—it becomes readily apparent that the structural and developmental metanarratives of class can no longer do quite the same job as before.

Among historians, the older belief that people's actions are best explained by their social locatedness, by their sociological identities, and by their belonging within "objective" social categories like class, understood in social structural or other materialist terms, has undergone extensive damage. Likewise, the counterclaim of the ensuing critique, that the basic categories of modern social understanding are not the "objective realities" so often assumed, but are instead historically constructed, is now also widely conceded. From within our contemporary skepticism about class, we can better appreciate the problematic implications of making it into a transhistorical category of analysis for industrial capitalist societies in general, whose logics of development had clear direction, with effects in politics and culture transparently understood. For example, we are better able to grasp the historical rootedness of the socialist political tradition in a particular era and its conditions—how, as a species of class-political agency with broader and convincing claims to national leadership, it was sustained by certain specific and finite, if large-scale, contingencies of history. Those histories involved a constellation of urban-industrial milieus and associated social structures, often demarcated geographically, residentially, and visually against the rest of society, supporting separate working-class cultures, and shaped by definite local and central government relations. In the industrializing parts of capitalist Europe, the formation of distinct proletarian worlds between the 1880s and 1920s permitted cultural and organizational solidarities to crystallize, which could become articulated successfully into the programs of socialist and Communist parties between the wars, with political effectivities lasting well down to the 1960s and beyond.

Historicized in this way, class politics may be regarded as a distinctive and historically located repertoire of languages for organizing the social world, which achieved their impressive purchase in the political life of capitalist societies during a long epoch from the 1880s to 1960s, yet possessed a far more variable, contingent, and contested relationship to the social histories we previously thought were driving the show. Once contextualized like this, we think, the politics of class becomes far more available for a discursive analysis. Yet so far, unfortunately, the possibility of the latter has been offered by polemicists on either side as a polar choice. Thus the "discursive approach to history" can either be embraced as the sophisticated and necessary response to the devastating consequences of an epistemological critique, or else it should be kept completely at bay, refused as self-indulgently theoreticist and hopelessly removed from the empirical study of actually existing societies. In turn, the "realist" alternative comes either celebrated as the grounded and reliable epitome of the historian's best practice or else dismissed as the "determinist fix," a naive reliance on outmoded solutions mired in empiricist conservatism.

Against these absolutisms, in the interests of dialogue and collaboration, we want to propose a pragmatics of good faith. On the one hand, those social historians still committed to a class-analytical approach might acknowledge—even if only strategically, and for a while—the intractable difficulties, methodologically and theoretically, of analyzing working-class politics as the expressive outcome of an economically located class interest and social-structural position. On the other hand, the advocates of "postmodernism" or "discursive history" might affirm the fruitfulness of the continuing practice of social history, if only for generating the carefully constructed and archivally grounded studies that they still require in order to "read." Such a pause for breath, or mutual suspension of disbelief, might stall the speed at which growing numbers of historians are treating social history as a set of outmoded practices deserving to be disavowed. For there has been a danger in recent polemics of disconnecting the rich and detailed social histories of class from the very explanations of political change they were designed to underwrite. There must surely be ways of bringing these discrete and allegedly antagonistic fields of work—of social historians holding to the ground of class, and "culturalist" or "discursive" historians insisting on the primacies of language—back into conversation.

Given the basic conundrum from which these disagreements descend—that of seeking to ascribe intersubjective unity to a social cate-

gory, especially one so divided by internal differences and fragmenta-
tions—it may help to see class formation as being as much a cultural and
political *postulate* as resting on demonstrable social facts. We might
approach class less as an observable or preexisting topography of structurally distributed social differences than as a set of emergent claims
about how the social world should best be understood. In that sense,
class entered history as the advocacy for a particular way of thinking
about social identity, and not just as a process creating new social positions defined by relation to the means of production or some other set of
objective or structural criteria. At this stage of the disagreements among
historians, we would argue, class discursively understood *has* come to
provide a better starting point for studying class formation than the classical ones of economics and social structure. For it was in discursive
terms that a new operational collectivity with powerful motivating
appeal and interpellative presence in social life, cultural practice, and
politics—namely, class in its actually available forms—came to be
defined: who got to be included, who formed the boundaries, who set
the tone, and who won the recognized voice.

Let us be clear: this would be a conceptual starting point, not a decision *for* certain kinds of history or sources and *against* others. Neither
economics nor social history could somehow cease to be studied. Capital
composition, accumulation regimes, labor markets, technologies of skill,
divisions of labor, workplace relations, wage systems, and apprentice-
ships would remain as important as they ever were, as too would neighborhoods and communities, families and households, personal relations
and sexualities, sport and recreation, and all of the rest. But languages of
class were inextricably embedded in all of those things. They were also
inscribed in the practices and cultures of everyday life, as well as in the
codifications and official statements of organizations, literature and the
press, and all other kinds of public talk. Thus the *discourse of class,* an insistence that class formed the organizing reality of emerging capitalist societies, together with the growth of specific practices and organizations
around that insistence, like trade unions and socialist parties, constitutively shaped those social histories from the start. In other words, the history of class was inseparable from the history of the category. Class
emerged historically as a set of discursive claims about the social world
seeking to reorder that world in terms of itself.

This *discursive move*—from assuming an objective reality of class to studying how the category of "class" came to be made, using all the programs and methods of social history, *as well as* the new cultural and intellectual accounts—can be extraordinarily fruitful. It frees analysis from the teleology of a class consciousness thought to be inscribed in the directional interest-based logics of class-collective experience. It also frees us from the need for alibis—from the search for special explanations when the idealized versions of class consciousness failed to arise. Rather than seeing working-class interests as a structurally given and agreed-upon basis for action, for example, we might treat the idea of "interests" itself as a problem, as the discursive effect of complex histories that first need to be mapped and explored. Instead of asking which working-class interests became reflected in which organizations and forms of action (one of labor history's classic problematics), we might examine how particular practices and institutions encouraged or hindered definite constructions of working-class interest. The transmission between interest and action was complex and two-way. As a discursive field, working-class interests were not reducible to any single overriding or essential contradiction of capital and labor. So far from such a contradiction being structurally constitutive for the rise of a labor movement in some necessary and straightforward fashion, labor movements were actually shaped from the field of force between the emergent conditions and their increasingly intense discursive articulation.

This returns us to the *pluralities* of language—to the many different forces acting on and through the lives of working people, the babble of interpellation, allowing them to recognize themselves in diverse possible ways. These indeterminate qualities of working-class identity, its nonfixities, recall us to the silences and exclusions that class appeals have always involved. How we see ourselves as a basis for action, how we become addressed as particular kinds of publics, is not fixed. We recognize ourselves variously—as citizens, as workers, as consumers, as parents, as lovers and sexual beings, as enthusiasts of sports and hobbies, as audiences for music and film, as believers in religious and other creeds, as generations, as objects of policy and surveillance, as subjects of race and nation, and so forth. Such recognitions are structured by power relations of various sorts. They are gendered by assumptions placing us as women or men.

At one level, this observation should perhaps not be especially controversial. The fragmentary, complex, nonfixed quality of identities or subject positions has not only become a commonplace of contemporary identity talk but retains license from older traditions of social theory too. But politics is usually conducted *as if* identities can be treated as stable and fixed. The operative question then becomes: how does identity settle and congeal; how is it worked upon; how does it acquire continuity over time; how is it fashioned into concentrated, resolute, or reasonably reliable shapes? How do some forms of identity begin to coalesce into more generalized and presumed forms of collective self-recognition, while others remain inchoate or unassimilable? That is, how is *agency* produced? Under what circumstances, in particular places and times, can identity's nonfixity become provisionally fixed, in such a way that individuals and groups can think of themselves and behave as a particular *kind* of collective agency, political or otherwise? How do people—in our case, workers—become shaped into acting subjects, understanding themselves in justified or possible ways?[35]

Politics is the effort at domesticating the infinitude of identity.[36] It is the attempt to hegemonize identity, to "order" it into a strong programmatic direction. If identity is to be considered decentered, then politics becomes precisely the process of trying to *create a center*. Moreover, this drive for coherence, to produce consistency and completeness, in whatever precise modalities but certainly via party-political and other programmatic interpellations, often in simplified and reassuring ways, entails simultaneous work on "society." Or to be more precise, it requires working on identity's social referents, on the systems of meanings and representations through which people organize their relationship to the material world, through which they manage their relationship to the social and historical conditions of their lives. Politics works on this imaginary field by seeking to make stable and unitary sense of the fragmentary, divided, and antagonistic aggregations of social relations and social spaces we call "society." Again: this is what has to happen before individuals and groups can organize their multiple and complex relations to the world into a strongly centered political identity capable of motivating action. For such collective action to occur, "society" itself has to be imagined, has to be visualized as the place where identity is bounded, as that in whose name things can be done.

## SO WHAT DOES "CLASS" ALLOW?

The power of the socialist political tradition was its capacity to harness and harmonize popular identities into a strongly centered idea of the working class—that is, to construct popular political agency around the discourse of class in all the classic materialist (gendered, skilled, nationally bounded, industrial) ways. This worked most successfully between the founding of socialist parties in the late nineteenth century and the rise of fascism in the 1930s, followed by another phase in the 1940s, when socialists and Communists joined larger coalitions of the Left, connecting class-political agency to broader democratic appeals. But whatever the period and place, socialist parties always contained a far richer sociology than a simple class-political reading tended to imply, whether in membership, voters, practices, or appeal. They appealed to workers, even on the most restricted definitions, highly unevenly. They also integrated much broader sections of the populace around the male, skilled, religious, and ethnic working-class core, whether these constituencies themselves met the criteria of working-classness, such as women, the unskilled, or national minorities, or were not working class at all, including dissenting intellectuals, parts of the professions, clerical and other white-collar layers, or shopkeepers and other small tradespeople in working-class neighborhoods. Socialist parties developed their public presence across a wide variety of "nonclass" issues and institutional fields, working through the public rhetorics of democratic citizenship, social justice, and egalitarianism as much as through the languages of socialism per se.[37]

Yet, despite this actual eclecticism, the programmatic centering of socialist practice around the notion of class remained clear enough. In its default loyalties—the priorities of campaigning, the syntax of official manifestos, the militants' rhetorical common sense—the socialist tradition was class-conscious to the core. But concentrating identity in that way had its costs. It encouraged a reduction *to* class. It involved silencings, exclusions, and neglects. Celebrating the working class presumed denigrating and disregarding others—expressing hostility toward not just other classes, but other categories of *workers* too. Distance was marked from any workers not organized into the parties, unions, and wider subcultural machineries of socialist affiliation—the rough and the unrespectable, the criminal, the frivolous, the sexually transgressive, the religiously devout, the ethnically different, and of course the feminine in her many possible incarnations. Elements of culture and subjectivity were similarly disowned—that is, any aspect of identity not easily disciplined into a highly centered notion of class-political agency. Crucially, socialist disregard for this kind of political space—the space of those "other" identities—provided openings for contrary labors of persuasion and affiliation to occur, coming from the state, from political rivals, from the churches, from commercial entertainment, and so forth. Sometimes that space of neglect widened into an arena of especially dangerous activist contestation where, under conditions of escalating societal crisis, right-wing populisms might win mass support. The fascisms of the 1920s and 1930s were one case of the latter. The contemporary racialized mobilizations against migrants and foreigners, scratching on the wounds of a deindustrialized social landscape that the decayed remnants of the socialist tradition can no longer organize, are another.

Consequently, while the existence of the working class might be postulated via analysis of production and its social relations, the collective agency or "unity" of that working class has always remained a never-attainable and always incomplete object of construction, a fictive agency, a contingency of political action. Now, the point of this argument, this way of regarding class, as a never-finished project of making, through a dialectic of discursive labor and actually existing forms and relations, we want to argue, should be precisely to *open a space for politics*—to allow us to understand much better, that is, the variable popularity of different political outlooks among the working class of different times and places. In the course of such an analysis, one combining discursive and earlier approaches, for instance, we might better understand the dynamics of socialism's twentieth-century rise and fall.

What we are suggesting is that there can be no *general* account of the ways in which groups of various kinds in various places achieve forms of collective agency with reach and efficacy into politics. Multiple contingencies overwhelm the persuasive possibility of any such general theory like that of Marx when it comes to understanding this process. We have something much more cautious in mind than that. While we certainly wish to argue that broad regularities of the production and circulation of goods, services, opportunities, and wealth under capitalism create conditions of deep inequality, we are not at the same time suggesting that deep inequality always and everywhere eventuates in radical politics. Yet it does sometimes, even if the processes by which this happens remain obscure and difficult to generalize. Somehow, in those circumstances and places where it does occur, a politics of the dispossessed comes to be "centered," expressly conceived in such a way as to allow and encourage collective affiliations on the part of the poor, the exploited, and the subordinated whose perceptions of their own situation remain variable, to say the least.

Examples abound. People come to find themselves in the same place politically, in the sense of making themselves available for some form of collective action, whether in response to a single event or circumstance or whether on the basis of more organized and sustained political mobilization, for all manner of reasons, some of them rationally managed and directed, but others definitely not. The resulting motivation might include rage, caprice, vindictiveness, revenge, and all manner of base desires, but also of course loyalty to principle, practical ethics of various kinds, formal beliefs, coherent alignment with a program or a creed, and a powerful sense of common justice. These motives are only in part awarded by individuals' position in a structure and their perception of it. To grasp the rest we have to address the discursive framing and construction of their subjectivities. Naturally enough, the processes we are seeking to describe are complex and historically contingent. They are not reducible to the sometimes polarized analytics of structuralism and poststructuralism, to the closed and canonical worlds of reductive Marxism or to the strategies of exclusionary versions of discourse theory. In effect, we need *both* Rudé and Hobsbawm *and* Scott (and much else besides).[38]

As we see it, "centering" is not a general sign expressing the possibility of action and politics, or a descriptor for the normal course of politics. On the contrary, we see centering as no more than a recognition of the highly contingent *processes* by which agency is produced in different cultural climates, geographical locations, wider polities, and of course conjunctures. Our claims for a pluralized analytical practice are made precisely in the hope that, for example, attention to structural matters as well as to discursive ones will illuminate the particularities of whatever politics we are studying or pursuing. In these terms, "centering" names the potential for collective agency, its aspiration, the coalescing and convergence of disparate groups and interests toward a common program or outlook, the cohering of hegemonies and the sharpening of their edge, even occasionally the gathering of a counterhegemonic impulse, to some degree consciously directed, to a greater degree not.

We would not like our argument here to be misconstrued. All the hard-won ground of social history—for instance, studies of family, neighborhood, and work, with their materialist analytic of social relations and means of production—should not now be abandoned. Yet once we start treating consciousness of class as an unstable, shifting, and indeterminate faculty, we also heighten the urgency of political and cultural analysis—discursive analysis of the "languages of class"—if we are to show how sociologically specified class capacities could be made to materialize in action and effects. As a collective identity, class presumed fixities and partialities of meaning that necessarily required silences, demarcations, and exclusions if its solidarities were to strengthen and grow. These are the boundaries that contemporary debates have been bringing into view. Not only feminist theorizing of gender, but also critiques of racialization and whiteness, and postcolonial analyses of empire's continuing metropolitan effects, have equipped us better than ever before to bring the universalizing claims of class analysis down to the ground.[39] By learning from the decomposition of class in the present, we can produce different histories of class and its valencies in the past.

We now have the chance to rethink what "class" entails or allows, *both* as a category of social historical analysis *and* as a basis for political mobilization. If, as we have argued, identity is mobile and not fixed, if it is not an effect or reflex of social circumstances and experience in that old materialist manner, and if the working class is divided in all sorts of ways, with no necessary unity in consciousness and shared experience, then what possible meanings remain for class as an operative political category, capable of moving masses of people into agency? How might it still be approached as a structural attribute of societies, and an essential means of grasping inequalities of distribution? How might we take the measure of contemporary "postmodernist" critiques, and join them to what is salvageable and enduring in the existing social history corpus, with its capacities for capturing the dynamics of stability and change in densely and intensively studied local contexts?

## POLITICS AGAIN

Through our discussion of those questions, we have chosen a particular entrance into a wide-reaching contemporary debate, where a variety of contentions have been unsettling the consensus one might have projected for a left-inclined social history as it emerged from the earlier legitimation fights of the 1970s. During the 1990s those recent contentions included not just the "defense of class" against "the end of social history," but a wider clash of historical epistemologies ("realists" versus "postmodernists"), philosophical disagreements ("politics of redistribution" versus "politics of recognition"), left versions of the culture wars, a range of debates over the linguistic turn, and so forth.[40]

Our own discussion has recurred most frequently to gender and the value of feminist critique, but other challenges to the materialist sufficiencies of labor history's older class-centered analytic should be added—the cultural politics of race and postcoloniality chief among them. Consumption and mass culture, themselves always "gendered" and "raced," add a further dimension to twentieth-century class formation, which until recently both left-wing political traditions and post-1960s social history had sorely neglected, but which a range of pioneering studies have since been addressing, with feminisms and cultural studies leading the way.[41] Of course, beginning in the 1980s the Right—especially in its Thatcherized notation—successfully captured the politics of consumption, creatively deploying languages of individualism, choice, and the market, hyping a consumerism expanded to embrace both the structural requirements of the post-Fordist economy and elaborate discourses of style. Only recently has the Left taken mass entertainment cultures and their popular pleasures seriously, led again by feminists. Much of contemporary politics has migrated to this ground, a terrain of crucial relevance for identity and subjectivity, a key site perhaps for a new politics of class.

Turning again to the "discursive move" outlined here, it would not be hard to imagine an analysis of the Thatcher or Reagan years that traversed those lines, presenting a picture not of a class-located conspiracy (one familiar temptation of older Left critiques), but of a dominant, briefly hegemonic "imaginary," which organized meaning and representation, and created identities, in a powerful political centering of the kind we have tried to describe. This was not a centering that banished dissent or counterimpulses completely from the field. That never happens, after all, short of fascism or wholly coercive regimes. But it was certainly one that profoundly disordered and disabled the possible forms of a Left response. Here, certainly, the sphere of state politics was not simply a vacancy. Nor was the exercise of a centralized power an illusion. In that sense, Katznelson's hopes for restoring party and other formal political concerns in historiography can be importantly realized, but now without any need of severance from the "social." As such an approach fully accepts, governmentality and its "regimes of truth" always need negotiation. They flow both ways, provoking silences as well as resistance and contestation.

The history of the making of the category of "class" is replete with examples of the latter, to be sure. At the very least, a vital contribution of social and labor history in the last thirty or forty years has been to recuperate them in subtle and well-grounded detail. That historiography does not stand utterly vitiated by its commitments to notions of class that we agree are no longer workable. Rich and complex historiographies cannot simply be obliterated ("almost moribund," as Joyce says of British labor history) by one kind of "postmodernist" fiat or another, as though they no longer matter.[42] Indeed, in Britain for a decade now, something called "old Labour" has stood negatively at the very center of the rhetorics of a Labour government and a party-political leadership determined to silence the social democratic voice of previous generations and sideline the discourses through which the Labour Party itself constructed a working-class politics of emancipation. *New* Labour amounts to a discursive maneuver to create a new center precisely on the ruins of its own past.

The communitarian discourses of Blairism, the largely empty rhetorics of "modernization" and "fairness," together with the fast-fix "Third Way," deliver permission for reinventing the party and evacuating its past. New Labour has bid "farewell to the working class" in every sense, seeking to expunge the "blue-collar, working-class, northern, horny-handed, dirty-overalled people" from its political imagination.[43] It convenes and interpellates a new political formation, whose discursive code is an infinitely flexible and "commonsense" but thin communitarianism. As Stuart Hall has said, the Labour government delivers some of what the Left thought it might want, but "the difficult truth seems to be that the Blair project, in its overall emphasis and key assumptions, is still essentially framed by and moving on terrain defined by Thatcherism."[44] Here, some notion of the "virtuous community"—an imagined nation, Middle England, the decent and the fair—is invoked, whose protection against asylum seekers, terrorists, single mothers, and welfare claimants authorizes policies so illiberal as to grace Thatcherism's high-water mark.

We introduce these brief (and no doubt tendentious) remarks on the Blair government to make a point. Writing a decade ago, Ira Katznelson spoke of labor history and labor historians as "making a difference."[45] This was not a claim, we think, that doing labor history could become a transformative political act in itself, a claim that through historiography the world could be directly made over. Rather his was a sense, shared we believe by many people interested in the history of the working class, that the manner in which the past is recuperated can have effects on perceptions of the present. This was the inspiration of the founders of social history in the 1960s, of Edward Thompson or Sheila Rowbotham for example, along with many others in Britain and North America: namely, that a knowledge of past struggles itself had a place in the finding and forming of present agency. In that sense, the past contributed to resistance, affording a potential node of opposition, if only by showing that it need not be like this. It can be different. Power can be resisted in its multiple, microphysical forms, as well as where it continues to be exercised in vast wedges as policy, policing, legislation, and force. Resistance has its identities and subjectivities too—plastic maybe, created involuntarily and on the move, without the reflexive fixity a former class analysis awarded them, yet occasionally convened around multiple refusals that the "class actors" of a previous generation would surely have found familiar.

# VI. CONCLUSIONS

## "CLASS" AND THE CRITIQUE OF SOCIAL HISTORY

When we began this project, we were moved by a sense of dismay at the rhetorics and strategies of closure that seemed to be accompanying the protracted debates over poststructuralist forms of analysis among historians. It is hard now to chart the detailed course of those controversies, which quickened between the later 1980s and early 1990s, but they were clearly connected with the complex reception of Foucault in the fields of history and the social sciences more widely, as well as with the impact of Derrida and deconstruction in literary disciplines. Cutting across those discussions were equally complex and uneven influences coming from feminism, from debates over gender, and from the new histories of sexuality. New convergences of history and anthropology were also occurring. And running through all of this was the impact of the newly emergent cross-disciplinary field of cultural studies.

This generalized "cultural turn" intensely affected the openness of scholarly work to the politics of gender, of sexuality, and of race, while putting into question habitual practices in a range of academic disciplines. Indeed, the resulting debates transgressed the frontier between the academy and politics all the time, often in mutually constructive and creative ways. We were ourselves ready participants in the extensive processes of rethinking about history, about theory, and about politics, which this entailed. Nothing in what we say is to be taken as opposition or regret concerning the fundamental necessity of the opening toward culture and the debates themselves. Nevertheless, some aspects of the handling of those intellectual transitions gave us pause. In particular, as we argued in chapter 4, some of the advocates of change seemed to be claiming not

just a different way of doing things, but one requiring sharp and unequivocal separation from the past. In seeking to distance their own understanding of historical studies from existing practices, they engaged in
polemics whose purpose seemed to be the disparaging and delegitimating
of earlier forms of work. They presented the choices involved as mutually excluding one another, grounded in contradictory and opposing
epistemologies.

For our own part, though, we wondered whether the boundaries
being drawn between old and new, between social and cultural, between
modern and postmodern, between structuralist and poststructuralist,
between Marx and not-Marx, were quite as uncrossable as some practitioners were presenting them, or whether they might be porous, nego-
tiable, commonly usable, and amenable to continuing redefinition. All
our instincts and past experience urged that final closures rooted in epistemological choices lacked overarching persuasiveness and staying
power. A politics of knowledge seeking finality or closure in that way
usually brings serious damage, both to general civility and to the other
kinds of conversation still taking place. More to the point, such intended
closures simply do not last, whether against Marxism per se, within
Marxism, or against or within any other system of thought or intellectual
tradition. One of the reasons for this, of course, is that the actual practices of a scholarly discipline are always and everywhere more complex,
more contradictory, and less unified than any successful ratifying of a
common epistemological standpoint would require. Intended acts of
intellectual closure will never succeed in fully silencing the opposition.
They can never banish the other practitioners from the field. In historiography and other aspects of intellectual life, at least, one's opponents
can usually be expected to stay around.

In history especially, for good or ill, few practitioners actually begin
with a self-conscious prior declaration of epistemological intent. The
"habitus" of historiography cannot be reduced to a set of positions originating in theories of knowledge, but includes motivations of much less
clarity embracing political belief, temporal contingencies, practical
affiliations, and subjectivities of all sorts. Philosophers insist upon the priority of theories of knowledge, while historians and others try to wrestle
with contingency and with the bewildering forms in which the worlds of
past and present tend to reveal themselves and become available. We

recognize, of course, the significance in any discipline of clear reflection on the various ways in which knowledge is composed and renders itself recuperable and useful. Questions of epistemology cannot be ignored or wished away. Yet reliance on epistemology as the provider of permission for one kind of analysis as against another, we believe, invites closure, encourages polemic, and damages conversation. It leads to destructive bitterness of a sustained and potentially voracious kind. One such episode exploded across the field of social history in the late 1970s through the debates reaching their crescendo in the infamous History Workshop encounter between Edward Thompson, Richard Johnson, and Stuart Hall in late 1979.[1] Another equally, if not more, embittering series of fights accompanied the turning to culture ten years later.

In this book, we have been focusing our discussion around the concept of "class," which in so many respects figured in the social historiography of the 1960s and 1970s as a central term. We have been trying, in particular, to puzzle our way through the question of what exactly the culturalist critiques of the social historian's predominant practices may now have established. Using the writings of Joan Scott and Gareth Stedman Jones as our principal examples, we have tried at some length to assess what those critiques have accomplished and enabled, and what they have not been able to do, or at least do not seem yet to be doing.

So here we say "yes" to the emblematic critique of social historiography without at the same time conceding hegemonic status to the critics' associated epistemological claims. Instead, we want to ask: what, if any, are the analytical limits of the poststructuralist register; and what, if any, are the conditions of usable traffic between social history and cultural history, and how might these best be addressed? It is not enough, in our view, simply to press questions of epistemology to the limit, though that was probably unavoidable during the difficult and contentious process of opening up the space where these matters might first be discussed. But rather, we need to consider the possible ways in which discussion of "the social" might now be readmitted. In addition, we wanted to pose the question of the present-day valency of class. This was not just a matter of whether classes exist any more or how they are produced. It was also a matter of what classes do or are supposed to do, and the work they are supposed to perform for the analysis of social historians and how that may have changed.

The kind of explanatory work that "class" was asked to perform during the heyday of social history in the 1960s and 1970s, in relation to the salient problematics of various periods and national fields, might be shown in many particular ways. To take one especially strong and elaborate illustration, from the early 1960s until well into the 1980s debates among British historians over the sources of the mid-Victorian social and political stability after the crisis-ridden first half of the nineteenth century remained heavily linked to social histories of working-class formation, often grounded in a particular community study or studies of particular trades or categories of workers. The resulting historiography embraced an extremely wide repertoire of approaches, which included at least the following: the long trek of British social historians through the "aristocracy of labor" as a field of manipulated class divisions; the whole moment of "social control"; more sophisticated arguments from the concept of "cultural hegemony," including ideas of class negotiation and the winning of consent; the focus of culture and civil society in reproducing power relations between classes; and the operation of structures behind people's backs, usually with a nod toward materialist determination but only in the final instance. A similar array of explanatory perspectives organized around the master category of class might be distinguished for other periods of British history too, such as the epoch of the Industrial Revolution covered by Edward Thompson's *Making of the English Working Class* and the vast associated historiographies, or the late Victorian and Edwardian nexus of the "decline of Liberalism" and the "rise of Labour." Other national fields might be described in comparable ways.[2]

Across the manifold differences and disagreements within these respective fields, "class" provided an important common terrain, even a kind of default understanding. The bitter divisions between "culturalists" and "structuralists" in the late 1970s and early 1980s included no retreat from the shared assumptions of class analysis per se, after all. Those arguments did not begin to problematize the vitality of the concept itself, but rather sought ever more sophisticated ways of embedding its uses in readings of all the noneconomic relations that complicated its appearance and functioning. However deep the divisions among social historians employing different forms of class analysis, none disputed that class was a terrain on which power decisively inscribed itself and through which questions of popular political agency (whether of conformity or resistance) should primarily be engaged.

So here also the main battles had raged over underlying differences concerning epistemology or the constitution of knowledge, driven in Britain in particular by the later 1970s impact of Louis Althusser's thought and the passions it raised. The bitterness of those disagreements, their line-drawing exclusivities, derived not from contest over the ontologies of class per se, but from arguments around "reading for the best Marx."[3] The destructiveness of those debates whose most spectacular moment came in 1979 lay entirely on the grounds of epistemology and of "correct" readings inside the Marxist canon. Responses to Althusser's discovery of an "epistemological break" in Marx's oeuvres provided the fault line around which the Thompson-Johnson confrontation organized itself. That debate formed self-consciously around questions of truth, and the participants on either side, Thompson chief among them, took great pains in ascribing bad politics explicitly to false epistemology.[4]

The shared class-analytical terrain notwithstanding, in other words, social history was hardly any straightforwardly consensual field. Yet in the meantime poststructuralist critiques have proceeded precisely to essentialize the history of class by implying a unitary consensual field of historiography specifically organized around common materialist assumption and shared epistemological error. The associated maneuver that then "decenters the social" compresses significant differences and consigns them to the same sphere of epistemological impossibility: "the social" cannot be recuperated, therefore all social histories depart from validity. What disappears is not just the valency of class but with it an entire field of historiography for which class and the relations of class are judged to have been fundamental. The critical assault on Thompsonian epistemology has become the talismanic form of this purging, classically conducted by Joan Scott invoking theorists like Derrida and Foucault. But Thompsonian epistemology, as we have just argued, by no means encompassed the whole complex field of the social history of class. Scott's attack on Thompson disposes of Thompson on experience, but only by a very dubious extension does it dispose of all possible Marxisms. This is what we mean by the epistemological essentialism of some poststructuralist critique and its claims.

Too many of the postmodernist or poststructuralist injunctions to move on from a self-evidently inadequate and now superseded historiography rest on easy and sometimes sloppy conflations in this way. For some, it now seems enough to brand the social historiography of class as "Marxist" at its foundation—a fact that should surprise at least some of us inside the field, who in the wider precincts of the profession during the 1960s and 1970s certainly encountered nothing remotely resembling the kind of Marxist predominance now routinely ascribed to the discussions of class of the time.[5] The cognate suggestion by Patrick Joyce that a fixation with class had disfigured the social historians' project over the years is no more convincing. For it is surely wrong to suppose that the class emphasis in social history across three or more decades delivered essentially a Marxist historiography as its central product. Systematic Marxisms in history writing have surely been harder to find than that.

## THE MARX OF SOCIAL HISTORY

In one way or another, the presence of Marx has shadowed our discussion throughout this book. We began by exploring the impact of the Anglo-Marxist group of historians in chapter 2, finding their influence homologous with the broadly materialist commitments of the larger movement toward social history during the 1960s and 1970s. At various points, we have also recurred more extensively to the importance of Edward Thompson, though again by emphasizing the generalized and pragmatic qualities of his Marxist affiliations in common with the wider corpus of left-inclined social historiography. Certainly until the 1970s, we would argue, most of the interest in Marxist approaches among social historians was likely to take that kind of "pretheoretical" form. Often mediated via the writings of historians like Edward Thompson or Eric Hobsbawm, it was inspired more by certain general working assumptions and the associated politics of knowledge than by any intensive first-hand reading of Marx himself.

Furthermore, when that sustained critical encounter with Marx's own writings *did* begin to develop in the thinking of many younger social historians during the 1970s, it soon took directions carrying them away from the more obvious classical grounds of Marxist thought. Inspired by feminisms, by the reception of Foucault's works and those of other poststructuralist thinkers, by deconstruction and other strands of literary theory, by theories of ideology and subjectivity, by psychoanalytic theory, by cultural anthropology, by cultural studies, and by a variety of other intellectual currents feeding into what we have summarized as the cultural turn, our own broad cohort came to develop an ambivalent and underexplicated relationship to the Marxist outlook we had earlier spent so many efforts trying to clarify. Some of that clarification had proceeded through bodies of thought whose affiliations remained avowedly inside the Marxist tradition. The long engagement with the ideas and legacies of Antonio Gramsci provided the best example of that sort. But by the mid-1980s, the kind of Marxism resulting from such a searching process of theoretical innovation and review was a peculiarly agnostic and distanced one—a "Marxism without guarantees," as Stuart Hall called it.[6] In large degree, it ceased to matter whether and how far one claimed a Marxist identity in any primary or formal manner. That identity remained unresolved in the background: not repudiated or disavowed necessarily, but also not recuperable in its earlier 1970s form.

After 1989, that silence grew. It had a variety of forms—sometimes embarassment and shame, sometimes a sense of loss and defeat, sometimes genuine uncertainty or confusion, and sometimes of course overt disavowal. Disposals of Marxism quickly followed upon the end of Communism and the more generalized crisis of socialism across the globe. As a continuing source of theory and ideas, or of broad intellectual inspiration for historians, the Marxist tradition now became practically delegitimated, all too glibly disparaged and dismissed. The tones varied from the gloating of anti-Marxist veterans and the procapitalist triumphalism of the new neoliberal marketeers to the more measured reflections of philosophical liberals and radical democrats, not to speak of the large numbers of workaday historians now relieved of the need to bother about one troublesome body of theory at least, or the somewhat disingenuous prescriptions of those post-Marxists who had never particularly read Marx in the first place. Amid the rather ridiculous belief that the demise of Soviet-style socialism somehow refuted the value of a plural and complex intellectual tradition, ill-considered rejections of Marxism as an entire body of thought were not hard to find. For postmodernists among historians, "Marxism" became a name for everything that now seemed to have been superseded or cast aside.

However, there were more careful attempts to take stock. In an important 1993 essay, "A Postmaterialist Rhetoric for Labor History," William Sewell acknowledged the productive strength of labor history while attacking the "broad and complacent materialist perspective [that] dominates the field." For unless that "largely unexamined materialist common sense is more widely and vigorously contested," he insisted, "labor history is destined to suffer from continuing intellectual doldrums."[7] In Sewell's estimation, "labor historians are too easily satisfied by explanations that identify a 'material' cause—say declining control over the process of production—but are highly skeptical of explanations that identify cultural causes—say shifts in political or religious discourse." His essay's principal purpose was to contest the "materialist rhetorical common sense" that he alleged underpinned labor history's pivotal concept of proletarianization.[8] He wanted to deconstruct the idea that the economy is "material" and to offer an alternative figuration of the object of social history in general. This last was inclusive in a welcome way, referring to feminist politics, to Foucault, to Gramsci and others, in an account of the expanded sense of the political that they provided. Sewell's was a stimulating piece not lacking in the generosities sometimes wholly missing from other contributions to these debates.

Yet at some key points Sewell's argument slid too easily between cognate but far from identical positions. What started life in his essay as labor history's "largely unexamined materialist common sense"—a rhetoric said to reside in the unreflected assumptions and scholarly reflexes of the field—quickly took more substantive form. His encoding of production and exchange as "material," as well as his references to economic reductionism as the central analytical procedure of the materialist trope, placed his object of critique pretty firmly within a "Marxist" orbit. By this means, accordingly, a single seamless movement connected an undertheorized labor historiography to the analytics and scholarly practices of a fully articulated materialist economic reductionism. Labor history became doubly convicted: weakened, we are told, by its refusal of theoretical engagement and its reluctance to move beyond commonsense materialism, it was nevertheless forced to bear the burden of grand narrative, of imperious reductionist maneuvering, of a systematic privileging of the "economic" in its causal schema, and so on. Yet it is hard to believe that any scholarly field can be both theoretically weak and conceptually evasive on the one hand, and fully committed to a reductive materialist standpoint on the other. In our own view, labor history was simply messier and more interesting than these criticisms allowed. And in any case it is hard to think of a body of work in labor history, or in social history more broadly for that matter, in which the logics of such a thoroughly reductive and sectarian Marxism held sway. Who wrote it and when?

This slippage from describing an operative "common sense" here to attributing a comprehensively theorized analytical procedure of economism there, unfortunately, seems to have characterized poststructuralist criticisms of Marxist historiography more generally. Thus the work of the early Marxists in the field of British social history was also, like Sewell's labor history, underspecified in theoretical terms, so much so that its prevailing methods are now no longer easily distinguishable from those of much broader bodies of work. The inheritors of the allegedly "totalizing" versions of class provided by Thompson and others were actually quite timid in making such claims for their own work in which, as often as not, a much more eclectic slew of methods tended to be in play.[9] Surely the argument cannot be sustained that the whole genre of British social history generated since the 1960s was marked by some totalizing Marxist modernism with its full range of derivative reductions. Yet this, too, seemed to be one of the central positions of Patrick Joyce's polemical essay "The End of Social History?" To counterpose a social history so misunderstood against other possible kinds of history—cultural, postmodern, or some other—is not enough unless the full range of social history's eclecticism as a field can also be properly recognized and given its due.

There can be no warrant for essentializing social history as a unitary practice in that way, reducing its contradictory world of culture and ideas and identities as well as of class itself to the mere reflections of a given economic structure and its social formation. That can only be interpreted as a maneuver intended to harden the postulated distinction between past practices and postmodern innovations—between an "old" social history and a "new" cultural history liberated from all metanarratives and all reductive modernisms. Once accomplished, that maneuver can then allow Marxism, as well as associated variants of Enlightenment reason, to be definitively banished in favor of what claims to be a nontotalizing and wholly nonreductive practice. Social history is thereby convicted of the essentializing consequences of its commitment to metanarrative foundationalism, which is itself held to have been incorrigibly grounded in a version of Marxist reductionism. That is surely tendentiously oversimplifying.

The "social" in social history cannot be treated simply as a code word for economic reductionism, or as a shorthand for the most schematized version of Marx's historical materialism, or as a synonym for those old and self-evidently superseded declarations that "social being" determines "social consciousness" and that the economic base invariably precedes its cultural superstructure. To do this would be to essentialize a complex field of historical writing into little more than the reflex of an underspecified Marxism on whose conceptual axioms it is wrongly alleged to have been founded. The question of social history is a much bigger one than this, as is the question of social class. And so, too, of course is the question of Marxism itself.

Here we need again to refer to the essay by Gareth Stedman Jones we discussed extensively in chapter 4. His has been perhaps the clearest and strongest statement of closure against a previous project of social history that had previously been deemed to possess political as well as more immediately historiographical importance. "From the end of the 1970s," he flatly wrote, "the Marxist approach to history, which had flourished in Britain and elsewhere for over two decades, entered a period of abrupt and terminal decline."[10] The decline of the "Marxist approach to history," on this reckoning, was permanent and irreversible. From terminal decline there is little prospect of return. But of whose death exactly was this the notice? The Marxist approach to history, no less, a single unnuanced thing, and one vitiated, we suppose, by its essential conventions of thought and understanding. These were defined by Stedman Jones in the most abbreviated way, verging on the peremptory, and were then used in the context of the political events surrounding the fall of the Berlin Wall and its aftermath to dispose root-and-branch of the tradition of thought and the social historiography said to be formed around it.

Stedman Jones left no space anywhere between the discursive approach to history he propounded and the most reductionist versions of economistic Marxism. In common with Sewell's critique, a slippage occurred somewhere between citation of Thompson's underdeveloped deference to certain general propositions drawn from Marx, on the one hand, and ascription of a fully fledged, canonical, and sectarian theory of history, on the other. But with the exception of *The Povery of Theory* and some other polemical works, Thompson's history writing constantly negotiated the particular forms of its Marxian inspiration, before eventually moving in the 1980s toward something closer to what we would now call a post-Marxism in the loose generic sense, if again on a similarly underexplicated theoretical basis.[11] As for the broader corpus of apparently Thompsonian social history, works of a truly or systematically reductive kind were very few on the ground. In fact, social historiography was replete with examples of *practical* analysis of the material world that certainly did not succumb to the relentless logics of economism Stedman Jones and others now claimed to find.

It is precisely the pluralities of this approach in Britain and elsewhere that have generated such a complex and usable historiography as well as some of the most ferocious contests inside the field itself. The idea that either this broad universe of social historiography since the 1960s or the rather more specific forms of Marxist articulation within it could ever have amounted to a single thing, or ever be plausibly described as such, we find a disingenuous reduction of its own. Given the passionate disagreements even within the more specifically and avowedly Marxist sector of discussions, and the fruitfulness of the debates surrounding them—what Perry Anderson referred to as *Arguments within English Marxism*—it is really astonishing that during a more recent phase of historiographical innovation this should all have become so completely effaced.[12] So we feel we need to say in our own not uncertain terms: history writing inspired by Marxism in Britain was *always* a field of theoretical contest and practical, that is to say nonreductive, unorthodoxy.

Yet these important pluralized differences within the Marxian approach are now somehow totally refused and forgotten. The undeniable difficulties in Marxism on which these differences rested are permitted no possibility of interesting or productive answer. Contradictory practices and statements to be found in the archive of Marx's own work are scrupulously neglected, though they are surely pertinent here. In particular, we should not allow the recurrent tensions between canonical statements of a materialist determinism on the one hand, and much messier substantive analyses of actual historical struggles on the other, to be so easily conflated.

So Marxism, too, has been a much more complicated field than current critics of social historiography allow. It is not our place here to demonstrate this in any detail, but "The Working Day," chapter 10 of the first volume of *Capital,* offers a fine example. Here, in a lengthy, layered, and complex account, Marx addressed changes in the length of the working day in the 1840s and after.[13] This was no canonical account in which class interests and class positions predefined the political forms and legislative interventions that composed this historical arena. In fact, Marx vacillated in the priority he awarded to the economic sphere, to the political context, and to the legislative moment. He declined to dissolve the contradictory behavior of the state into a neat reductive story; and even at the end of this extraordinary chapter of historical analysis we are left in some doubt as to Marx's view of the causal weight of the various factors bearing on the determination of the length of the working day. Such a forceful and nuanced account surely cannot be collapsed into a simplified set of reductive meanings, thus to be essentialized as the "Marxist approach to history." Yet it is now exactly through such a procedure, such a collapsing of complex meanings, that such an approach is said to be incorrigibly vitiated by the alleged consensuality of its essential reductions.

Among social historians in Britain, with few exceptions, the disciplined orthodoxies of *Soviet* Marxism and its dependents, and the Stalinized versions of the theory of history with which these were associated, have had little place. On the contrary, in Britain it was entirely to be expected that differences in reading Marx resulted in differences in writing history. Here Marxism amounted to a complex and plural field of meanings embracing few reductionists in the party-orthodox or sectarian senses and containing plenty who sought further to de-essentialize its procedures. Attempts to retheorize Marxism, through Althusser or Gramsci, were not simply responses to recurrent crises within a larger political world. This Marxism has been habitually, though not invariably, more inclusive and less self-enclosed than is sometimes supposed. The history of Marxism in the social historical field in Britain cannot plausibly be represented as the long march of a reductive orthodoxy through the historical archive. The history of the working class has unquestionably framed an important body of Marxist work within this British social historiography, but it surely distorts the latter's complexities to insist that it emerged as the intellectual reflection of a highly centered Marxist orthodoxy.

## THE IMPORTANCE OF NOT IGNORING STRUCTURES

With this book we are not proposing a detailed program for any new or alternative methodology. Nor have we presented any comprehensive and systematic survey of the field. We would never claim to have touched in detail every possible base or to have outlined entire bibliographical fields. Instead, we are offering an intervention. We chose to proceed "symptomatically" by considering a focused selection of salient texts. Our primary intent is to free debate from the exclusionary forms in which for the past fifteen years it has often been cast. Certainly we are hoping to influence historians' practices but want to do so in a nonprogrammatic spirit that seeks to embrace as much as possible from the innovative historical work now being done. We want to depolemicize a field of debate riven across some years by magisterial statements of closure and defensive responses thereto. For this purpose, we think the time has finally become more propitious.

To repeat: our own method has been interventionist and not comprehensive. We want to show that different analytical registers might be combined without compromising each other and indeed to their mutual advantage. This might also be accomplished, we think, without in the process establishing any new orthodoxy. Out of the options released by this pluralized agenda, for example, it ought to be possible to imagine projects that combine poststructuralist understandings of the kind advocated by Joan Scott *together with* the approaches classically associated with social history, some of them concerned with structures and processes operating independently of their discursive rendition, or producing "regularities" as we have been calling them—for example, political economy, dissections of the labor process, analysis of labor markets, ethnographies of the workplace, mappings of community, or microhistorical reconstructions of everyday life. From a contemporary point of view, why should it not be possible to combine a political economy of globalized sweatshop labor with all the associated studies of discourse, identity, culture, and subjectivity?

We make this plea for pluralism not without examples in mind. We might mention, for instance, the work over many years of Andrew Ross, whose own trajectory reflects the kinds of combination we are suggesting. Beginning his career in the 1980s with a critical study of poetry in the United States, he followed this first with a densely argued book on the relationship of intellectuals to popular culture since the 1940s, and then with several further volumes of reflections on the contemporary interface between science, technology, and cultural understandings. Throughout that time, he was also involved editorially with one of the several pioneer journals of cultural studies in the United States, *Social Text,* which has certainly been identified with a "constructionist" approach to social analysis, sometimes extremely controversially so.[14] Most recently, on the other hand, Ross has also been heavily involved in campaigning against contemporary forms of globalized sweatshop labor, seeking in several key books to explore the interrelations among mass entertainment cultures, new patterns of consumer capitalism, and the cheap labor circuits and transnationalized forms of political economy that lie behind them. Along the way, he also published a detailed ethnography of Celebration, Florida, the Disney Corporation's new planned surburban community, which again sought to combine readings of the cultural meanings of the new urbanism with a social critique of the reworking of the American Dream and structural analysis of the regional economies of property development and control.[15]

While Ross himself may be no historian by disciplinary affiliation, his efforts at grasping both the economics and the cultural meanings of globalized sweatshop production restate one of our main questions, to which we have returned again and again in this book: how does the historian's practice converge to a politics of the present day? There were clear and confident answers for that question in an earlier period: during the heyday of social history those inspired by Thompson rested their case on the way working people processed their experience of exploitation over generations to produce in the end a collective consciousness of class, which then could serve as the foundation of radical or revolutionary politics. This of course drew its authority from a reading of the texts associated with the "early" Marx and in particular his 1844 Manuscripts. And it is exactly this notion of experience, as we have seen, that Joan Scott and others have comprehensively demolished. But if, as we have argued, this demolition did not at the same time remove all possible Marxisms from methodological acceptability, then what are the other possibilities? What other regularities might there be that connect the present with the past with regard to the main themes of this book?

Like Marx, Edward Thompson approached his project by thinking about continuity. He saw the formation of class-collective agency as a long struggle against patterns of exploitation inherent to industrial capitalist production, whose effects accumulated through history. The brute ontologies of working-class circumstances over time, and the necessity of their conditions of exploitation, delivered a sense of continuity grounded in the unavoidable experience of class relations. This made it possible confidently to connect the struggles of a past working class with present-day exigencies, whose logics of persistence were taken to be given by the capitalist conditions of production. So the genealogies of class inherent in Thompson's method rendered continuity an unproblematic concept.

This strategy was not always pursued by other practitioners with quite the sweep of the imperious grand narrative of Thompson's magnum opus. A lower-range register could be commonly employed. Much of the work published in the early years of *History Workshop Journal* sought to derive far more modest or local forms of collective agency for present-day purposes from careful and sympathetic reconstructions of the historical experience of quite particularized communities. Continuity assembled by recuperating the history of a group, whether work-centered or residentially based, whether defined by ethnic, social, gender, sexual, or some other coordinates of identity, could in this way be considered strategic for raising the group's self-awareness in the present time. That might even enable political and other forms of collective action.[16]

The process of establishing continuities with the past in this way becomes fundamental for the possibilities of collective organization in the present. These politicized purposes of social history were intensely pursued through a variety of the working contexts fashioned by the broad cohorts inspired by the example of Thompson and others during the 1960s and 1970s, from the Labour History Society and its new regional equivalents and the History Workshop movement in Britain, to the Mid-Atlantic Radical Historians Organization and its journal in the United

States.[17] History Workshops in particular were replete with such reconstructions of class-based or other experiences, whose resonance for the present remained rhetorically vital yet mostly unproblematized. In the meantime, as we have seen, precisely those projections of continuity have been called radically into question. As deployed by historians such as Joan Scott, poststructuralist thought disrupts those genealogies of class and by extension damages other assumptions about how agency in the sense of emancipatory politics might be created.

The earlier thinking about continuity as a narrative of class experience invoked agency in two distinct ways: first, by deriving the possibilities for revolutionary agency in the past from an argument about the collective dynamics of working-class self-making; second, by claiming that the process of recuperating historical experiences of that kind could serve to create radical political agency for the present. Both hopes now stand disrupted by poststructuralist critique. In Scott's identitarian world, or a world in which the construction and refashioning of political subjectivities are taken to offer the main ground of politics, the former labors of recuperating past experience of class can no longer converge to agency in the former way. In Thompsonian practice, Scott argues, the project of recuperating class was already vitiated by the consequences of its preexisting structuralist commitments, which worked to silence or marginalize other kinds of voices and suppress the possibility of recognizing other interests. Her critique likewise severs the available narratives of class from present political possibilities. Yet acknowledging the force and necessity of that critique should not preclude all possible forms of continuing thought on the subject. It should be possible, we think, to conceive of class in ways that are not vitiated or contaminated by error. Class affiliations and the structured regularities working to produce them ought, on the contrary, to provide one of the necessary bases from which to explain the possibilities for generating forms of collective agency, whether historically or in our own world.

This is the primary question for us: what power does class have to produce agency in the present; and how might this depend on historical understandings of class as well as on the continuities carrying these forward to a later time? That is, with class reconfigured along the lines of our argument, how far can we imagine a practice of social history that might contribute to our understanding of the formation of agency in the contemporary world? How do solidarities eventuate in politics over time? How does political agency attain something more than a capacity for occasional disruptions, for intermittent or sporadic effects in politics, something more than isolated or punctual explosions of presence? How does it eventuate in political continuities with an efficacy for change? And last but not least: how might that agency reconnect with an aspiration to change not just this or that piece of legislation or the recognition under law of previously disregarded identities, profoundly important though these have to remain, but also the state, the practices of government, and even the system of private ownership in the economy?

Marx's working class arose materially out of the process of production, called into being by the necessities of capitalist accumulation. In his conception it was to be rendered a majority class by the expansion of that production on an international scale. It was imagined as a reflex of the material relations of the economic system itself. It did not choose to be created. It was an inevitable outcome of processes occurring beyond the reach of the actions of the individuals and groups composing the class and initially, at least, beyond their comprehension. Consciousness was brought to the working class, or created as a condition of its own self-making, as Thompson would have it, by forces that lie beyond its own reach, that is, by structural necessities entailed by the development of capitalism itself and its "laws of motion."

Some version of this kind represented structural analysis in its earlier hegemonic and well-tried form. It permitted contingency, national difference, and variable politics according to circumstance. But it did not permit departure from the central axiom that contradictions arising between the forces and social relations of production would inevitably create social conflict. The principal notation of that conflict, moreover, would be a clash of classes conceived in world-historical terms if not on a literally world-historical scale. This describes the canonical version of structuralism from an orthodox Marxist perspective. Its omissions were legion, and by now extremely well-known. Marx was weak on empire, on women, mainly despised the peasantry, disdained the claims of many nationalities, and excluded from the account those elements of social formations marginalized by history (like the landed aristocracy) or those whose actions were considered marginal to the main event (the petite bourgeoisie).

We intend smuggling back none of this older conceptual baggage by reintroducing a structural register of analysis. But we remain convinced of the importance of conceptualizing the regularities through which, under conditions of the capitalist economy, the interconnected inequalities of money, power, and position are created and secured. We are not seeking sovereign status for a structuralist analytic but rather insist that the analysis of the field of inequality in general cannot be omitted or subsumed into discursive accounts of its condition, essential though these will have to remain. Yet at the same time, crucially, our redeployed understanding of class owes little to the production process itself in the older orthodox or productiv*ist* Marxist sense. We seek instead to emphasize the wider repertoire of ways in which dispossession, disempowerment, vulnerability, and poverty now tend to be created under contemporary capitalisms. We accept that the commonalty or universality of class experience in the Thompsonian notation can no longer be used to provide the unifying thread for such arguments. That classical model of an underlying class formation and the processes by which class comes to consciousness of itself, thereby forming the necessary basis for a progressive politics, has certainly gone, whether or not, and to what degree, it ever sufficiently described class and class formation in the actually existing industrializing world. In that Thompsonian story of working-class formation the shift from being to consciousness was not only thought to be inevitable but also invariably benign. Historically, it was certainly taken to be a good thing.

So what we cannot argue is that the common *experiences* of class inequality form a general basis for agency in the present, precisely because in different times and in different cultures inequality is handled discursively and becomes discursively maintained, becoming constructed in *un*common ways. If we remove the unifying notion of shared experience and replace it with contingent discursive constructions in that way, then the expectation of class consciousness as a recurrent figuration ceases to be available. Yet in full recognition of these consequences, we would still argue for the necessity—theoretically, heuristically, strategically—of acknowledging the persistence of class as a prediscursive or nondiscursive formation. Structural regularities in the processes by which rich and poor are created under conditions of capitalism remain vitally important, even while the discursive negotiation and the discursive defenses remain extremely variable, because such regularities nevertheless define one particularly decisive terrain where political intervention can occur. Then, of course, all the difficult questions arise about the relative importance of this particular terrain for political intervention as opposed to others. If for classical Marxists and the mainstream of the social historiography of class such regularities tended to provide the materialist bottom line in that hardened structuralist sense, that is not the ground on which we are now trying to think.

In other words, simply by postulating the existence of such structural regularities—which in our own notation we are taking to be fundamental to understanding class in its contemporary formations—we are *not* logically required to embrace the further assumption that these regularities necessarily translate into solidarities and forms of consciousness that we can then describe as class consciousness traditionally understood, in the canonical and time-honored way. Quite the contrary, for the manner in which political awareness is raised is profoundly contingent and variable. Our entire argument in this book presumes that it cannot be regarded as merely the expressive reflex of structural change. Thus: in postulating the meaningful importance of class as one continuing ground for politics we are *not* asking that it be rewarded hegemonic status. By seeking to reintroduce structural regularity, in this case of the production of inequalities under capitalism, we are not arguing for the abandonment of the more recent poststructuralist understanding or to reclaim for structure its old primacy. What we *are* saying is that in any analysis that we would consider comprehensive, we cannot imagine that both cultural and structural understandings would not need to be in play. They certainly need not be at war. If we really want to understand the contemporary forms of inequality of goods and power, we need to take our analysis across a range of contexts and terrains, using a variety of methods and assumptions, and thinking within more than a single register.

## MORE THAN ONE REGISTER

We regard the critical impact of the cultural turn on historians' thinking as constructive, beneficial, and wholly unavoidable, as we have repeatedly said during the course of this book. Moreover, no interventions had more effect in this regard than the essays of Joan Scott between the mid-1980s and early 1990s.[18] Yet even as they helped open such vital space for innovative thinking about "gender as a useful category of historical analysis," or more broadly about the importance for historians of post-structuralist theory, Scott's injunctions have not always resulted in analyses that proved as richly or ambitiously contextualized vis-à-vis the whole society as the best examples of the social history they wanted to supersede. Indeed, once it departs from the ground of pure critique, Scott's own historical writing seems either drawn down in Foucauldian fashion to the microworlds of the discursive economy where subjectivities are made, or else remains in a mode of critical exegesis practically indistinguishable from established genres of the history of ideas.[19]

Yet why should the critique of the earlier structuralist or materialist social histories acquire this particular consequential logic? In contrast to the latter, we are arguing that the study of class—or the social contexts, relations, and practices which that term was deployed by social historians to connote—requires attention to larger and more extensive transpersonal regularities and the forms of institutional action that work consciously and unconsciously to help shape or disrupt them. So far, the particular analytical strategies advocated by Scott have not only failed to engage that wider set of contexts but actually seem to occlude them. In arguing this, we are not seeking to counterpose our own "macro" ambitions against Scott's "micro" account in the manner of some earlier facile polemics. Rather we are trying to find or invent a nonexclusive language or set of terms that can precisely allow such polemical juxtapositions to be transcended. For that purpose we have arrived contingently at the expression of "register." In our usage, this is not meant to be theorized into a complex and elaborate conceptual program. It serves rather as an enabling metaphor, an escape from the essentializing epistemologies hitherto impeding our field.

In seeking to reaffirm the importance of class, moreover, we are not trying to mirror the claim raised so effectively by Scott that every discourse, every discursive practice, every effect is gendered in some way. In recalling discussion to a contextual ground of societal analysis, no such universal claims for class, its discourses, or its politics need be entailed. A generation ago some predominant but now vitiated forms of thinking about social history encouraged us to think in exactly those terms, for example, by subsuming and subordinating women within them, and Scott's lasting service was to have rendered such reductions inadmissible. That gendered critique of an older model of class analysis and its reductions has become the broadly accepted consensual ground for feminist and other radical historians seeking to understand the emancipatory possibilities of social change during the nineteenth and twentieth centuries. But a continuing attention to class and its forms of realization, appropriately specified and historicized, can nevertheless profoundly illuminate the ways in which gender needs to be approached and understood. Practicing a gender history without attention to what we are calling *larger regularities* in this sense, whether conceptualized in structural, social, or some other terms, can make very little sense.

Keeping these purposes in mind, therefore, what questions can a poststructuralist register of analysis like Joan Scott's *not* easily or fluently address? For example, how within a poststructuralist theoretical register might we deal with the systemic production of poverty as opposed to its microsubjective, individually localized, or identitarian consequences? Poststructuralism has been at its most productive when forcing us to confront the complex machineries of meaning through which poverty comes to be understood, all the complex modalities of its social and cultural construction. It points us to the realm of representations and languages and to all the ways in which bits and pieces of meaning are consciously and unconsciously worked into systems of practice, as well as into the ways of understanding the world and how it works. The poststructuralist challenge has made it impossible to approach questions of poverty without dealing with the discursive relations and practices surrounding and shaping its actually existing manifestations. That we now need to approach poverty as a discursive formation is for us beyond dispute. However, that does not exhaust all the registers of possible or necessary approach.

For example, can the poststructuralist register deal sufficiently with the question of how people enter the condition of being poor, with the processes that produce and reproduce poverty as well as those that discursively secure such a condition of being? Again, this is not intended as a way of smuggling back in the structuralisms of social history past, or of reintroducing the simple binaries of years ago, such as most obviously that of economy versus culture. We are suggesting, on the contrary, that there are ways of dealing with these questions in different registers that can emphatically avoid the exclusion of one from another. We do not actually have to choose between them, between investigating the political economy of class, the production of economic inequalities, and the regularities of economic distribution in a particular society, on the one hand, and reading the discursive forms through which they are represented, made accessible, and become understood, on the other.

Thus we can address the factory as a site of accumulation and capital formation, or as a place for the production of commodities for exchange, as a place of technological innovation, as a site of the division of labor and the practice of labor discipline, as an outcome of the commitment of capital as well as the operation of local land markets and wage determinations, all of which bear consequences for surrounding populations and their forms of governance. Or we can treat the factory as a locus of gender, ethnic, and cultural divisions and distinctions, as a site of conflicts arising around these as well as between capital and labor. Or we can approach the factory discursively by seeking to understand all the ways in which it has the capacity to shape and inform the social and cultural imaginary. Or we can seek to do all of these things and more.

Why should any one of these varying analytics be preferred exclusively, or be treated as more useful and legitimate than the others? By what possible criteria might we be able to tell a trade union organizer or shop-floor militant that it is more important to grasp the factory's social and cultural construction than to understand the logistics of the company's order book and wage rolls, the structured regularities of production and distribution, the complex coordinates of the local and regional labor markets, or the imposed infrastructure of the labor process, work rules, and rhythm of the working day? A willingness to pose this question does *not* require us to believe that any of those factors could ever somehow claim their immunity from discursive analysis. Indeed, they positively require discursive analysis in order to be properly understood. Yet it also seems the height of naïveté to pretend that there are no differences in how these respective issues need to be addressed. To organize her fellow workers into an effective collective agency for securing concrete improvements in wages and the conditions of work, a trade union militant would surely need to be equipped with some structuralist appreciation for how those conditions become defined and secured. Understanding the factory's discursive architecture would definitely be a vital help, indeed an essential priority for the most effective trade union efforts. But to discharge their tasks effectively such organizers need other kinds of knowledge too.

The point, surely, is that these different objects and purposes of analysis, each requiring its respective strategies and registers, should ideally be undertaken *together*. The factory is self-evidently a unit of economic production. It exists in a chain of circulation of commodities and money from the local through the national to the global and back. At the same time, it provides a microworld of culture, a site where the particular cultural coordinates of local time and place obtain, operate, and intersect. The factory—or any other locus of production—provides both an economic and a cultural setting in these terms. Each of these faculties deserves a different register of analysis. This is not to say that the economic dimensions of the factory can only be approached by economic analysis and are somehow unavailable for cultural and discursive approaches. Here the metaphor of "register" is *not* being proposed in order to reproduce the boundaries of older competing essentialisms or polemical position-taking. Rather, what we are arguing is that the same object—in this case the factory—should be amenable to a range of varying analytical approaches.

Finding the ways to encourage the generous and collaborative exchange of ideas across different analytical registers is the most urgent of the challenges now facing an engaged historiography. It has become the crucial priority for social and cultural historians seeking an understanding of the politics of the contemporary world and possibly even an access to the means of changing them. To allow such collaborative traffic between registers to get under way, we would argue, the type of epistemological argument that reigned so prescriptively across the debates of social and cultural historians for much of the later 1980s and the 1990s will need to be moved away from the center. Arguments strictly licensed and regulated by immaculately consistent epistemological standpoints communicate very badly with one another, not least when particular forms of politics are deemed to derive from, or be entailed by, one particular epistemology as against another. In their most negative and destructive consequences, the polemical confrontations of the 1990s operated precisely to exclude the possibility of benign intellectual traffic between opposing registers of analysis in exactly that way.

In trying to de-essentialize what we are calling "registers," to refuse epistemological polarizations and hierarchies, we are canvasing a revival of conceptual pluralism in practice, by means of what we have described as a pragmatics of good faith.[20] If this means acknowledging that there are indeed some structures that operate "behind people's backs," that those structures display regularities over time and place, and that they are amenable to common analytical approaches deriving from disciplines such as economics or sociology, then this is only to place those structures into an empirical and analytical register distinct from identity, culture, and language. It may be that we can know them only through their discourses and ours, but this scarcely alters their materiality. If our main illustration here has been the production of poverty—that is, actually existing forms of resource shortage and maldistribution—then we can acknowledge the necessary discursive terms of the available strategies for studying this without at the same time denying the materiality of the relevant structures themselves. For the obvious regularities of wealth and poverty in various capitalisms across different times and places certainly do exist outside attempts discursively to understand them. Discourse may provide the limits of our ability to talk about things, but discursive constructions cannot exhaust the world's field of precultural or noncultural settings and actualities.

So where does this leave the social historical work of the earlier time—that is, before Joan Scott's and Gareth Stedman Jones's interventions of the 1980s, before the cultural turn, before the diffusion of the influence of Foucault? That social historical work at its best, we would argue, was not abjectly dependent on Marxist structuralism in the older canonical way that poststructuralist attacks have alleged. At the same time, social historians would simply never have considered for a moment abandoning the ground of "material life." Such a withdrawal was not *thinkable* within the conceptual framing of the field at the time. Nevertheless, from within that materialist framing (the framing implied by Hobsbawm's concept of the "history of society") social historians remained open throughout the 1970s in response to an extremely wide variety of challenges (especially through readings of Gramsci and the energizing impact of feminism) to questions of culture in the broadest sense of the term, embracing women, families, sexualities, education, sport and recreation, disease and medicine, professionalization, media, art and design, religion, and so forth. There may well have been notable, even strategic omissions and silences, but what field has ever been free of these?

Is it possible, now, to envisage a hybrid history capable of retaining a version of a materialist perspective while recognizing in its practice the necessity of the discursive moment? We have tried to propose a non-polemical, mutually supportive grouping of registers of analysis precisely to enable ways of doing history in such a conceptually pluralist manner. That would be a practice free of master narrative, free of the reductions inherent in such narrative; but also a practice in which the discursive would not be allowed to overwhelm the structural, or delegitimate it, and vice versa. By envisaging a "sociocultural" history in this way (which might even be called a history that remains Marxist in some recognizable ways), we have no wish to recuperate the central theoretical axioms of the older social history field as some have previously described them, but rather to recognize that the best of the social history produced since the 1960s remained open to analysis arising in different and sometimes contradictory theoretical spheres.

The *practice* of that social history, as opposed to the intervening postmodernist or poststructuralist allegations about its essentialist predilections, was plural and expansive in its willingness to broach new questions affecting new fields in new ways. The most critical and creative versions of that social history have also shown themselves capable of merging and collaborating with the new forms of analysis that the new cultural history freshly allowed. A generous and pluralist historical practice embracing a variety of ways of looking at the world, past and present, can surely be envisaged once we emerge from the moment of delegitimating polemic. That is the primary intention behind our book: to pull the field out of its disabling polemics and to bring together the best analyses from whatever conceptual source.

# NOTES

*Preface*

1. Geoff Eley and Keith Nield, "Why Does Social History Ignore Politics?" *Social History* 5 (1980): 249–72.

2. See Richard Johnson, "Thomson, Genovese, and Socialist-Humanist History," *History Workshop Journal* 6 (Autumn 1978): 79–100.

3. On the other hand, some people clearly *had* been thinking about the piece. Fourteen years later Ira Katznelson featured it rather centrally in a programmatic article marking his retirement as editor of *International Labor and Working-Class History*. His article launched a special Roundtable called "What Next for Labor and Working-Class History?" with responses from each of the journal's board members. See Ira Katznelson, "The 'Bourgeois' Dimension: A Provocation about Institutions, Politics, and the Future of Labor History" (with responses by Lizabeth Cohen, Geoffrey Field, Helmut Gruber, Michael Hanagan, Bruce Levine, David Montgomery, Mary Nolan, Anson Rabinbach, Judith Stein, Louise A. Tilly, and Sean Wilentz), *International Labor and Working-Class History* 46 (Fall 1994): 7–32, 33–92. We respond to Katznelson's article in chapter 5 of this volume.

4. See the conference report by Kelly Boyd and Rohan McWilliam in *Social History* 20 (January 1995): 93–100.

5. Geoff Eley and Keith Nield, "Starting Over: The Present, the Post-Modern, and the Moment of Social History," *Social History* 20 (1995): 355–64; Eley and Nield, "Farewell to the Working Class?" and "Reply: Class and the Politics of History," *International Labor and Working-Class History* 57 (Spring 2000): 1–30, 76–87; Geoff Eley, "Is All the World a Text? From Social History to the History of Society Two Decades Later," in Terence J. McDonald (ed.), *The Historic Turn in the Human Sciences* (Ann Arbor: University of Michigan Press, 1996), 193–243; Eley, "Problems with Culture: German History after the Linguistic Turn," *Central European History* 31 (1998): 197–227; Eley, "Between Social History and Cultural Studies: Interdisciplinarity and the Practice of the Historian at the End of the Twentieth Century," in Joep Leerssen and Ann

Rigney (eds.), *Historians and Social Values* (Amsterdam: Amsterdam University Press, 2000), 93–109; Keith Nield, "A British Debate. Under the Sign of the Social: Bringing Politics Back In?" *Tijdschrift voor Sociale Geschiedenis* 23 (1997): 182–96; Nield, "Under the Sign of Liberalism: The End of History and the New World Order," in Simon Groenveld and Michael Wintle (eds.), *Under the Sign of Liberalism: Varieties of Liberalism in Past and Present* (Zutphen: Walburg Pers, 1997), 133–45.

*Chapter 1*

1. Alaine Touraine, *L'après socialisme* (Paris: Grasset, 1983); André Gorz, *Farewell to the Working Class* (London: Pluto Press, 1982). For the West German debate at this same time, Rolf Ebbighausen and Friedrich Tiemann, eds., *Das Ende der Arbeiterbewegung in Deutschland? Ein Diskussionsband zum sechzigsten Geburtstag von Theo Pirker* (Opladen: Westdeutscher Verlag, 1984). The British equivalent began earlier, actually before the election of Thatcher in 1979, in the 1978 Marx Memorial Lecture by Eric Hobsbawm. See Eric Hobsbawm et al., *The Forward March of Labour Halted?* (London: Verso, 1981). For the general context of these debates, see Michael Schneider, "In Search of a 'New' Historical Subject: The End of Working-Class Culture, the Labor Movement, and the Proletariat," *International Labor and Working-Class History* 32 (Fall 1987): 46–58.

2. The debate in Britain began in the newly established (and short-lived) Labour Party discussion journal *New Socialist* (from 1981 until its independence was effectively curtailed in the mid-1980s) and was then taken up by the CPGB theoretical journal *Marxism Today,* which coined the slogan of "New Times" and pioneered a New Left revisionism until its discontinuation in 1991. See James Curran, ed., *The Future of the Left* (Cambridge: Polity, 1984); Stuart Hall and Martin Jacques, eds., *New Times: The Changing Face of Politics in the 1990s* (London: Lawrence and Wishart, 1991); Eric Hobsbawm, *Politics for a Rational Left: Political Writing, 1977–1988* (London: Verso, 1989); Stuart Hall, *The Hard Road to Renewal* (London: Verso, 1988).

3. Stuart Hall and Martin Jacques, "Introduction," in Hall and Jacques, eds., *New Times,* 11.

4. The fullness of possible citations here would be huge. For an indication, see Stuart Hall, "Ethnicity: Identity and Difference," and Paul Gilroy, "One Nation under a Groove: The Cultural Politics of 'Race' and Racism in Britain," both in Geoff Eley and Ronald Grigor Suny, eds., *Becoming National: A Reader* (New York: Oxford University Press, 1996), 337–49, 250–69.

5. See David Roediger, *The Wages of Whiteness: Race and the Making of the American Working Class* (London: Verso, 1991); *Towards the Abolition of Whiteness: Essays on Race, Politics, and Working-Class History* (London: Verso, 1994); and "Race and the Working-Class Past in the United States: Multiple Identities and

the Future of Labor History," *International Review of Social History* 38 (1993), Suppl.: 127–43. See also Alexander Saxton's *The Rise and Fall of the White Republic: Class Politics and Mass Culture in Nineteenth-Century America* (London: Verso, 1990), which appeared just before Roediger's book; anthropologist Ruth Frankenberg's *White Women, Race Matters: The Social Construction of Whiteness* (Minneapolis: University of Minnesota Press, 1993), and Toni Morrison's extended essay, *Playing in the Dark: Whiteness and the Literary Imagination* (Cambridge: Harvard University Press, 1992). Later monographs included Noel Ignatiev, *How the Irish Became White* (New York: Routledge, 1995); Neil Foley, *The White Scourge: Mexicans, Blacks, and Poor Whites in Texas Cotton Culture* (Berkeley: University of California Press, 1997); Matthew Frye Jacobson, *Whiteness of a Different Color: European Immigrants and the Alchemy of Race* (Cambridge: Harvard University Press, 1998); Matt Wray and Annalee Newitz, eds., *White Trash: Race and Class in America* (New York: Routledge, 1997).

6. For Britain, see especially Laura Tabili, *"We Ask for British Justice": Workers and Racial Difference in Late Imperial Britain* (Ithaca: Cornell University Press, 1994); and on the broader terrain of citizenship, Kathleen Paul, *Whitewashing Britain: Race and Citizenship in the Postwar Era* (Ithaca: Cornell University Press, 1997). For a searching review of Tabili, drawing out the general historiographical context, see Laura Lee Downs, *Social History* 22, no. 2 (May 1997): 202–7. For France, see Gérard Noiriel, *The French Melting Pot: Immigration, Citizenship, and National Identity* (Minneapolis: University of Minnesota Press, 1996).

7. Joan W. Scott, "On Language, Gender, and Working-Class History," *International Labor and Working-Class History* 31 (Spring 1987): 1–13, with responses by Bryan D. Palmer (14–23), Christine Stansell (24–29), and Anson Rabinbach (30–36). Scott's "Reply to Criticism" was in *International Labor and Working-Class History* 32 (Fall 1987): 39–45.

8. Ira Katznelson and Aristide R. Zolberg, eds., *Working-Class Formation: Nineteenth-Century Patterns in Western Europe and the United States* (Princeton: Princeton University Press, 1986). The editors' regret at the exclusion was expressed in note 2.

9. J. Carroll Moody and Alice Kessler-Harris, eds., *Perspectives on American Labor History: The Problems of Synthesis* (De Kalb: Northern Illinois University Press, 1990), 55–79, 217–34. But only thirteen of the sixty-seven participants at the original conference (Northern Illinois University, October 1984) were women.

10. Ava Baron, ed., *Work Engendered: Toward a New History of American Labor* (Ithaca: Cornell University Press, 1991); Laura L. Frader and Sonya O. Rose, eds., *Gender and Class in Modern Europe* (Ithaca: Cornell University Press, 1996); Lenard R. Berlanstein, ed., *Rethinking Labor History: Essays on Discourse and Class Analysis* (Urbana and Chicago: University of Illinois Press, 1993). See also

Patrick Joyce, ed., *The Historical Meanings of Work* (Cambridge: Cambridge University Press, 1989); and Sonya O. Rose, "Gender and Labor History: The Nineteenth-Century Legacy," *International Review of Social History* 38 (1993), Suppl.: 145–62.

11. Kathleen Canning, *Languages of Labor and Gender: Female Factory Work in Germany, 1850–1914* (Ithaca: Cornell University Press, 1996; repr., Ann Arbor: University of Michigan Press, 2002); "Gender and the Politics of Class Formation: Rethinking German Labor History," in Geoff Eley, ed., *Society, Culture, and the State in Germany, 1870–1930* (Ann Arbor: University of Michigan Press, 1996), 105–41; "Feminist Theory after the Linguistic Turn: Historicizing Discourse and Experience," *Signs* 19 (1994): 368–404. Joan Scott's challenge was raised initially in 1986 in the *American Historical Review* with "Gender: A Useful Category of Historical Analysis," which was then reprinted in *Gender and the Politics of History* (New York: Columbia University Press, 1988), 28–50.

12. Joyce, "Introduction," in *Class* (Oxford: Oxford University Press, 1995), 5.

13. See Lewis H. Siegelbaum and Ronald Grigor Suny, eds., *Making Workers Soviet: Power, Class, and Identity* (Ithaca: Cornell University Press, 1994). A majority of essays consider particular categories of workers (Heather Hogan on St. Petersburg metalworkers, Hiroaki Kuromiya on Donbas miners, Diane Koenker on printers, Chris Ward on cotton workers, Daniel Orlovsky on white-collar workers) or particular locations (S. A. Smith on St. Petersburg, 1905–17, Stephen Kotkin on Magnitogorsk in the 1930s). Several explore the broader discourse of class identity in particular periods (Mark Steinberg, "Vanguard Workers and the Morality of Class" before the Revolution; Gabor Rittersporn on the changing categories of Bolshevik social address, and Sheila Fitzpatrick on labor-management relations, both on the 1930s). A twelfth essay, "The Iconography of the Worker in Soviet Political Art" by Victoria E. Bonnell, departs from the social historical ground of the main volume but barely remarks on the gendered dimensions of the material, although the same author had published a similar treatment of women elsewhere: "The Representation of Women in Early Soviet Political Art," *Russian Review* 50 (1991): 267–88.

14. The volume originated in a conference at Michigan State University in November 1990, conceived deliberately in response to discussions in other fields, including especially Katznelson and Zolberg's *Working-Class Formation* and Joan Scott's general proposals. Commentators from outside the field framed the conference discussions with this in mind, including Michael Burawoy, Kathleen Canning, Geoff Eley, David Montgomery, Sonya Rose, and William Sewell, Jr. An extraordinarily stimulating level of discussion was achieved in the conference itself, which addressed questions of nationality and religion as well as gender.

15. Something of the same gap, between the acknowledgment of theory and the practice of the detailed analysis, is present in another book Joyce published around the same time, where Scott, Riley, and others are generously cited in the introduction, while the detailed reading of the two lives that organize the book (Edwin Waugh and John Bright) proceeds conspicuously without gender. See Patrick Joyce, *Democratic Subjects*, 6.

16. See Patrick Joyce, *Work, Society, and Politics: The Culture of the Factory in Later Victorian England* (Brighton: Harvester, 1980).

17. These quotations are taken from 10f. and 16 of the introduction to Joyce, ed., *Class.* It's only fair to quote one of the passages in full (10f.): "In liberal as well as right historiography class is still a central term. When its Marxist framework is challenged, it none the less remains unscathed as part of professional common sense. In fact, the more the notion is questioned the more it appears to become entrenched in this common sense. Numerous textbooks and monographs continue to be written in which classes are still historical actors, albeit without their historical roles. As an adjective, 'class' sends millions marching up and down the pages of history, complete with 'working-class' values, 'middle-class' politics, and so on. As a narrative principle it gives these actors their various parts in the resulting stories of past and present. Perhaps it is time to look for new actors and new narratives?" Joyce's earlier work on factory paternalism was in *Work, Society, and Politics.* For his subsequent claims for the superordinate status of populist notions of "people," "citizens," and "nation," see *Visions of the People: Industrial England and the Question of Class, 1840–1914* (Cambridge: Cambridge University Press, 1991) and *Democratic Subjects;* and for a useful general statement, "A People and a Class: Industrial Workers and the Social Order in Nineteenth-Century England," in M. L. Bush, ed., *Social Orders and Social Classes in Europe since 1500: Studies in Social Stratification* (London: Longman, 1992), 199–217. Our comment shouldn't be taken as hostility to theories of narrativity as such. Joyce himself has deployed these to interesting effect, but see especially Margaret R. Somers, "Narrativity, Narrative Identity, and Social Action: Rethinking English Working-Class Formation," *Social Science History* 26 (1992): 591–630.

18. "The discursive approach to history" is the description used by Gareth Stedman Jones in his important retrospective essay, "Anglo-Marxism, Neo-Marxism and the Discursive Approach to History," in Alf Lüdtke, ed., *Was bleibt von marxistischen Perspektiven in der Geschichtsforschung?* (Göttingen: Wallstein Verlag, 1997), 149–209, also published in a shortened version as "The Determinist Fix: Some Obstacles to the Further Development of the Linguistic Approach to History in the 1990s," *History Workshop Journal* 42 (Autumn 1996): 19–35. The revisionist historiography of class had its starting points in the early 1980s, burgeoning into full-blown controversy by the end of the decade. The

ball was set rolling by Gareth Stedman Jones, "Rethinking Chartism," in *Languages of Class: Studies in English Working-Class History, 1832–1982* (Cambridge: Cambridge University Press, 1983), 90–178, an essay whose earliest versions dated back to 1977.

19. The complexities of this process and the subtleties of the thinking involved, not to speak of the extraordinarily ramified nature of the associated debates, can easily become oversimplified in any summary description. For examples of the revisionist historiography in a later nineteenth-century British context, whose authors were either students or colleagues of Stedman Jones, see Eugenio F. Biagini and Alastair J. Reid, eds., *Currents of Radicalism: Popular Radicalism, Organized Labour, and Party Politics in Britain, 1850–1914* (Cambridge: Cambridge University Press, 1991); Eugenio F. Biagini, *Liberty, Retrenchment, and Reform: Popular Liberalism in the Age of Gladstone, 1860–1880* (Cambridge: Cambridge University Press, 1992); Alastair J. Reid, *Social Classes and Social Relations in Britain, 1850–1914* (Cambridge: Cambridge University Press, 1992); Miles Taylor, *The Decline of English Radicalism, 1847–1860* (Oxford: Oxford University Press, 1995); *Speaking for the People: Party, Language, and Popular Politics in England, 1867–1914* (Cambridge: Cambridge University Press, 2002). For a somewhat different but related strand of work emphasizing "histories of the social," see Patrick Joyce, *The Rule of Freedom: Liberalism and the Modern City* (London: Verso, 2003); Patrick Joyce, ed., *The Social Question: New Bearings in History and the Social Sciences* (London: Routledge, 2002).

20. See especially Lawrence Stone, "History and Post-Modernism," *Past and Present* 131 (May 1991): 217–18.

21. Geoff Eley and Keith Nield, "Starting Over: The Present, the Postmodern, and the Moment of Social History," *Social History* 20 (1995): 356.

22. Joan W. Scott, "The 'Class' We Have Lost," *International Labor and Working-Class History* 52 (Spring 2000): 73.

23. See the conference report by Kelly Boyd and Rohan McWilliam, *Social History* 20 (1995): 93–100.

24. See Eley and Nield, "Starting Over," and "Farewell to the Working Class?" *International Labor and Working-Class History* 57 (Spring 2000): 1–30, together with our "Reply: Class and the Politics of History," 76–87.

## Chapter 2

1. For a bibliographical overview dating from this time, see Geoff Eley, "Some Recent Tendencies of Social History," in George Iggers and Harold Parker, *International Handbook of Historiography: Contemporary Research and Theory* (Westport, Conn.: Greenwood, 1980), 55–70.

2. The precursor of *Annales* was the *Revue de synthèse historique* founded in

1900 by the philosopher of history Henri Berr (1863–1954) to open a dialogue between history and social science. Febvre (1878–1956) and Bloch (1866–1944) joined the *Revue* in 1907 and 1912 respectively, publishing their first major works and collaborating in Strasbourg before launching the new journal and moving to Paris. In 1946, the journal changed its name to *Annales: économies, sociétés, civilisations*. For good introductions, see Peter Burke, *The French Historical Revolution. The "Annales" School, 1919–1989* (Cambridge: Polity, 1999); François Dosse, *New History in France: The Triumph of Annales* (Urbana: University of Illinois Press, 1984); Troian Stoianovich, *French Historical Method: The "Annales" Paradigm* (Ithaca: Cornell University Press, 1976); Stuart Clark, ed., *The "Annales" School: Critical Assessments,* 4 vols. (London: Routledge, 1999); Carole Fink, *Marc Bloch: A Life in History* (Cambridge: Cambridge University Press, 1989); Matthias Middell, "The *Annales,*" in Stefan Berger, Heiko Feldner, and Kevin Passmore, eds., *Writing History: Theory and Practice* (London: Arnold, 2003), 104–17.

3. For the two emblematic examples, see E. H. Hunt, *British Labour History, 1815–1914* (London: Weidenfeld and Nicolson, 1981); Eric Hobsbawm, *Labouring Men: Studies in the History of Labour* (London: Weidenfeld and Nicolson, 1967).

4. Versions of this analysis, stressing the different institutional locations of social history, the varying relations among the disciplines, and the specific connections (enabling and inhibiting) with the surrounding political culture, especially the supports available from the national labor movements, work for other national historiographies too. Thus the post-1945 strength of the Communist Party in Italy endowed Marxist approaches to the social history of the working class with a dominance comparable to that in France. In Scandinavia, with half a century of largely continuous social democratic government after the 1930s, progressivist public cultures provided particularly strong sustenance for the social history departures of the 1960s—on the one hand, via the pioneering investigations of reform-driven social expertise inaugurated earlier in the century (in demography, public health, family policy, and so forth); on the other hand, via the popular institutional histories of the labor movement. In most countries in Europe, the democratic upswing after 1918 (however short-lived in some cases) created the essential starting points, including new universities, new chairs of history, new journals, and a general refounding of intellectual life. The potentials for social history coalesced most successfully in the converging initiatives of reform-minded social investigators and the labor movement's own chroniclers and archivists, usually with a tenuous relationship to academic history departments, where traditional state-centered perspectives reigned supreme.

5. For a brief conspectus of these antecedents, see Geoff Eley, "The Gen-

erations of Social History," in Peter N. Stearns, ed., *Encyclopedia of European Social History: From 1350 to 2000*, vol. 1 (New York: Charles Scribner's Sons, 2001), 3–12, and *A Crooked Line: From Cultural History to the History of Society* (Ann Arbor: University of Michigan Press, 2005), 63–65. See also Maxine Berg, *A Woman in History: Eileen Power, 1889–1940* (Cambridge: Cambridge University Press, 1996).

6. See, for instance, two of the earliest general accounts of British social history "from below": G. D. H. Cole and Raymond Postgate, *The Common People, 1746–1938* (London: Methuen, 1938), and Arthur Leslie Morton, *A People's History of England* (London: Lawrence and Wishart, 1938). The former retained its place until the 1960s.

7. But see here Miles Taylor, "The Beginnings of Modern British Social History?" *History Workshop Journal* 43 (Spring 1997): 155–76, which perversely exaggerates the influence of the Cambridge historians and other conservative figures in the prehistories of social history.

8. Harold Perkin, *The Origins of Modern English Society, 1780–1880* (London: Routledge and Kegan Paul, 1969).

9. See Edward P. Thompson, *The Making of the English Working Class* (London: Gollancz, 1963).

10. John Foster, *Class Struggle in the Industrial Revolution* (London: Methuen, 1974).

11. Here is the famous explication from Thompson's preface: "By class I understand an historical phenomenon, unifying a number of disparate and seemingly unconnected events, both in the raw material of experience and in consciousness. I emphasize that it is an *historical* phenomenon. I do not see class as a 'structure,' nor even as a 'category,' but as something which in fact happens (and can be shown to have happened) in human relationships. . . . More than this, the notion of class entails the notion of historical relationship. Like any other relationship, it is a fluency which evades analysis if we attempt to stop it dead at any given moment and anatomize its structure. . . . The relationship must always be embedded in real people and in a real context. . . . And class happens when some men, as a result of common experiences (inherited or shared), feel and articulate the identity of their interests as between themselves, and as against other men whose interests are different from (and usually opposed to) theirs. The class experience is largely determined by the productive relations into which men are born—or enter involuntarily. Class-consciousness is the way in which these experiences are handled in cultural terms: embodied in traditions, value systems, ideas, and institutional forms. If the experience appears as determined, class-consciousness does not. We can see a *logic* in the responses of similar occupational groups undergoing similar experiences, but we cannot predicate any *law*. Consciousness of class arises in the

same way in different times and places, but never in *just* the same way." Thompson, *Making,* 9–10.

12. In addition to Perkin, *Origins,* see the following: Geoffrey Best, *Mid-Victorian Britain, 1851–1870* (London: Fontana, 1971); Arthur Marwick, *The Deluge: British Society and the First World War* (Boston: Little, Brown, 1965) and *The Nature of History* (London: Macmillan, 1970); John Vincent, *Formation of the Liberal Party, 1857–1868* (New York: Scribner, 1967).

13. See these works by Hobsbawm: *Labouring Men; Primitive Rebels: Studies in Archaic Forms of Social Movement in the Nineteenth and Twentieth Centuries* (Manchester: Mancehester University Press, 1959); (with George Rudé), *Captain Swing: A Social History of the Great English Agricultural Uprising of 1830* (London: Lawrence and Wishart, 1968); *Bandits* (London: Weidenfeld and Nicolson, 1969); *The Age of Revolution, 1789–1848* (London: Weidenfeld and Nicolson, 1962); *Industry and Empire: From 1750 to the Present Day* (London: Weidenfeld and Nicolson, 1968).

14. For one good snapshot of the climate of discussion on the eve of the so-called linguistic turn, just before the axiomatic materialism of the social history wave started to founder, see the works of R. S. Neale, which open an idiosyncratic but intelligent window onto the range of approaches to class analysis on offer during the 1970s. See R. S. Neale, *Class in English History, 1680–1850* (Oxford: Blackwell, 1981); ed., *History and Class: Essential Readings in Theory and Interpretation* (Oxford: Blackwell, 1983); *Writing Marxist History: British Society, Economy, and Culture since 1700* (Oxford: Blackwell, 1985).

15. For the "labor aristocracy thesis," see Robert Gray, *The Aristocracy of Labour in Nineteenth-Century Britain, c. 1850–1900* (London: Macmillan, 1981); and for the critique of Thompson's work launched from the Birmingham Center for the Contemporary Cultural Studies, see among other texts Richard Johnson, "Thompson, Genovese, and Socialist-Humanist History," *History Workshop Journal* 6 (Autumn 1978): 96–119.

16. See the following: Eric Hobsbawm, "The Historians' Group of the Communist Party," in Maurice Cornforth, ed., *Rebels and Their Causes: Essays in Honour of A. L. Morton* (London: Lawrence and Wishart, 1979), 21–47; Bill Schwarz, "'The People' in History: The Communist Party Historians' Group, 1946–56," in Richard Johnson, Gregor McLennan, Bill Schwarz, and David Sutton, eds., *Making Histories: Studies in History-Writing and Politics* (London: Hutchinson, 1982), 44–95; Dennis Dworkin, *Cultural Marxism in Postwar Britain: History, the New Left, and the Origins of Cultural Studies* (Durham: Duke University Press, 1997), 10–44; David Parker, "The Communist Party and Its Historians, 1946–89," *Socialist History* 12 (1997): 33–58; Harvey J. Kaye, *The British Marxist Historians: An Introductory Analysis* (Oxford: Polity, 1984). Other members of the group (not all of whom kept their Marxist affiliations) included

the archaeologist Vere Gordon Childe, the classicists George Thomson and Benjamin Farrington, the ancient historians John Morris and E. O. Thompson, the medievalists Edward Miller and Gordon Leff, early modernists Eric Kerridge and M. E. James, the economic historian John Habbakuk, and the labor historian Henry Collins.

17. See Maurice Dobb, *Studies in the Development of Capitalism* (London: Routledge and Kegan Paul, 1946, rev. ed. 1963), together with the anthology of the associated debate edited by Rodney Hilton, *The Transition from Feudalism to Capitalism* (London: New Left Books, 1976). Dobb was born in 1900, Hill and Rudé in 1910, Kiernan in 1913, Saville and Hilton in 1916, Hobsbawm in 1917, Dorothy Thompson in 1923, and Edward Thompson in 1924. Raphael Samuel, the baby of the group, was born in 1938.

18. For Dona Torr, see her *Tom Mann and His Times* (London: Lawrence and Wishart, 1956); John Saville, ed., *Democracy and the Labour Movement: Essays in Honor of Dona Torr* (London: Lawrence and Wishart, 1954); David Renton, *Dissident Marxism: Past Voices for Present Times* (London: Zed Books, 2004), 104–21, and "Opening the Books: The Personal Papers of Dona Torr," *History Workshop Journal* 52 (Autumn 2001): 236–45.

19. See *Age of Revolution,* followed by *The Age of Capital, 1848–1875* (London: Weidenfeld and Nicolson, 1975); *The Age of Empire, 1875–1914* (London: Weidenfeld and Nicolson, 1987); *The Age of Extremes, 1914–1991: A History of the World* (London: Michael Joseph, 1994).

20. Kiernan's works include *British Diplomacy in China, 1880 to 1885* (Cambridge: Cambridge University Press, 1939); *The Revolution of 1854 in Spanish History* (Oxford: Clarendon, 1966); *The Lords of Human Kind: European Attitudes Towards the Outside World in the Imperial Age* (London: Weidenfeld and Nicolson, 1969); *Marxism and Imperialism: Studies* (London: Routledge and Kegan Paul, 1974); *America, the New Imperialism: From White Settlement to World Hegemony* (London: Zed Press, 1978); *State and Society in Europe, 1550–1650* (Oxford: Blackwell, 1980); *The Duel in History: Honour and the Reign of Aristocracy* (Oxford: Oxford University Press, 1988); *Tobacco: A History* (London: Radius, 1991). See Harvey J. Kaye, "V. G. Kiernan, Seeing Things Historically," in Kaye, *The Education of Desire: Marxists and the Writing of History* (New York: Routledge, 1992), 65–97.

21. Rudé's major works included *The Crowd in the French Revolution* (Oxford: Oxford University Press, 1959); *Wilkes and Liberty: A Social Study of 1763 to 1774* (Oxford: Oxford University Press, 1962); *The Crowd in History: A Study of Popular Disturbances in France and England, 1730–1848* (New York: Wiley, 1964); (with Eric Hobsbawm), *Captain Swing; Protest and Punishment: The Story of Social and Political Protestors Transported to Australia, 1788–1868* (Oxford: Oxford

University Press, 1978). Also see Harvey J. Kaye, "George Rudé, All History Must Be Studied Afresh," in Kaye, *The Education of Desire,* 31–64.

22. For Raphael Samuel's early works, see Samuel, ed., *Village Life and Labour* (London: Routledge and Kegan Paul, 1975); ed., *Miners, Quarrymen, and Salt Workers* (London: Routledge and Kegan Paul, 1977); "History Workshop, 1966–80," in Samuel, ed., *History Workshop: A Collectanea, 1967–1991. Documents, Memoirs, Critique, and Cumulative Index to History Workshop Journal* (Oxford: History Workshop, 1991). For Edward Thompson: *Making of the English Working Class;* with Eileen Yeo, eds., *The Unknown Mayhew: Selections from the Morning Chronicle, 1849–1850* (London: Merlin, 1971); *Whigs and Hunters: The Origin of the Black Act* (London: Allen Lane, 1975); with Douglas Hay, Peter Linebaugh, John G. Rute, E. P. Thompson, and Cal Winslow, *Albion's Fatal Tree: Crime and Society in Eighteenth-Century England* (London: Allen Lane, 1975); *Customs in Common: Studies in Traditional Popular Culture* (London: Merlin, 1991).

23. Edward P. Thompson, "The Peculiarities of the English," in Thompson, *The Poverty of Theory and Other Essays* (London: Merlin, 1978), 35–91, and *William Morris: From Romantic to Revolutionary* (New York: Pantheon, 1976; orig. ed. 1955); Raymond Williams, *Culture and Society, 1780–1950* (London: Hogarth, 1958) and *The Long Revolution* (Harmondsworth: Penguin Books, 1961).

24. G. Mingay, *English Landed Society in the Eighteenth Century* (London: Routledge, 1963); F. M. L. Thompson, *English Landed Society in the Nineteenth Century* (London: Routledge, 1963). John Saville was a leading mover of the Society for the Study of Labour History founded in 1960. With Asa Briggs, he coedited the successive volumes of *Essays in Labour History* (London: Macmillan, 1960, 1971; Croom Helm, 1977), and between the 1950s and 1990s he published prolifically on labor history. By the time he retired from editing the *Dictionary of Labour Biography,* the project had reached its tenth volume (London: Macmillan, 2000).

25. For Thomas Hodgkin see Anne Summers, "Thomas Hodgkin (1910–1982)," *History Workshop Journal* 14 (Autumn 1982): 180–82. His main works were *Nationalism in Colonial Africa* (London: F. Muller, 1956); *Nigerian Perspectives: An Historical Anthology* (Oxford: Oxford University Press, 1960); *Vietnam: The Revolutionary Path* (London: Macmillan, 1981). See also his essay "The Revolutionary Tradition in Islam," *History Workshop Journal* 10 (Autumn 1980): 138–50. For Basil Davidson, see Christopher Fyfe, ed., *African Studies since 1945: A Tribute to Basil Davidson* (London: Longman, 1976).

26. See Christopher Hill, Rodney Hilton, and Eric Hobsbawm, "*Past and Present:* Origins and Early Years," *Past and Present* 100 (August 1983): 3–14.

27. Trevor Aston, ed., *Crisis in Europe, 1560–1660* (London: Routledge and Kegan Paul, 1965).

28. One key essay by a leading *Annales* historian, Pierre Vilar, "The Age of Don Quixote," *New Left Review* 68 (July–August 1971): 59–71, was not translated until much later. For the subsequent course of the general debate, see Geoffrey Parker and Lesly M. Smith, eds., *The General Crisis of the Seventeenth Century* (London: Routledge and Kegan Paul, 1978).

29. By 1987, only five of the thirty-three titles in the *Past and Present Publications* series published by Cambridge University Press fell after the French Revolution, and it was not until the 1980s that the accent moved more toward the modern era. For the periods between the late Middle Ages and the French Revolution, in contrast, *Past and Present* became the premier English-language journal for social history during its heyday in the 1960s and 1970s.

30. The early case was the so-called Anderson-Nairn debate of the mid-1960s. See Perry Anderson, "Origins of the Present Crisis," *New Left Review* 23 (January–February 1964): 26–53; Tom Nairn, "The English Working Class," *New Left Review* 24 (March–April 1964): 43–57. Edward Thompson famously replied in "The Peculiarities of the English," *Socialist Register 1965* (London: Merlin, 1965), 311–62. Anderson's riposte came as "Socialism and Pseudo-Empiricism: The Myths of Edward Thompson," *New Left Review* 35 (January–February 1968): 2–42. Thompson revived and extended these polemics in *The Poverty of Theory and Other Essays;* Anderson replied in his *Arguments within English Marxism* (London: Verso, 1980). For a commentary, see Keith Nield, "A Symptomatic Dispute? Notes on the Relation between Marxian Theory and Historical Practice in Britain," *Social Research* 47 (1980): 479–506. For the general context, see Dworkin, *Cultural Marxism,* 125–82; Paul Corner, "Marxism and the British Historiographical Tradition," in Zygmunt G. Baranski and John R. Short, eds., *Developing Contemporary Marxism* (London: Macmillan, 1985), 89–111.

31. See, for example, the various works of Harvey J. Kaye, beginning with *British Marxist Historians* and continuing through his various editions of the writings of Victor Kiernan and others. See Harvey J. Kaye, ed., *History, Classes, and Nation-States: Selected Writings of V. G. Kiernan* (Oxford: Polity, 1988); Victor G. Kiernan, *Poets, Politics, and the People,* ed. Kaye (London: Verso, 1990); Kiernan, *Imperialism and Its Contradictions,* ed. Kaye (New York: Routledge, 1995); George Rudé, *The Face of the Crowd: Studies in Revolution, Ideology, and Popular Protest,* ed. Kaye (New York: Wheatsheaf, 1988); Kaye and Keith McClelland, eds., *E. P. Thompson: Critical Perspectives* (Oxford: Polity, 1990); Kaye, *The Education of Desire: Marxists and the Writing of History* (New York: Routledge, 1992).

32. See Thompson, *Making.* The literature on Thompson's work and influence is now enormous, but see especially Kaye and McClelland, eds., *E. P. Thompson;* Bryan D. Palmer, *E. P. Thompson: Objections and Oppositions* (London: Verso, 1994).

33. Thompson, *Making,* 12.

34. The older Anglo-Marxist generation was very supportive of the workshops: Christopher Hill and a fellow board member of *Past and Present,* Joan Thirsk, presided over sessions of History Workshop 3 (November 1968), including "The English Countryside in the Nineteenth Century," where Thompson was also a key speaker; at History Workshop 4 (November 1969), "The Nineteenth-Century Working Class" Eric Hobsbawm delivered a famous talk, "The New Working-Class World, 1880–1914." The first workshop, "A Day with the Chartists" (March 1967), had drawn around fifty participants; by the third workshop, there were some two hundred fifty; History Workshop 4 drew six hundred; History Workshop 6 on "Childhood in History: Children's Liberation" (May 1972) drew some two thousand. For these and other details, see Samuel, ed., *History Workshop, 1967–1991,* 92–107.

35. *Albion's Fatal Tree,* 13. For the wider research, see the following collections of essays: J. S. Cockburn, ed., *Crime in England* (London: Methuen, 1977); V. A. C. Gatrell, Bruce Lenman, and Geoffrey Parker, eds., *Crime and the Law: The Social History of Crime in Western Europe since 1500* (London: Europa, 1980); John Brewer and John Styles, eds., *An Ungovernable People: The English and Their Law in the Seventeenth and Eighteenth Centuries* (London: Hutchinson, 1980).

36. In the 1980s the international range of the invited participation broadened. The long-term core included David William Cohen, Alf Lüdtke, Hans Medick, and Gerald Sider. The initial Göttingen round table, "Work Processes" in 1978, produced a volume edited by Robert Berdahl et al., *Klassen und Kultur: Sozialanthropologische Perspektiven in der Geschichtsschreibung* (Frankfurt am Main: Syndikat, 1982); the second met in Paris in 1980, leading to Hans Medick and David Sabean, eds., *Interest and Emotion: Essays on the Study of Family and Kinship* (Cambridge: Cambridge University Press, 1984); the third and fourth meetings in Bad Homburg in 1982–83, "Domination/*Herrschaft,*" culminated in Alf Lüdtke, ed., *Herrschaft als soziale Praxis: Historische und social-anthropologische Studien* (Göttingen: Vandenhoeck und Ruprecht, 1991); the fifth and sixth round tables extended from 1985 through 1989 and eventually led to Gerald Sider and Gavin Smith, eds., *Between History and Histories: The Making of Silences and Commemorations* (Toronto: University of Toronto Press, 1997). See David William Cohen, *The Combing of History* (Chicago: University of Chicago Press, 1994), 1–23.

37. After *Strikes in France, 1830–1968,* with Edward Shorter (Cambridge: Harvard University Press, 1974) and *The Rebellious Century, 1830–1930,* with Louise Tilly and Richard Tilly (Cambridge: Harvard University Press, 1975), Charles Tilly produced successively *The Contentious French* (Cambridge: Harvard University Press, 1986) and *Popular Contention in Great Britain, 1758–1834* (Cambridge: Harvard University Press, 1995). These were quantitative histo-

ries of changing "repertoires of contention" and the rise of modern mass politics, whose argument was succinctly summarized in numerous particular essays. See, for example, "How Protest Modernized in France, 1844–55," in William O. Aydelotte, Allan G. Bogue, and Robert William Fogel, eds., *The Dimensions of Quantitative Research in History* (Princeton: Princeton University Press, 1972), 210–24; "Britain Creates the Social Movement," in James Cronin and Jonathan Schneer, eds., *Social Conflict and the Political Order in Modern Britain* (New Brunswick: Rutgers University Press, 1982), 21–51; "Contentious Repertoires in Britain, 1754–1834," *Social Science History* 17 (1993): 253–80. Tilly's corpus also includes a programmatic textbook, *From Mobilization to Revolution* (Reading, Mass.: McGraw-Hill, 1978), and the macroanalytical *European Revolutions, 1492–1992* (Oxford: Blackwell, 1993), rejoining collective action to capitalism and state making. Most recently, see Tilly, *Contention and Democracy in Europe, 1650–2000* (Cambridge: Cambridge University Press, 2004).

38. William H. Sewell, Jr., "Whatever Happened to the 'Social' in Social History?" in Joan W. Scott and Debra Keates, eds., *Schools of Thought: Twenty-Five Years of Interpretive Social Science* (Princeton: Princeton University Press, 2001), 210.

39. Sewell, "Whatever Happened," 213.

40. Sewell, "Whatever Happened," 211.

41. One scorching critique of social historians' simplistic and untheoretical use of "modernization theory," which concentrated its fury overwhelmingly against U.S. specialists on France (including Charles Tilly, Peter Stearns, Louise Tilly, Joan Scott, and others), gave insufficient recognition to this difference between the meta-analytical frameworks social historians used to situate their particular studies, which could often be explicated quite perfunctorily if at all, and the substantive richness of the particular studies themselves. See Tony Judt, "A Clown in Regal Purple: Social History and the Historians," *History Workshop Journal* 7 (Spring 1979): 66–94.

42. In the U.S. context of the 1960s, for example, key influences on the social histories of class formation included David Montgomery, Herbert Gutman, and Stephan Thernstrom. See David Montgomery, *Beyond Equality: Labor and the Radical Republicans, 1862–1867* (New York: Knopf, 1967); Montgomery, *Workers' Control in America: Studies in the History of Work, Technology, and Labor Struggles* (Cambridge: Cambridge University Press, 1979); Herbert G. Gutman, *Work, Culture, and Society in Industrializing America: Essays in Working-Class and Social History* (New York: Knopf, 1976); Stephan Thernstrom, *Poverty and Progress: Social Mobility in a Nineteenth-Century City* (Cambridge: Harvard University Press, 1964); Thernstrom, *The Other Bostonians: Poverty and Progress in the American Metropolis, 1880–1970* (Cambridge: Harvard University Press, 1973). One key emblematic volume was Stephan Thernstrom and Richard Sen-

nett, eds., *Nineteenth-Century Cities: Essays in the New Urban History* (New Haven: Yale University Press, 1969). Histories of slavery followed their own rhythm, while the emergence of Black history during the 1960s and 1970s hugely complicated this story. For its wider intellectual resonance among social historians of a Thompsonian stripe, the work of Eugene G. Genovese deserves special mention, especially *Roll, Jordan, Roll: The World the Slaves Made* (New York: Vintage, 1972).

43. *Social History* 1 (1976).

44. Sewell, "Whatever Happened," 209: "After rising to a position of hegemony in the historical profession in the United States and in most other countries by the end of the 1970s, social history has since been displaced as the leading edge of historical scholarship by cultural history. Many established social historians, myself included, have effectively stopped doing social history and taken up cultural history instead. Most important, perhaps, current graduate students don't show much interest in social history." While accurately describing this aspect of the zeitgeist, Sewell probably overstates his case. Social history established its greatest general dominance by the end of the 1970s in France and the United States. In Britain, most history departments remained far more recalcitrantly wedded to the old distinctions within the discipline; in West Germany, the various tendencies of social history remained embattled well into the 1990s; and similar stories of uneven and partial advance would certainly need to be told, country by country, elsewhere. Moreover, in the United States social history was not so much entirely abandoned during the 1990s as reconfigured in new hybrid combinations with cultural history.

45. Elizabeth Fox-Genovese and Eugene Genovese, "The Political Crisis of Social History: A Marxian Perspective," *Journal of Social History* 10 (1976): 205–20; Gareth Stedman Jones, "From Historical Sociology to Theoretical History," *British Journal of Sociology* 27 (1976): 35–69; Lawrence Stone, "History and the Social Sciences in the Twentieth Century," in Charles F. Delzell, ed., *The Future of History* (Nashville: Vanderbilt University Press, 1977), 3–42; Judt, "Clown in Regal Purple."

46. The most extensive and divisive debate among social historians in Britain during the later 1970s surrounded Richard Johnson, "Thompson, Genovese, and Socialist-Humanist History," but involved disagreements *within* an avowedly Marxist paradigm. That debate reached an ugly climax in Oxford at History Workshop 13 in November 1979, where Edward Thompson unleashed an intemperate polemic against the Birmingham Center for Contemporary Cultural Studies during a plenary session with Johnson and Stuart Hall. What seems so striking in retrospect about this occasion, which concentrated so dramatically the attention of not only social historians in Britain but also the broader intellectual Left, was how little it foreshadowed the equally bitter political and his-

toriographical disagreements of the coming decade, through which the validity of the class-centered materialist perspectives themselves were brought so radically into question. This Oxford debate was published in Raphael Samuel, ed., *People's History and Socialist Theory* (London: Routledge, 1981), 376–408.

47. See William H. Sewell, Jr., *Work and Revolution in France: The Language of Labor from the Old Regime to 1848* (Cambridge: Cambridge University Press, 1980), 8–10.

48. Sewell, "Whatever Happened," 213.

49. The emblematic collection here was Lynn Hunt, ed., *The New Cultural History* (Berkeley: University of California Press, 1989), especially Hunt's own "Introduction: History, Culture, and Text," 1–22, and the essays by Suzanne Desan, "Crowds, Community, and Ritual in the Work of E. P. Thompson and Natalie Davis," 47–71, and Aletta Biersack, "Local Knowledge, Local History: Geertz and Beyond," 72–96. Apart from Thompson's *Making,* key influences included Natalie Zemon Davis, *Society and Culture in Early Modern France* (Stanford: Stanford University Press, 1975); Carlo Ginzburg, *The Cheese and the Worms: The Cosmos of a Sixteenth-Century Miller* (Baltimore: Johns Hopkins University Press, 1980); Clifford Geertz, *The Interpretation of Cultures* (New York: Basic Books, 1973). The Hunt volume is dedicated "To Natalie Zemon Davis, inspiration to us all"; Davis had also been "commentator at large" at the originating conference, "French History: Texts and Culture," held at Berkeley on 11 April 1987 during the visit of Roger Chartier to the History Department there. See Roger Chartier, *Cultural History: Between Practices and Representations* (Ithaca: Cornell University Press, 1988), and his "Text, Printing, Readings," in Hunt, ed., *New Cultural History,* 154–75. The salient Frenchness of this cultural turn among North American historians was palpable.

50. See especially Raymond Williams, *Marxism and Literature* (Oxford: Oxford University Press, 1977); Stuart Hall, Dorothy Hobson, Andrew Lowe, and Paul Willis, eds., *Culture, Media, Language* (London: Hutchinson, 1980). The first of Foucault's works was translated in 1965, *Madness and Civilization,* plus *The Order of Things* in 1970 and *Archaeology of Knowledge* in 1972. By the end of the 1970s all were available apart from volumes 2 and 3 of *The History of Sexuality,* which were yet to be published in France: see *The History of Sexuality, Vol. 1: An Introduction* (New York: Pantheon, 1978); *The Use of Pleasure: Vol. 2 of The History of Sexuality* (New York: Vintage, 1985); *The Care of the Self: Vol. 3 of The History of Sexuality* (New York: Vintage, 1986). See also two collections of interviews and essays: Michel Foucault, *Language, Counter-Memory, Practice: Selected Essays and Interviews,* ed. D. F. Bouchard (Oxford: Blackwell, 1977); Colin Gordon, ed., *Power/Knowledge: Selected Interviews and Other Writings, 1972–1977, by Michel Foucault* (Brighton: Harvester, 1980). The reception of Foucault among historians was only fully under way by the mid-1980s.

51. The speed of the shift from the social to the cultural can easily be exaggerated. For example, a comprehensive forum sponsored by the British journal *History Today* on the state of the discipline in 1984–85, which solicited short commentaries from specialists under thirteen "What is . . . ?" headings for different types of history, had no separate section for cultural history. The latter fell somewhere between "What Is the History of Art?" "What Is Intellectual History?" and "What Is the History of Popular Culture?" See Juliet Gardner, *What Is History Today . . . ?* (Atlantic Highlands, N.J.: Humanities Press International, 1988).

52. Gareth Stedman Jones, *Outcast London: A Study in the Relationship between Classes in Victorian Society* (Harmondsworth: Peregrine Books, 1976). See also Stedman Jones, "History in One Dimension," *New Left Review* 36 (March–April 1966): 48–58; "The Pathology of British History," *New Left Review* 46 (November–December 1967): 29–43, reprinted as "History: The Poverty of Empiricism," in Robin Blackburn, ed., *Ideology in Social Science: Readings in Critical Social Theory* (London: Fontana, 1972), 96–115; and "From Historical Sociology to Theoretical History."

53. Gareth Stedman Jones, *Languages of Class: Studies in English Working-Class History, 1832–1982* (Cambridge: Cambridge University Press, 1983).

54. Joan W. Scott, *Gender and the Politics of History* (New York: Columbia University Press, 1988).

55. In early modern European history, for example, Peter Burke and Bob Scribner exemplified the movement from social to cultural history especially well: Burke's early works were self-consciously indebted to approaches drawn from sociology, while his later ones equally clearly modeled themselves on the cultural disciplines; Scribner began his career as the leading social historian of the urban Reformation in Germany, and then moved on to an inventive exploration of the latter's cultural field of meanings. For Burke, compare his *Tradition and Innovation in Renaissance Italy: A Sociological Approach* (London: Fontana, 1974) and *Sociology and History* (London: Allen and Unwin, 1980) with the recent *What Is Cultural History?* (Cambridge: Polity, 2004) and *Varieties of Cultural History* (Ithaca: Cornell University Press, 1997). Compare Robert W. Scribner's pioneering "Civic Unity and the Reformation in Erfurt," *Past and Present* 66 (1975): 29–60, with his slightly later "Reformation, Carnival, and the World Turned Upside-Down," *Social History* 3 (1978): 281–329; also *For the Sake of Simple Folk: Popular Propaganda for the German Reformation* (Cambridge: Cambridge University Press, 1981) and *Popular Culture and Popular Movements in Reformation Germany* (London: Hambledon Press, 2003).

56. Clark's work self-consciously recast Thompson's analysis in *The Making* using the new language of gender history. See Anna Clark, *The Struggle for the Breeches: Gender and the Making of the British Working Class* (Berkeley: University

of California Press, 1995); Sonya Rose, *Limited Livelihoods: Gender and Class in Nineteenth-Century England* (Berkeley: University of California Press, 1992); Kathleen Canning, *Languages of Labor and Gender: Female Factory Work in Germany, 1850–1914* (Ithaca: Cornell University Press, 1996; repr., Ann Arbor: University of Michigan Press, 2002).

57. See Harry Braverman, *Labor and Monopoly Capital* (New York: Monthly Review Press, 1974); Annette Kuhn, "Structures of Patriarchy and Capital in the Family," and Veronica Beechey, "Women and Production: A Critical Analysis of Some Sociological Theories of Women's Work," in Annette Kuhn and AnnMarie Wolpe, eds., *Feminism and Materialism: Women and Modes of Production* (London: Routledge and Kegan Paul, 1978), 42–67, 155–97; Michèle Barrett, *Women's Oppression Today: The Marxist/Feminist Encounter*, rev. ed. (London: Verso, 1988), 152–86. For the impact of Althusser, see E. Ann Kaplan and Michael Sprinker, eds., *The Althusserian Legacy* (London: Verso, 1993), and Gregory Elliott, *Althusser: The Detour of Theory* (London: Verso, 1987).

58. There is no satisfactory intellectual history of the impact of Marxist ideas in British intellectual life during the 1970s. For some valuable mapping, see Stuart Hall, "Cultural Studies and the Centre: Some Problematics and Problems," in Stuart Hall, Dorothy Hobson, Andrew Lowe, and Paul Willis, eds., *Culture, Media, Language: Working Papers in Cultural Studies, 1972–79* (London: Hutchinson, 1980), 15–47, and Perry Anderson, *In the Tracks of Historical Materialism* (London: Verso, 1983).

59. See Dworkin, *Cultural Marxism;* Williams, *Marxism and Literature;* Hall et al., eds., *Culture, Media, Language.*

60. Terry Lovell, ed., *British Feminist Thought* (Oxford: Blackwell, 1990), 21–22.

61. See Ellen Meiksins Wood, *The Retreat from Class: A New "True" Socialism* (London: Verso, 1986); Bryan D. Palmer, *Descent into Discourse: The Reification of Language and the Writing of Social History* (Philadelphia: Temple University Press, 1990), 120–44; Neville Kirk, "In Defence of Class: A Critique of Recent Revisionist Writing upon the Nineteenth-Century English Working Class," *International Review of Social History* 32 (1987): 2–47. See also Ellen Meiksins Wood and John Bellamy Foster, eds., *In Defense of History: Marxism and the Postmodern Agenda* (New York: Monthly Review Press, 1997).

62. See Eley, *Crooked Line,* 90–148.

63. See Jean-François Lyotard, *The Postmodern Condition* (Manchester: Manchester University Press, 1984), xxiv.

64. Kate Ellis, "Stories Without Endings: Deconstructive Theory and Political Practice," *Socialist Review* 19 (1989), 38.

65. Stuart Hall, "Some Problems with the Ideology/Subject Couplet," *Ideology and Consciousness* 3 (1978): 120.

66. Sewell, "Whatever Happened," 216.

67. See Ann Laura Stoler, *Carnal Knowledge and Imperial Power: Race and the Intimate in Colonial Rule* (Berkeley: University of California Press, 2002), and *Race and the Education of Desire: Foucault's History of Sexuality and the Colonial Order of Things* (Durham: Duke University Press, 1995); Anne McClintock, *Imperial Leather: Race, Gender, and Sexuality in the Colonial Conquest* (New York: Routledge, 1995); Paul Gilroy, *There Ain't No Black in the Union Jack: The Cultural Politics of Race and Nation* (London: Hutchinson, 1987), and *The Black Atlantic: Modernity and Double Consciousness* (Cambridge: Harvard University Press, 1993).

68. Compare Leonore Davidoff and Catherine Hall, *Family Fortunes: Men and Women of the English Middle Class, 1780–1850* (London: Hutchinson, 1987), with Catherine Hall, *White, Male, and Middle-Class: Explorations in Feminism and History* (Cambridge: Polity, 1992), and *Civilising Subjects: Metropole and Colony in the English Imagination, 1830–1867* (Cambridge: Polity, 2002).

69. See Lynn Hunt, *Revolution and Urban Politics in Provincial France: Troyes and Reims, 1786–1790* (Stanford: Stanford University Press, 1978), and *Family Romance of the French Revolution* (Berkeley: University of California Press, 1992); Joan W. Scott, *The Glassworkers of Carmaux: French Craftsmen and Political Action in a Nineteenth-Century City* (Cambridge: Harvard University Press, 1974), and *Gender and the Politics of History;* William H. Sewell, Jr., *Structure and Mobility: The Men and Women of Marseille, 1820–1870* (Cambridge: Cambridge University Press, 1985), and *Work and Revolution;* Judith R. Walkowitz, *Prostitution and Victorian Society: Women, Class, and the State* (Cambridge: Cambridge University Press, 1980), and *City of Dreadful Delight: Narratives of Sexual Danger in Late-Victorian London* (Chicago: University of Chicago Press, 1992).

70. Canning, *Languages of Gender and Labor;* Lenard R. Berlanstein, ed., *Rethinking Labor History: Essays on Discourse and Class Analysis* (Urbana: University of Illinois Press, 1993); Jacques Rancière, *The Nights of Labor: The Workers' Dream in Nineteenth-Century France* (Philadelphia: Temple University Press, 1989); Donald Reid, "The Night of the Proletarians: Deconstruction and Social History," *Radical History Review* 28–30 (1984): 445–63; Patrick Joyce, *Work, Society, and Politics: The Culture of the Factory in Victorian England* (Brighton: Harvester, 1980), *Visions of the People: Industrial England and the Question of Class, 1840–1914* (Cambridge: Cambridge University Press, 1991), and *Democratic Subjects: The Self and the Social in Nineteenth-Century England* (Cambridge: Cambridge University Press, 1994).

71. Robert Gray, *The Factory Question and Industrial England, 1830–1860* (Cambridge: Cambridge University Press, 1996); Clark, *Struggle;* Rose, *Limited Livelihoods.* See also Patrick Joyce, ed., *The Historical Meanings of Work* (Cambridge: Cambridge University Press, 1989).

72. Palmer, *E. P. Thompson,* 159, 194 n. 5.

73. David Mayfield, "Language and Social History," *Social History* 16 (1991): 355.

74. Mayfield, "Language and Social History," 355. See also William H. Sewell, Jr., "How Classes Are Made: Critical Reflections on E. P. Thompson's Theory of Working-Class Formation," and Robert Gray, "History, Marxism, Theory," in Kaye and McClelland, eds., *E. P. Thompson,* 50–77, 153–82.

75. See Geoff Eley and Keith Nield, "Why Does Social History Ignore Politics?" *Social History* 5 (1980): 249–72.

76. In attempting this amid the height of the polemical anxieties surrounding the implications of the linguistic turn for historians, David Mayfield and Susan Thorne, "Social History and its Discontents: Gareth Stedman Jones and the Politics of Language," *Social History* 17 (1992): 165–88, managed to provoke a small storm of furious controversy. While subsequently the purposes and value of that debate became commonly dismissed by historians less interested in theory per se, it at least sought to grapple with the dilemmas—analytical, epistemological, political, ethical—that the earlier project of an ambitious social history now faced. For an example of such a dismissal, whose tendentious misdescriptions speak volumes about its author's own no-nonsense innocence of the issues concerned, see Richard J. Evans, *In Defence of History* (London: Granta, 1997), 297–301. The full roster of contributions provoked by Mayfield and Thorne's article was as follows: Jon Lawrence and Miles Taylor, "The Poverty of Protest: Gareth Stedman Jones and the Politics of Language—A Reply," *Social History* 18 (1993): 1–15; Patrick Joyce, "The Imaginary Discontents of Social History—A Note of Response," *Social History* 18 (1993): 81–85; Mayfield and Thorne, "Reply," *Social History* 18 (1993): 219–33; Anthony Easthope, "Romancing the Stone: History-Writing and Rhetoric," *Social History* 18 (1993): 235–49; James Vernon, "Who's Afraid of the Linguistic Turn? The Politics of Social History and Its Discontents," *Social History* 19 (1994): 81–97; Neville Kirk, "History, Language, Ideas, and Postmodernism: A Materialist View," *Social History* 19 (1994): 221–40; Joyce, "The End of Social History?" *Social History* 20 (1995): 73–91; Kelly Boyd and Rohan McWilliam, "Historical Perspectives on Class and Culture," *Social History* 20 (1995): 93–100; Geoff Eley and Keith Nield, "Starting Over: The Present, the Postmodern, and the Moment of Social History," *Social History* 20 (1995): 355–64; Joyce, "The End of Social History? A Brief Reply to Eley and Nield," *Social History* 21 (1996): 96–98; Marc W. Steinberg, "Culturally Speaking: Finding a Commons between Poststructuralism and the Thompsonian Perspective," *Social History* 21 (1996): 193–214.

77. See Palmer, *Descent into Discourse;* Wood, *Retreat from Class;* Wood and Foster, eds., *In Defense.*

*Chapter 3*

1. See Christopher Lloyd, *Explanation in Social History* (Oxford: Blackwell, 1986), 260–62.

2. See Peter Novick, *That Noble Dream: The "Objectivity Question" and the American Historical Profession* (Cambridge: Cambridge University Press, 1988), 610. Stone's statement came in a letter to *Harper's* in April 1984 responding to an ill-informed broadside by Gertrude Himmelfarb against the relativistic consequences of the new social history of all kinds. See Gertrude Himmelfarb, "Denigrating the Rule of Reason: The 'New History' Goes Bottom Up," *Harper's* 268 (April 1984): 88. Stone's letter followed in the June issue, 4–5.

3. Jean-François Lyotard, *The Postmodern Condition: A Report on Knowledge* (Minneapolis: University of Minnesota Press, 1984); Jürgen Habermas, "Modernity—An Incomplete Project," in Hal Foster, ed., *The Anti-Aesthetic: Essays on Postmodern Culture* (Port Townsend, Wash.: Bay Press, 1983), 3–15.

4. Any full account of the diffusion of thinking about postmodernism would require far more detail than we can devote here. For a characteristically magisterial conspectus, see Perry Anderson, *The Origins of Postmodernity* (London: Verso, 1998), which tracks the initial coinage among Spanish-speaking and Luso-Brazilian literary intellectuals in the 1930s through isolated usages of the 1940s and 1950s to the contemporary explosion of interest. Hans Bertens, *The Idea of the Postmodern: A History* (London: Routledge, 1995), traces more detailed etymologies to the writings of literary critic Ihab Hassan in the 1960s and 1970s and architectural critics Robert Venturi, Charles Jencks, and Robert Stern in the later 1970s. Andreas Huyssen, "Mapping the Postmodern," *New German Critique,* 33 (Fall 1984): 5–52, is a crucial early essay. See also Margaret A. Rose, *The Post-Modern and the Post-Industrial: A Critical Analysis* (Cambridge: Cambridge University Press, 1991), 3–20. Good early general accounts covering the arts, popular culture, and cultural commentary can be found in Linda Hutcheon, *The Politics of Postmodernism* (London: Routledge, 1989), and Steven Connor, *Postmodernist Culture: An Introduction to Theories of the Contemporary* (Oxford: Blackwell, 1989). For the arts, see especially Brian Wallis, ed., *Art After Modernism: Rethinking Representation* (Boston: New Museum of Contemporary Art, New York, in assoc. with David R. Godine, 1984); and Russell Ferguson, Martha Gever, Trinh T. Minh-ha, and Cornel West, eds., *Discourses: Conversations in Postmodern Art and Culture* (Cambridge, Mass.: New Museum of Contemporary Art, New York and MIT Press, 1990). Key early debates occurred at a conference at the London Institute of Contemporary Art in May 1985, when Lyotard presented his ideas. See Lisa Appignanesi, ed., *Postmodernism. ICA Documents* (London: Free Association Books, 1989); also Lisa Appignanesi, ed., *Ideas from France: The Legacy of French Theory. ICA Documents* (London:

Free Association Books, 1989), based on seminars and a conference at the ICA in November–December 1984.

5. See Fredric Jameson, "Postmodernism, or, The Cultural Logic of Late Capitalism," *New Left Review* 146 (July–August 1984): 59–92. This formed the opening chapter of a later book-length discussion, also incorporating other essays of the 1980s: *Postmodernism, or, The Cultural Logic of Late Capitalism* (Durham: Duke University Press, 1991).

6. See especially David Harvey, *The Condition of Postmodernity: An Enquiry into the Origins of Cultural Change* (Oxford: Blackwell, 1989); Scott Lash and John Urry, *The End of Organized Capitalism* (Madison: University of Wisconsin Press, 1987); Alan Lipietz, *Mirages and Miracles: The Crisis of Global Fordism* (London: Verso, 1987); Ash Amin, ed., *Post-Fordism: A Reader* (Oxford: Blackwell, 1994); Rose, *The Post-Modern and the Post-Industrial*, 21–39. See also the much earlier views of Daniel Bell, *The Cultural Contradictions of Capitalism* (London: HarperCollins, 1976).

7. Here see especially Foster, ed., *Anti-Aesthetic;* Andrew Ross, ed., *Universal Abandon? The Politics of Postmodernism* (Minneapolis: University of Minnesota Press, 1988); E. Ann Kaplan, ed., *Postmodernism and Its Discontents: Theories, Practices* (London: Verso, 1988); Dick Hebdige, *Hiding in the Light: On Images and Things* (London: Routledge, 1988); Dick Hebdige, "After the Masses," in Nicholas B. Dirks, Geoff Eley, and Sherry B. Ortner, eds., *Culture/Power/History: A Reader in Contemporary Social Theory* (Princeton: Princeton University Press, 1994), 222–35; Jim Collins, *Uncommon Cultures: Popular Culture and Post-Modernism* (New York: Routledge, 1989).

8. See especially Angela McRobbie, "Postmodernism and Popular Culture," in Appagnanesi, ed., *Postmodernism*, 165–79; Lorraine Gammon and Margaret Marshment, eds., *The Female Gaze: Women as Viewers of Popular Culture* (London: Women's Press, 1988); Linda J. Nicholson, ed., *Feminism/Postmodernism* (New York: Routledge, 1990); Judith Butler, "Contingent Foundations: Feminism and the Question of 'Postmodernism,' " in Judith Butler and Joan W. Scott, eds., *Feminists Theorize the Political* (London: Routledge, 1992), 3–21; Imelda Whelehan, *Modern Feminist Thought: From the Second Wave to "Post-Feminism"* (New York: New York University Press, 1995), 194–215.

9. McRobbie, "Postmodernism and Popular Culture," 168.

10. See especially Linda Nicholson and Steven Seidman, eds., *Social Postmodernism: Beyond Identity Politics* (Cambridge: Cambridge University Press, 1995), where however only four of the fourteen contributors were actually sociologists by teaching position, two of them (R. W. Connell and Ali Rattansi) formed mainly outside the United States. See also *Theory, Culture, and Society*, 5, no. 2–3 (June 1988): Special Issue on Postmodernism; Craig Calhoun, ed., *Social Theory and the Politics of Identity* (Oxford: Blackwell, 1994); Pauline Marie

Rosenau, *Post-Modernism and the Social Sciences: Insights, Inroads, and Intrusions* (Princeton: Princeton University Press, 1992). Among sociologists in Britain there was much less resistance to ideas of the postmodern: for instance, the many works of Zygmunt Baumann, including *Legislators and Interpreters: On Modernity, Postmodernity, and Intellectuals* (Cambridge: Polity, 1987), and *Intimations of Postmodernity* (London: Routledge, 1991); Barry Smart, *Modern Conditions, Postmodern Controversies* (London: Routledge, 1992), and *Postmodernity* (London: Routledge, 1992); Scott Lash, *Sociology of Postmodernism* (London: Routledge, 1990); Bryan Turner, ed., *Theories of Modernity and Postmodernity* (London: Sage, 1990); Roy Boyne and Ali Rattansi, eds., *Postmodernism and Society* (London: Macmillan, 1990).

11. Among an enormous literature, see especially Iain Chambers and Lidia Curti, eds., *The Post-Colonial Question: Common Skies, Divided Horizons* (London: Routledge, 1996).

12. It did appear adjectivally in the very last and somewhat residual category, "Global Culture in a Postmodern Age." It registered in only two of the forty essay titles, again as an untheorized descriptor: Cornel West's "The Postmodern Crisis of the Black Intellectuals" and Homi K. Bhabha's "Postcolonial Authority and Postmodern Guilt." See Cary Nelson and Lawrence Grossberg, eds., *Marxism and the Interpretation of Culture* (Urbana: University of Illinois Press, 1988); Lawrence Grossberg, Cary Nelson, and Paula Treichler, eds., *Cultural Studies* (New York: Routledge, 1992).

13. For examples of critical grappling with Foucault's ideas, see Jeffrey Weeks, "Foucault for Historians," *History Workshop Journal* 14 (Autumn 1982): 106–19; Patricia O'Brien, "Michel Foucault's History of Culture," in Lynn Hunt, ed., *The New Cultural History* (Berkeley: University of California Press, 1989), 25–46; Rachel Harrison and Frank Mort, "Patriarchal Aspects of Nineteenth-Century State Formation: Property Relations, Marriage and Divorce, and Sexuality," in Philip Corrigan, ed., *Capitalism, State Formation, and Marxist Theory* (London: Routledge, 1980), 79–109; Laura Engelstein, "Combined Underdevelopment: Discipline and the Law in Imperial and Soviet Russia," *American Historical Review* 98, 2 (1993): 338–53; Rudy Koshar, "Foucault and Social History: Comments on Combined Underdevelopment," *American Historical Review* 98, 2 (1993): 354–63; Jan Goldstein, "Forming Discipline with Law: Problems and Promises of the Liberal State," *American Historical Review* 98, 2 (1993): 376–81; Jan Goldstein, ed., *Foucault and the Writing of History* (Cambridge: Harvard University Press, 1994).

14. Kenneth Barkin, "Bismarck in a Postmodern World," *German Studies Review* 18 (1995): 246.

15. At the same time, the scale of this "threat" was hugely inflated. As recently appointed editor of *Central European History,* the flagship journal of Ger-

man historians in North America, Barkin acknowledged that of the hundred or more submissions he had received during the previous two years barely five had "a postmodern slant." "Bismarck in a Postmodern World," 243. Barkin's article and the response, Michael Geyer and Konrad H. Jarausch, "Great Men and Postmodern Ruptures: Overcoming the 'Belatedness' of German Historiography," *German Studies Review* 18 (1995): 253–74, also prompted an Internet discussion initiated by Diethelm Prowe, which extended from August through October 1995. See http://www2.h-net.msu.edu/~german/discuss/pomo/.

16. Gertrude Himmelfarb, *On Looking into the Abyss: Untimely Thoughts on Culture and Society* (New York: Vintage, 1994), 131ff. A previous volume of Himmelfarb's essays, *The New History and the Old: Critical Essays and Reappraisals* (Cambridge: Harvard University Press, 1987), had grown from her *Harper's* article of April 1984, "Denigrating the Rule of Reason," one of the earliest shots in this particular culture war. See note 2 above.

17. Lawrence Stone, "History and Post-Modernism," *Past and Present* 131 (May 1991): 217–18. The place of publication, to which of course Stone had privileged access, gave this ignorant and inflammatory squib particular resonance.

18. Thus in 1987 major assessments appeared by John Toews in the *American Historical Review* and Donald Kelley and Alan Megill in the *Journal of the History of Ideas*. In 1989 an issue of the *American Historical Review* was wholly given over to what the editor called "the problems that critical theory has posed for grounding the truth value of historical statements," including an exchange between David Harlan and David Hollinger on literary theory and the philosophy of language, an article by Alan Megill on the status of "explanation" in historical writing, and a forum, "The Old History and the New," originating as the opening session at the American Historical Association's annual meeting in December 1988. Debates also occurred in the *Journal of Modern History* and *History and Theory,* the latter centering on the writings of F. R. Ankersmit. Hayden White's salience also grew around this time, and Hunt, ed., *New Cultural History,* appeared in 1989. See John E. Toews, "Intellectual History after the Linguistic Turn: The Meaning and the Irreducibility of Experience," *American Historical Review* 92 (1987): 879–907; Donald R. Kelley, "Horizons of Intellectual History: Retrospect, Circumspect, Prospect," *Journal of the History of Ideas* 48 (1987): 143–69; Alan Megill, "The Reception of Foucault by Historians," *Journal of the History of Ideas* 48 (1987): 117–40; David Harlan, "Intellectual History and the Return of Literature," *American Historical Review* 94, no. 3 (1989): 581–609; David Hollinger, "The Return of the Prodigal: The Persistence of Historical Knowing," *American Historical Review* 94, no. 3 (1989): 610–21; Harlan, "Reply to David Hollinger," *American Historical Review* 94, no. 3 (1989): 622–26; Alan Megill, "Recounting the Past: Description, Explanation, and

Narrative in Historiography," *American Historical Review* 94, no. 3 (1989): 627–53; Theodore S. Hamerow, Gertrude Himmelfarb, Lawrence W. Levine, Joan W. Scott, John E. Toews, "AHR Forum: The Old History and the New," *American Historical Review* 94, no. 3 (1989): 654–98; Robert Darnton, "The Symbolic Element in History," *Journal of Modern History* 58 (1986): 218–34; Dominick LaCapra, "Chartier, Darnton, and the Great Symbol Massacre," *Journal of Modern History* 60 (1988): 95–112; James Fernandez, "Historians Tell Tales: Of Cartesian Cats and Gallic Cockfights," *Journal of Modern History* 60 (1988): 113–27; F. R. Ankersmit, "Historical Representation," *History and Theory* 27 (1988): 205–28, and "Historiography and Postmodernism," *History and Theory* 28 (1989): 137–53. Hayden White's *Metahistory: The Historical Imagination in Nineteenth-Century Europe* (Baltimore: Johns Hopkins University Press, 1973), followed by *Tropics of Discourse: Essays in Cultural Criticism* (Baltimore: Johns Hopkins University Press, 1978), had long appeared, but his ideas were not taken up extensively by historians until the mid-1980s. His new influence was registered by *The Content of the Form: Narrative Discourse and Historical Representation* (Baltimore: Johns Hopkins University Press, 1987). See also Thomas L. Haskell, "The Curious Persistence of Rights Talk in the 'Age of Interpretation,'" *Journal of American History* 74 (1987): 984–1012; and Robert F. Berkhofer, Jr., "The Challenge of Poetics to (Normal) Historical Practice," *Poetics Today* 9 (1988): 435–52.

19. Jane Caplan, "Postmodernism, Poststructuralism, and Deconstruction: Notes for Historians," *Central European History* 22, 3–4 (1989): 266. Caplan's sober and careful disentangling of these three terms laid out the necessary distinctions just as various other historians were busily scrambling them.

20. Joan W. Scott, "Introduction," *Gender and the Politics of History* (New York: Columbia University Press, 1988), 7–8. Scott's article, "Gender: A Useful Category of Historical Analysis," was published originally in *American Historical Review* 91, no. 4 (1986): 1053–75, and then reprinted in *Gender and the Politics of History*, 28–50.

21. In addition to the attacks by Himmelfarb and Stone, see the response to Ankersmit by Perez Zagorin, "Historiography and Postmodernism: Reconsiderations," *History and Theory* 29 (1990): 263–74, together with the rejoinder, F. R. Ankersmit, "Reply to Professor Zagorin," 275–96. Bryan D. Palmer's book-length polemic, *Descent into Discourse: The Reification of Language and the Writing of Social History* (Philadelphia: Temple University Press, 1990), predates the crystallizing of postmodernism into a central term of historiographical conflict. While nodding to the debates of the 1980s, Palmer denied their usefulness for characterizing contemporary capitalism: "I take poststructuralism to be the ideology of postmodernism, and it is the impact of this theoretical implosion on the writing of social history that is addressed in what follows." See vii, 219 n.

5. For another early critique of poststructuralist influences, see Michael Ermarth, "Mindful Matters: The Empire's New Codes and the Plight of Modern European Intellectual History," *Journal of Modern History* 57 (1985): 506–27.

22. For Ankersmit, see *Narrative Logic: A Semantic Analysis of the Historian's Language* (The Hague: M. Nijhoff, 1983); "Historiography and Postmodernism" and "Reply to Professor Zagorin;" *History and Tropology: The Rise and Fall of Metaphor* (Berkeley: University of California Press, 1994). For Kellner, *Language and Historical Representation: Getting the Story Crooked* (Madison: University of Wisconsin Press, 1989); "Narrativity and History: Post-Structuralism and Since," *History and Theory* 26 (1987): 1–29. See also Ankersmit and Kellner's jointly edited *A New Philosophy of History* (Chicago: University of Chicago Press, 1995). Patrick Joyce traveled from the social history of *Work, Society, and Politics: The Culture of the Factory in Later Victorian England* (Brighton: Harvester, 1980), through the broadened culturalism of *Visions of the People: Industrial England and the Question of Class, 1848–1914* (Cambridge: Cambridge University Press, 1991), to a theoretically rationalized intellectual history in *Democratic Subjects: The Self and the Social in Nineteenth-Century England* (Cambridge: Cambridge University Press, 1994). See also his edited reader, *Class* (Oxford: Oxford University Press, 1995), and the edited volume, *The Social in Question: New Bearings in History and the Social Sciences* (London: Routledge, 2002). It is unclear whether Berkhofer would embrace the "postmodernist" label, but his *Beyond the Great Story: History as Text and Discourse* (Cambridge: Harvard University Press, 1995) is one of the strongest expositions of the pertinent viewpoints so far. For Alun Munslow, see *Deconstructing History* (London: Routledge, 1997) and his edited volume *The Routledge Companion to Historical Studies* (London: Routledge, 2000); and for Keith Jenkins, *Rethinking History* (London: Routledge, 1991) and *On "What Is History?": From Carr and Elton to Rorty and White* (London: Routledge, 1995). Munslow coedits the new journal *Rethinking History: The Journal of Theory and Practice,* and Jenkins edited *The Postmodern History Reader* (London: Routledge, 1997).

23. See Richard J. Evans, *In Defence of History* (London: Granta, 1997). The London Institute of Historical Research sponsored a series of debates around these issues in the Autumn 2001 issue of its online journal *History in Focus.* See Patrick K. O'Brien, "An Engagement with Postmodern Foes, Literary Theorists, and Friends on the Borders of History," together with Alun Munslow's reply. See also the associated site *Continuous Discourse: History and Its Postmodern Critics,* where Evans replies to a series of critical commentaries. The website can be accessed at http://ihr.sas.ac.uk/ihr/Focus/. For the debate in *Social History,* see the detailed citations in chapter 2, note 76, in the present book.

24. Only six of the thirty-two books listed by Jenkins in his recommendations for further reading are authored by historians qua disciplinary affiliations,

as opposed to philosophers, literary theorists, and sociologists. While more of the recommended articles originated with historians in disciplinary terms (we count sixteen out of twenty-seven), that also suggests the paucity of book-length exemplifications and the difficulties of translating postmodernist prescriptions into monographs of the usual kind. See Jenkins, ed., *Postmodern History Reader,* 436–38. Much of the early discussion of poststructuralism's implications for history was conducted by nonhistorians, from Derek Attridge, Geoff Bennington, and Robert Young, eds., *Post-Structuralism and the Question of History* (Cambridge: Cambridge University Press, 1987), to Elizabeth Deeds Ermarth's influential *Sequel to History: Postmodernism and the Crisis of Time* (Princeton: Princeton University Press, 1992).

25. In the absence of any explicit avowal by the authors themselves, we are a little hesitant in citing the following as instances of the new postmodern sensibility, but these works come to mind: Matt K. Masuda, *The Memory of the Modern* (New York: Oxford University Press, 1996); Susan A. Crane, *Collecting: Historical Consciousness in Early Nineteenth-Century Germany* (Ithaca: Cornell University Press, 2000); Peter Fritzsche, *Stranded in the Present: Modern Time and the Melancholy of History* (Cambridge: Harvard University Press, 2004). Despite their impressive creativity and ambition, though, the writing of each of these authors remains inside the essay form. Moreover, this paucity of book-length monographs generated under the sign of postmodernism contrasts with the wider contexts of contemporary interdisciplinarity, which by now has inspired an extremely rich and extensive body of monographic literature, particularly in relation to cultural studies, the full range of humanities disciplines, and historical anthropology. In particular, the old distinction between "social" and "cultural" history has become increasingly meaningless and mobile.

26. Keith Jenkins, "Introduction," in Jenkins, ed., *Postmodern History Reader,* 28.

27. We used this phrase in an earlier (and not very successful) effort at encouraging such a dialogue. See Geoff Eley and Keith Nield, "Farewell to the Working Class?" *International and Working-Class History* 57 (Spring 2000): 18; Eley and Nield, "Reply: Class and the Politics of History," *International and Working-Class History* 57 (Spring 2000): 83.

28. This same argument can be applied to the character and composition of "the archive" itself: how certain materials find their way into an actual archive and others don't, how those materials are organized and made available, how they are made to authorize certain kinds of knowledge and not others, all these faculties become every bit as subject to the labors of construction in the preceding sense as do the works of written history. Once the archive beomes associated with the contingent and the partial rather than the authoritative and the fixed, moreover, historians become much freer to find their sources beyond the

precincts of the physical repositories and officially sanctioned institutions we conventionally take "archives" to mean. This freeing of the historian's relationship to the possible types and locations of legitimate evidence during the past two decades has been immensely liberating. It has many complex sources, but intellectually we owe this above all to the slow reception and working-through of the ideas on the subject of the archive of Michel Foucault. See especially his essay "Nietzsche, Genealogy, History," in Michel Foucault, *Language, Counter-Memory, Practice: Selected Essays and Interviews,* ed. D. F. Bouchard (Oxford: Blackwell, 1977), 139–64. For further brilliant reflections, see Carolyn Steedman, *Dust: The Archive and Cultural History* (New Brunswick: Rutgers University Press, 2002), especially chapter 4, "The Space of Memory: In an Archive," 66–88. Also see Thomas Richards, *The Imperial Archive: Knowledge and the Fantasy of Empire* (London: Verso, 1993).

29. See, for example, O'Brien's claims that in practice "good" historians have always understood the importance of what postmodernists are now arguing: "Engagement with Postmodern Foes," 11, at http://ihr.sas.ac.uk/ihr/Focus/Whatishistory/obrien.html. This familiar rhetorical sidestep becomes radically disingenuous in Evans, *In Defence of History.*

30. Alun Munslow, "The Postmodern in History: A Response to Professor O'Brien," *History in Focus* 4 (Autumn 2001), at http://ihr.sas.ac.uk/ihr/Focus/Whatishistory/munslow1.html; Munslow, *Deconstructing History,* 163.

31. Munslow, "Postmodern in History," 3, 4. We might well demur here at Munslow's particular language. Historians are not supposed to "impose" their chosen frames or interpretations (what Munslow calls here "a personally chosen narrative form") onto their materials, after all. The historian's best practice involves a far more complex and careful process of reflectiveness and negotiation. Munslow implies a coerciveness in the relationship of historians to their materials, which the protocols of their discipline specifically require them to avoid. Subtle misdescriptions of this kind, and the resulting suspicion that postmodernist historians are insufficiently interested in how the best historians actually practice their work, are precisely what undermines the willingness of many historians to take postmodernist critiques seriously.

32. Munslow, "Postmodern in History," 5, 4f.

33. Munslow, *Deconstructing History,* 83.

34. Editorial, *History Workshop Journal* 10 (Autumn 1980): 1.

35. Jacques Derrida, "Like the Sound of the Sea Deep within a Shell: Paul De Man's War," *Critical Inquiry* 14 (1988): 606; Raymond Williams, *Marxism and Literature* (Oxford: Oxford University Press, 1977), 83–89.

36. Tony Bennett, "Text and History," in Peter Widdowson, ed., *Re-Reading English* (London: Methuen, 1982), 235.

37. Linda Nicholson and Steven Seidman, "Introduction," in Nicholson and Seidman, eds., *Social Postmodernism*, 26.

38. Of course, Lyotard himself had a far more philosophically grounded and abstract understanding of the nature of the metanarratives of modernity: "I will use the term *modern* to designate any science that legitimates itself with reference to a metadiscourse . . . making explicit appeal to some grand narrative, such as the dialectics of spirit, the hermeneutics of meaning, the emancipation of the rational or working subject, or the creation of wealth." By contrast, the "postmodern condition" became an "incredulity towards metanarratives" of that sort, or a distrust of any of the large-scale languages of explanation and justification that tend to be called upon for legitimating the governing practices of the modern world. See Lyotard, *Postmodern Condition*, xxii. Substantively, his most important historical claims concerned the transformations in the place of knowledge in society between the nineteenth and late twentieth centuries.

39. Here we are primarily making a point about concepts and approaches. The theoretical difficulties associated with using the concept of class for purposes of political analysis are clearly distinct from whatever may have been happening to the structural manifestations of class in actually existing early twenty-first-century capitalism, although of course they are intimately and intricately interconnected.

40. The earliest salvoes included Ellen Meiksins Wood, *The Retreat from Class: A New "True" Socialism* (London: Verso, 1986); Neville Kirk, "In Defence of Class: A Critique of Recent Revisionist Writing upon the Nineteenth-Century English Working Class," *International Review of Social History* 32 (1987): 2–47; Bryan D. Palmer, *Descent into Discourse: The Reification of Language and the Writing of Social History* (Philadelphia: Temple University Press, 1990), 120–44. More recently see Neville Kirk, ed., *Social Class and Marxism: Defences and Challenges* (Aldershot: Scolar Press, 1996); and Kirk, *Change, Continuity, and Class: Labour in British Society, 1850–1920* (Manchester: Manchester University Press, 1998).

41. Marc W. Steinberg, "Culturally Speaking: Finding a Commons between Poststructuralism and the Thompsonian Perspective," *Social History* 21 (1996): 194–95. Steinberg cites this argument as developed by Patrick Joyce in "The End of Social History," *Social History* 20 (1995): 84, and *Democratic Subjects*, 3. See also William Sewell, Jr., "Toward a Post-Materialist Rhetoric for Labor History," in Lenard R. Berlanstein, ed., *Rethinking Labor History: Essays on Discourse and Class Analysis* (Urbana: University of Illinois, 1993), 15–38.

42. Thompson's most elaborate and impassioned statement of this view was contained in Edward Thompson, "The Poverty of Theory: or an Orrery of Erros," in *The Poverty of Theory and Other Essays* (London: Merlin, 1978), 217–29.

43. Thompson himself certainly thought like this, and to that extent he and the maximalist postmodernist critics are the mirror image of each other. Thus Thompson rejected Harold Perkin's grand interpretation of British history on the grounds of his Weberianism in relation to class, just as he hated the work of John Foster on the grounds of its highly economistic or Leninist reading of Marx. Thompson devoted great polemical energies to doing what Patrick Joyce and other postmodernists wanted to do to him: namely, undermining the epistemological foundations of the legitimacy of a body of adversarial work.

44. "Judith Butler: Reanimating the Social," in Nicholas Gane, ed., *The Future of Social Theory* (London: Continuum, 2004), 58; also Judith Butler, "Merely Cultural," *New Left Review* 227 (January–February 1998): 33–44.

45. Nikolas Rose, "Governing the Social," in Gane, ed., *Future of Social Theory,* 181.

46. Rose, "Governing the Social," 179.

47. More recently Joyce seems to have tacitly conceded this misappropriation. As a programmatic concept the term has gone from his most recent book, *The Rule of Freedom: Liberalism and the Modern City* (London: Verso, 2003), appearing only incidentally as a "protean term" in his "Introduction" to Joyce, ed., *Social in Question,* 15.

48. Keith Jenkins, "Postmodernism," in Kelly Boyd, ed., *Encyclopedia of Historians and Historical Writing,* vol. 2 (London: Fitzroy Dearborn, 1999), 952.

49. Jenkins, "Postmodernism," 952.

50. Jenkins, *On "What Is History?"* 6. See also Patrick Joyce, "The Imaginary Discontents of Social History: A Note of Response to Mayfield and Thorne, and Lawrence and Taylor," *Social History* 20 (1995): 84: "Times have moved on, and historians simply have to learn to keep up with them."

51. In his programmatic advocacy of the "new history," for example, Alun Munslow distinguishes three such epistemologies, which he labels "reconstructionist or modernist," "constructionist or late-modernist," and "deconstructionist." Whereas the first two of these share an Enlightenment-derived analytical empiricism, the last exchanges the modernist heritage for a postmodernist "cultural," literary, or representational conception of the past. See Alun Munslow, *The New History* (Harlow: Pearson Education, 2003), 5–7. Yet, under the rubric of "situated knowledges," Munslow also recognizes the existence of a wider epistemological diversity, encompassing "race epistemologies, feminist epistemologies, gay epistemologies, and Marxist epistemologies." *New History,* 3. It is not clear why these other possibilities recede from consideration in the main body of his book. Similarly, the move from recognizing that in one important dimension history is an essentially literary activity to suggesting that history should be written primarily according to literary rules is a very big one. We can agree that historical writing should be subjected to the same readings and pro-

cedures of evaluation as a fiction or other literary text without concluding that this is all there is to say about the writing of history.

## Chapter 4

1. Edward P. Thompson, "Eighteenth-Century English Society: Class Struggle without Class?" *Social History* 3 (1978): 150.

2. Thompson, "Eighteenth-Century English Society," 147.

3. Huw Beynon, "Class and Historical Explanation," in M. L. Bush, ed., *Social Orders and Social Classes in Europe since 1500: Studies in Social Stratification* (London: Longman, 1992), 243; Edward P. Thompson, "The Peculiarities of the English," in Ralph Miliband and John Saville, eds., *The Socialist Register 1965* (London: Merlin, 1965), 357.

4. See Asa Briggs, ed., *Chartist Studies* (London: Macmillan, 1959); James Epstein and Dorothy Thompson, eds., *The Chartist Experience: Studies in Working-Class Radicalism and Culture, 1830–60* (London: Macmillan, 1982).

5. To back this claim up we can't hope to provide anything resembling a full bibliography in just a single note. The easiest and most effective way of confirming the point would be to consult a range of relevant journals for the 1970s and 1980s, including the *Bulletin of the Society for the Study of Labour History, Llafur, Social History,* and *History Workshop Journal,* whose articles, review sections, and inventories of research in progress will quickly provide such a detailed map.

6. David Crew, *Town in the Ruhr: A Social History of Bochum, 1870–1914* (New York: Columbia University Press, 1979); Mary Nolan, *Social Democracy and Society: Working-Class Radicalism in Düsseldorf, 1890–1920* (Cambridge: Cambridge University Press, 1981); Donald H. Bell, *Sesto San Giovanni: Workers, Culture, and Politics in an Italian Industrial Town, 1880–1922* (New Brunswick: Rutgers University Press, 1986); Louise A. Tilly, *Politics and Class in Milan, 1881–1901* (New York: Oxford University Press, 1992); Reginald E. Zelnik, *Labor and Society in Tsarist Russia: The Factory Workers of St. Petersburg, 1855–1870* (Stanford: Stanford University Press, 1971); Ronald Grigor Suny, *The Baku Commune, 1917–1918: Class and Nationality in the Russian Revolution* (Princeton: Princeton University Press, 1973).

7. William H. Sewell, Jr., *Structure and Mobility: The Men and Women of Marseille, 1820–1870* (Cambridge: Cambridge University Press, 1985); Joan W. Scott, *The Glassworkers of Carmaux: French Craftsmen and Political Action in a Nineteenth-Century City* (Cambridge: Harvard University Press, 1974); Patrick Joyce, *Work, Society, and Politics: The Culture of the Factory in Victorian England* (Brighton: Harvester, 1980); Gareth Stedman Jones, *Outcast London: A Study in the Relationship between Classes in Victorian Society* (Harmondsworth: Peregrine Books, 1976).

8. See Sewell, *Structure and Mobility,* and the extremely influential article that long preceded it, "Social Change and the Rise of Working-Class Politics in Nineteenth-Century Marseille," *Past and Present* 65 (1974): 75–109. Sewell's dissertation was completed in 1971 (University of California, Berkeley), but unlike Scott's his book was not published until much later, in fact *after* his own earlier book, *Work and Revolution in France: The Language of Labor from the Old Regime to 1848* (Cambridge: Cambridge University Press, 1980), had played a key role in announcing the so-called cultural turn. This intellectual itinerary endowed the materialist analytic of *Structure and Mobility* with a notable ambivalence it would have lacked if published a decade earlier.

9. See Sewell, *Work and Revolution,* 6–7.

10. Sewell sees this limitation as intrinsic to the form of the local study: "Part of the problem, clearly, is that the process of ideological development transcended local communities. To explain the content of the ideology of Marseille's workers in 1848, for example, we would have to look both at the intellectual development of socialist theory in the course of the 1840s and at the revolutionary agitation of the Parisian workers in the spring of 1848, because these were the major sources of the ideas taken up by Marseille's workers. Although certain aspects of economic, demographic, and social structure can be studied most profitably at the local level, a history of workers' ideology can scarcely avoid taking a national perspective." Sewell, *Work and Revolution,* 7. But there is nothing that inheres in the form of the local study per se to prevent analysis of politics or ideology in the local setting, in this case the emergence of democratic socialism in Marseille during the 1848 revolution. Sewell regrets that while he could track the spread of this new ideology as a social historian, he could not explain its character. Yet if "explaining its shape and content seemed to lie beyond [his] powers as a social historian," we would argue, this resulted more from the type of questions he chose to ask. One consequence of the materialist epistemology guiding the new social history was to demote politics into more of an epiphenomenon.

11. Joyce, *Work, Society, and Politics,* 315.

12. This difference of approach may have reflected different readings of Marx, although neither Joyce nor the others displayed a particularly clear or elaborate debt in this direction. Thus Joyce specifically invoked the mature Marx's theoretical distinction between the "formal" and the "real" subjection of labor, in which the latter became the key achievement of the labor process characteristic of modern industry, which secured the employer's direct control over production. Joyce's usage was heavily influenced by a brilliant deployment of this distinction by Stedman Jones in a 1975 article: "England's First Proletariat: 'Class Struggle and the Industrial Revolution,'" *New Left Review* 90 (March–April 1975): 35–69. In keeping with the political sensibilities of the

late sixties, Scott and Sewell seemed more influenced by the younger Marx's couplet of "being" and "consciousness" and the associated distinction between "class in itself" and "class for itself."

13. Joyce, *Work, Society, and Politics,* xvii.

14. Stedman Jones, *Outcast London,* 337.

15. Stedman Jones, *Outcast London,* 349. In explaining the minority persistence of post-Chartist radicalism and early signs of support for socialism in some parts of Lancashire and Yorkshire, Joyce mirrored this argument. Greater evidence of resistance against the pervasiveness of the factory-based paternalism could be found in the woollen and worsted towns of the West Riding of Yorkshire, where workers kept larger measures of craft control against the spread of mechanization. Similarly, radicalism and independence persisted among workers in Lancashire where trade unions and friendly societies offered countervailing social and institutional resources—namely, among the surviving craft trades, where "non-factory skilled and craft workers" could be "most effectively sealed from [the effects of the paternalist politics]." See Joyce, *Work, Society, and Politics,* 302.

16. In fact, in this respect Stedman Jones's argument is somewhat overdrawn. In light of the continuing appeal of popular liberalism, and given the exclusionary effects of an extremely narrow franchise, the successes of broad-based progressivist politics of various kinds between the 1890s and 1914 were actually quite significant.

17. See Stedman Jones's first chapter, "London as an Industrial Center," in *Outcast London,* 19–32. The quoted phrase is from 19.

18. Gareth Stedman Jones, "Working-Class Culture and Working-Class Politics in London, 1870–1900: Notes on the Remaking of a Working Class," *Journal of Social History* 7 (1974): 460–508, reprinted in Gareth Stedman Jones, *Languages of Class: Studies in English Working-Class History, 1832–1982* (Cambridge: Cambridge University Press, 1983), 179–238.

19. Stedman Jones, "Introduction," in *Languages of Class,* 11.

20. For a careful and sophisticated critique of Stedman Jones, which situates its analysis of politics *precisely* in the sort of densely researched social history we are seeking to recuperate in this book, see Marc Brodie, *The Politics of the Poor: The East End of London, 1885–1914* (Oxford: Oxford University Press, 2004); also Brodie, "Free Trade and Cheap Theatre: Sources of Politics for the Nineteenth-Century London Poor," *Social History* 28 (October 2003): 346–60.

21. Stedman Jones, "Introduction," in *Languages of Class,* 10–11.

22. Stedman Jones, "Introduction," in *Languages of Class,* 23–24. Here Stedman Jones was talking specifically about the Labour Party in the twentieth century, but the argument has a general applicability. For the extended form of the discussion, see "Why Is the Labour Party in a Mess?" *Languages of Class,* 239–56.

23. Stedman Jones, "Introduction," in *Languages of Class,* 23–24.

24. See the following works by Patrick Joyce: *Visions of the People: Industrial England and the Question of Class, 1840–1914* (Cambridge: Cambridge University Press, 1991); *Democratic Subjects: The Self and the Social in Nineteenth-Century England* (Cambridge: Cambridge University Press, 1994); *The Rule of Freedom: Liberalism and the Modern City* (London: Verso, 2003). We should emphasize as strongly as possible here that no judgment is being made of the quality of the books concerned. In fact, they remain remarkably impressive within their own terms, that is, as sophisticated, challenging, and insightful historical explorations within the chosen genres of analysis. Thus in describing *Democratic Subjects* as an exercise in intellectual history, we are not rejecting it on those grounds, and on the contrary find it extremely illuminating *as such.* Likewise, in its combination of theoretical facility and rich knowledge of the relevant sources and subject matters, *The Rule of Freedom* qualifies as one of the most original contributions to the historiography of liberalism for a long time. Its discussions of the complex dialectics of governmentality and resistance, for example, as well as much else besides, cannot be ignored by any social historian of the period (for instance, 183–89). In characterizing these works, we are not seeking to dismiss or diminish them, but rather to isolate some of the consequences of their chosen approach.

25. All three were in a kind of intimate and self-reflexive dialogue with social history, in which they'd earlier occupied leading roles. See Stedman Jones, *Languages of Class;* Scott, *Gender and the Politics of History* (New York: Columbia University Press, 1988); Sewell, *Work and Revolution.* While fundamentally informed by social categories of analysis, their subsequent works are intellectual histories in the formal sense (histories of ideas based on readings of published texts). See Gareth Stedman Jones and Ian Patterson, eds., *Charles Fourier: The Theory of the Four Movements* (Cambridge: Cambridge University Press, 1996); Joan W. Scott, *Only Paradoxes to Offer: French Feminists and the Rights of Man* (Cambridge: Harvard University Press, 1996); William Sewell, Jr., *A Rhetoric of Bourgeois Revolution: The Abbé Sieyes and What Is the Third Estate?* (Durham: Duke University Press, 1994). Stedman Jones is working on "changes in European social and political thought in the aftermath of the French Revolution." See the Contributor's Note (252) to Stedman Jones, "The Determinist Fix: Some Obstacles to the Further Development of the Linguistic Approach to History in the 1990s," *History Workshop Journal* 42 (Autumn 1996): 19–35.

26. To the best of our knowledge, Stedman Jones has neither replied to critics of the essay on Chartism nor taken his analysis of Chartist language any further. He reiterates the argument in Gareth Stedman Jones, "Anglo-Marxism, Neo-Marxism, and the Discursive Approach to History," in Alf Lüdtke, ed.,

*Was bleibt von marxistischen Perspektiven in der Geschichtsforschung?* (Göttingen: Wallstein Verlag, 1997), 173–82, the full text from which Stedman Jones, "Determinist Fix," was excerpted.

27. Robert Gray, "The Deconstruction of the English Working Class," *Social History* 11 (1986): 367. Among the other critiques, see especially James Epstein, "Rethinking the Categories of Working-Class History," *Labour/Le Travail* 18 (Fall 1986): 195–208; David Mayfield and Susan Thorne, "Social History and Its Discontents: Gareth Stedman Jones and the Politics of Language," *Social History* 17 (1992): 165–88. Among subsequent contributions postdating Stedman Jones's intervention, which also carry the discussion further, see especially Anna Clark, *The Struggle for the Breeches: The Making of the British Working Class, 1780–1850* (Berkeley: University of California Press, 1995); Paul Pickering, "Class Without Words: Symbolic Communication in the Chartist Movement," *Past and Present* 112 (1986): 144–62; James Epstein, "Understanding the Cap of Liberty: Symbolic Practice and Social Conflict in Early Nineteenth-Century England," *Past and Present* 112 (1989): 75–118, and *Radical Expression: Political Language, Ritual, and Symbol in England, 1790–1850* (New York: Oxford University Press, 1994); John Smail, "New Languages for Labor and Capital: The Transformation of Discourse in the Early Years of the Industrial Revolution," *Social History* 12 (1987): 49–72; Marc W. Steinberg, "Culturally Speaking: Finding a Commons between Post-Structuralism and the Thompsonian Perspective," *Social History* 21 (1996): 193–214, and "'The Labour of the Country is the Wealth of the Country': Class Identity, Consciousness, and the Role of Discourse in the Making of the English Working Class," *International Labor and Working-Class History* 49 (Spring 1996): 1–25. See also Richard Biernacki, *The Fabrication of Labor: Germany and Britain, 1640–1914* (Berkeley: University of California Press, 1995), which proposes a mode of cultural analysis based on nonlinguistic practices; and James Epstein, *In Practice: Studies in the Language and Culture of Popular Politics in Modern Britain* (Stanford: Stanford University Press, 2003), which brings together that author's valuable reflections on these issues over the years, including the essay mentioned earlier in this note, "Rethinking the Categories."

28. Joan W. Scott, "On Language, Gender, and Working-Class History," in *Gender and the Politics of History*, 67. Stedman Jones's only direct rejoinder to Scott, which grudgingly admits the "incompleteness" of an approach that leaves out gender, merely accuses her of "continued adherence to an essentialist notion of class," in which a post-Foucauldian stress on power relations replaces the Marxist stress on relations of production. See Stedman Jones, "Anglo-Marxism," 177 n. 39. This is surely tendentious, missing Scott's meaning and distorting the theoretical effects of *Gender and the Politics of History*.

29. James Vernon, *Politics and the People: A Study in English Political Culture, c.*

*1815–1867* (Cambridge: Cambridge University Press, 1993), 6. See also Pickering, "Class Without Words"; Epstein, "Understanding the Cap of Liberty," and *Radical Expression*. To dismiss these proposals as just a new version of the old economism, in which political cultures are approached as "simply mirrors of social experience," is certainly a blunt reduction of a complex and imaginative analytic, a striking example of the epistemological line-drawing we're trying to transcend. See Stedman Jones, "Anglo-Marxism," 181 n. 44.

30. Michael Sonenscher, *Work and Wages: Natural Law, Politics, and the Late Eighteenth-Century French Trades* (Cambridge: Cambridge University Press, 1989); Biernacki, *Fabrication of Labor;* Robert Gray, *The Factory Question and Industrial England, 1830–1860* (Cambridge: Cambridge University Press, 1996). William Reddy's *The Rise of Market Culture: The Textile Trade and French Society, 1750–1900* (Cambridge: Cambridge University Press, 1984) and *Money and Liberty in Modern Europe: A Critique of Historical Understandings* (Cambridge: Cambridge University Press, 1987) were important transitional texts. More generally, see Patrick Joyce, ed., *The Historical Meanings of Work* (Cambridge: Cambridge University Press, 1989).

31. The projects assembled in Ava Baron, ed., *Work Engendered: Toward a New History of American Labor* (Ithaca: Cornell University Press, 1991), and Laura L. Frader and Sonya O. Rose, eds., *Gender and Class in Modern Europe* (Ithaca: Cornell University Press, 1996), had genealogies independent of Scott's influence during the 1980s. See especially Sonya O. Rose, "'Gender at Work': Sex, Class, and Industrial Capitalism," *History Workshop Journal* 21 (Spring 1986): 113–31. For work on the welfare state, see Elizabeth Wilson, *Women and the Welfare State* (London: Methuen, 1977); Anna Davin, "Imperialism and Motherhood," *History Workshop Journal* 5 (Spring 1978): 9–65; Jane Lewis, *The Politics of Motherhood: Child and Maternal Welfare in England, 1900–1939* (London: Croom Helm, 1980); Karen Offen, "Depopulation, Nationalism, and Feminism in Fin de Siècle France," *American Historical Review* 89 (1984): 648–76; Linda Gordon, ed., *Women, the State, and Welfare* (Madison: University of Wisconsin Press, 1990); Gisela Bock and Pat Thane, eds., *Maternity and Gender Policies: Women and the Rise of the European Welfare States, 1880–1950s* (London: Routledge, 1991); Seth Koven and Sonya Michel, eds., *Mothers of a New World: Maternalist Politics and the Emergence of Welfare States* (London: Routledge, 1993).

32. Kathleen Canning, "German Particularities in Women's History/Gender History," *Journal of Women's History* 5, no. 1 (Spring 1993): 102–14. In addition to the work collected in Baron, ed., *Work Engendered,* and Frader and Rose, eds., *Gender and Class,* see especially Sonya O. Rose, *Limited Livelihoods: Gender and Class in Nineteenth-Century England* (Berkeley: University of California Press, 1992); Clark, *Struggle for the Breeches.*

33. Canning, *Languages of Labor and Gender* (Ithaca: Cornell University Press, 1996; repr., Ann Arbor: University of Michigan Press, 2002).

34. David Crew, "Who's Afraid of Cultural Studies? Taking a 'Cultural Turn' in German History," in Scott Denham, Irene Kacandes, and Jonathan Petropoulos, eds., *A User's Guide to German Cultural Studies* (Ann Arbor: University of Michigan Press, 1997), 50.

35. Joan W. Scott, "The Evidence of Experience," in Terrence J. McDonald, ed., *The Historic Turn in the Human Sciences* (Ann Arbor: University of Michigan Press, 1996), 390.

36. "Evidence of Experience," 391.

37. "Evidence of Experience," 387.

38. Edward P. Thompson, *The Making of the English Working Class* (London: Gollancz, 1963), 12; Sheila Rowbotham, *Hidden from History: Three Hundred Years of Women's Oppression and the Fight Against It* (London: Pluto Press, 1973).

39. Scott, "Evidence of Experience," 384. The italics are ours.

40. Scott, "Evidence of Experience," 394–95. See Gayatri Chakravorty Spivak, "Subaltern Studies: Deconstructing Historiography," in *In Other Worlds: Essays in Cultural Politics* (New York: Routledge, 1987), 241.

41. Scott, *Only Paradoxes to Offer*.

42. Scott, *Only Paradoxes to Offer*, 11–12.

43. See especially Charles Sowerwine, *Sisters or Citizens? Women and Socialism in France since 1876* (Cambridge: Cambridge University Press, 1982); Helmut Gruber, "French Women in the Crossfire of Class, Sex, Maternity, and Citizenship," in Helmut Gruber and Pamela Graves, eds., *Women and Socialism / Socialism and Women: Europe between the Two World Wars* (New York: Berghahn, 1998), 279–320; Christine Bard and Jean-Louis Robert, "The French Communist Party and Women: From 'Feminism' to Familialism," in Gruber and Graves, eds., *Women and Socialism*, 321–47; Claire Duchen, *Women's Rights and Women's Lives in France, 1944–1968* (London: Routledge, 1994), and *Feminism in France: From May '68 to Mitterand* (London: Routledge, 1986); Christine Bard, "Proletarians of the Proletariat: Women's Citizenship in France," *International Labor and Working-Class History* 48 (Fall 1997): 49–67; Claire Goldberg Moses, "Debating the Present, Writing the Past: 'Feminism' in French History and Historiography," *Radical History Review* 52 (1992): 79–94.

44. Scott, *Only Paradoxes to Offer*, 16.

45. Scott, *Only Paradoxes to Offer*, 16.

46. Michel Foucault, *Remarks on Marx. Conversations with Duccio Trombadori* (New York: Semiotext(e), 1991), 154, 153, 150.

47. Foucault, *Remarks on Marx*, 154.

48. Foucault, *Remarks on Marx*, 154–56.

49. See Stedman Jones, "Determinist Fix" and "Anglo-Marxism." See fur-

ther his "Introduction" to Fourier, *Theory of the Four Movements,* vii–xxvi; Stedman Jones, "Introduction," in Karl Marx and Friedrich Engels, *The Communist Manifesto* (London: Penguin Books, 2002), 1–187; Stedman Jones, *An End to Poverty?* (London: Profile Books, 2004). Finally, see the text of the address given as one of a series of six sermons in King's College Chapel, Cambridge: Stedman Jones, "Faith in History," *History Workshop Journal* 30 (Autumn 1990): 62–67; and the interview conducted by Peter Schöttler, in Stedman Jones, *Klassen, Politik und Sprache: Für eine theorieorientierte Sozialgeschichte* (Münster: Westfälisches Dampfboot, 1988), 277–317.

50. The quoted phrase is taken from Edward Thompson's description of the shared assumption behind the Marxist tradition. See Stedman Jones, "Anglo-Marxism," 153; Edward Thompson, *The Poverty of Theory and Other Essays* (London: Merlin, 1978), 199–200.

51. Stedman Jones, "Anglo-Marxism," 172–73.

52. This is the distant echo of an earlier critique of the national intellectual culture mounted by the *New Left Review* in the mid-1960s. See Perry Anderson, "Origins of the Present Crisis," and Tom Nairn, "The British Political Elite," *New Left Review* 23 (January–February 1964): 26–53, 19–25; Nairn, "The English Working Class," *New Left Review* 24 (March–April 1964): 45–57; Nairn, "The Anatomy of the Labour Party," *New Left Review* 27 (September–October 1964): 38–65, and *New Left Review* 28 (November–December 1964): 33–62; Anderson, "Components of the National Culture," *New Left Review* 50 (July–August 1968): 3–57. For Stedman Jones's own contributions at this time, see Gareth Stedman Jones, "History in One Dimension," *New Left Review* 36 (March–April 1966): 48–58, and "The Pathology of British History," *New Left Review* 46 (November–December 1967): 29–43, reprinted as "History: The Poverty of Empiricism," in Robin Blackburn, ed., *Ideology in Social Science: Readings in Critical Social Theory* (London: Fontana, 1972), 96–115. Anderson's two essays, "Origins" and "Components," were reprinted in Perry Anderson, *English Questions* (London: Verso, 1992), 15–47, 48–104, together with two new reflections on each: "The Figures of Descent" and "A Culture in Contraflow," 121–92, 193–301. See also Gregory Elliott, *Perry Anderson: The Merciless Laboratory of History* (Minneapolis: University of Minnesota Press, 1998), 12–20, 46–53.

53. Stedman Jones, "Anglo-Marxism," 153. Here Stedman Jones is referring mainly to the English-speaking world, and in the primary instance to work in Britain. As we argued in chapter 2, the influence of the *Annales* school was also vital to the rise of social history in the English-speaking world, converging in many ways with ideas of the "Anglo-Marxists." Stedman Jones has also written specifically about that elsewhere in "The New Social History in France," in Colin Jones and Dror Warhman, eds., *The Age of Cultural Revolutions: Britain and France, 1750–1820* (Berkeley: University of California Press, 2002), 94–105.

54. Stedman Jones, "Anglo-Marxism," 183.

55. Stedman Jones, "Anglo-Marxism," 207–8.

56. Stedman Jones, "Anglo-Marxism," 208.

57. See especially Ellen Meiksins Wood, *The Retreat from Class: A New "True" Socialism* (London: Verso, 1986); Neville Kirk, "In Defence of Class: A Critique of Recent Revisionist Writing upon the Nineteenth-Century English Working Class," *International Review of Social History* 32 (1987): 2–47; Bryan D. Palmer, *Descent into Discourse: The Reification of Language and the Writing of Social History* (Philadelphia: Temple University Press, 1990), 120–44.

58. See the opening sentence of the first substantive section of *The Communist Manifesto*: "The history of all hitherto existing society is the history of class struggles." Marx and Engels, *Communist Manifesto*, 219.

59. Understanding these differences with any confidence is hampered by the absence of any full-scale or explicit debate. Both authors have confined themselves mainly to incidental references or an occasional note. See Scott, "On Language," 67; Stedman Jones, "Anglo-Marxism," 177 n. 39.

60. In developing our argument here we've found the writings of Ian Hacking extremely helpful. See *The Taming of Chance* (Cambridge: Cambridge University Press, 1990), and *The Social Construction of What?* (Cambridge: Harvard University Press, 2000).

61. Stedman Jones, "Anglo-Marxism," 205.

62. Such studies could also penetrate down to a level of grounded concreteness in the manner of the social and economic histories of particular industries or types of work.

63. See, for example, Gwyn A. Williams, "18 Brumaire: Karl Marx and Defeat," in Betty Matthews, ed., *Marx: A Hundred Years On* (London: Lawrence and Wishart, 1983), 11–37; Stuart Hall, "Rethinking the 'Base-and-Superstructure' Metaphor," in Jon Bloomfield, ed., *Class, Hegemony, and Party* (London: Lawrence and Wishart, 1977), 43–72.

64. Stedman Jones, "Anglo-Marxism," 205 n. 81.

65. See especially Eugenio F. Biagini and Alastair J. Reid, eds., *Currents of Radicalism: Popular Radicalism, Organized Labour, and Party Politics in Britain, 1850–1914* (Cambridge: Cambridge University Press, 1991); Eugenio F. Biagini, ed., *Citizenship and Community: Liberals, Radicals, and Collective Identities in the British Isles, 1865–1931* (Cambridge: Cambridge University Press, 1996); also, Stedman Jones, "Why Is the Labour Party in a Mess?" The most interesting monograph in this vein is Jon Lawrence, *Speaking for the People: Party, Language, and Popular Politics in England, 1867–1914* (Cambridge: Cambridge University Press, 1998).

66. Stedman Jones, "Anglo-Marxism," 207–8.

67. One of us has tried to write a general history of the European Left dur-

ing the nineteenth and twentieth centuries laying this more complex field of possibilities out: Geoff Eley, *Forging Democracy: The History of the Left in Europe, 1850–2000* (New York: Oxford University Press, 2002).

68. Stedman Jones, "Anglo-Marxism," 206–7.

69. See especially Clark, *Struggle for the Breeches;* Pickering, "Class Without Words"; Epstein, "Understanding the Cap of Liberty," and *Radical Expression;* Smail, "New Languages"; Steinberg, "Culturally Speaking" and " 'The Labour of the Country."

70. Stedman Jones, "Anglo-Marxism," 206.

71. Stedman Jones, "Anglo-Marxism," 208.

72. Patrick Joyce, "Introduction," in Joyce, ed., *Class* (Oxford: Oxford University Press, 1995), 3.

## Chapter 5

1. Geoff Eley and Keith Nield, "Why Does Social History Ignore Politics?" *Social History* 5 (May 1980): 249–71.

2. See here Geoff Eley, *A Crooked Line: From Cultural History to the History of Society* (Ann Arbor: University of Michigan Press, 2005), which itself built on Eley, "Is All the World a Text? From Social History to the History of Society Two Decades Later," in Terrence McDonald, ed., *The Historic Turn in the Human Sciences* (Ann Arbor: University of Michigan Press, 1996), 193–243; and Nicholas B. Dirks, Geoff Eley, and Sherry B. Ortner, "Introduction," in Dirks, Eley, and Ortner, eds., *Culture/Power/History: A Reader in Contemporary Social Theory* (Princeton: Princeton University Press, 1994), 3–45.

3. For excellent discussions of the state's presence inside the social, see Paul W. Werth, "Through the Prism of Prostitution: State, Society, and Power," *Social History* 19 (1994): 1–15; Kathleen Canning, "State, Social Body, and Public Sphere: Regulating Female Factory Labor during the 1890s," *Languages of Labor and Gender: Female Factory Work in Germany, 1850–1914* (Ithaca: Cornell University Press, 1996; repr., Ann Arbor: University of Michigan Press, 2002), 126–69; Kathleen Canning, "Social Body, Body Politics: Recasting the Social Question in Germany, 1875–1900," in Laura L. Frader and Sonya O. Rose, eds., *Gender and Class in Modern Europe* (Ithaca: Cornell University Press, 1996), 211–37. For recent state theory, see Bob Jessop, *State Theory: Putting Capitalist States in Their Place* (Cambridge: Polity, 1990); Stanley Aronowitz and Peter Bratsis, eds., *Paradigm Lost: State Theory Reconsidered* (Minneapolis: University of Minnesota Press, 2002); and Timothy Mitchell, "The Limits of the State: Beyond Statist Approaches and Their Critics," *American Political Science Review* 85 (1991): 77–96.

4. We're thinking here of the disproportionate anger provoked by Richard

Johnson's important article, "Edward Thompson, Eugene Genovese, and Socialist-Humanist History," *History Workshop Journal* 6 (Autumn 1978): 79–100, in which he proposed the name "culturalism" for the perspectives deriving from Thompson's and Genovese's work.

5. Michel Foucault, *Power/Knowledge: Selected Interviews and Other Writings, 1972–1977,* ed. Colin Gordon (New York, 1980), 60.

6. Dirks, Eley, and Ortner, "Introduction," 5.

7. Quintin Hoare and Geoffrey Nowell-Smith, eds., *Selections from the Prison Notebooks of Antonio Gramsci* (London: Lawrence and Wishart, 1971), 238.

8. See Perry Anderson, "The Antinomies of Antonio Gramsci," *New Left Review* 100 (November 1976–January 1977): 5–78.

9. See Karl Marx, "Preface" to *A Contribution to the Critique of Political Economy* (1859), in Marx, *Early Writings,* ed. Lucio Colletti (Harmondsworth: Penguin Books, 1975), 424–28.

10. Michel Foucault, *The History of Sexuality, Volume I: An Introduction* (New York: Vintage, 1980), 92.

11. Paul Rabinow, ed., *The Foucault Reader: An Introduction to Foucault's Thought* (New York: Pantheon, 1984), 63–64.

12. Rabinow, ed., *The Foucault Reader,* 65.

13. Rabinow, ed., *The Foucault Reader,* 60.

14. Foucault, *Power/Knowledge,* 80–81.

15. Foucault, *Power/Knowledge,* 81 (emphasis in original).

16. Foucault, *History of Sexuality,* 94–95.

17. Foucault, *History of Sexuality,* 95–96.

18. Indeed, in various writings Gayatri Chakravorty Spivak actually concedes as much, acknowledging the potentially immobilizing effects of a "discursive approach." Precisely in order to allow politics to be conducted, epistemological critique will need to be suspended; and because the consequences of epistemological consistency for the taking of political action may be disabling, we are justified pragmatically ("strategically") in proceeding on extradiscursive ground. See Spivak, "Subaltern Talk: Interview with the Editors," in Donna Landry and Gerald MacLean, eds., *The Spivak Reader* (London: Routledge, 1996), 287–308; Spivak, "The New Subaltern: A Silent Interview," in Vinayak Chaturvedi, ed., *Mapping Subaltern Studies and the Postcolonial* (London: Verso, 2000), 324–41; Spivak, "Teaching for the Times," in Jan Nederveen Pieterse and Bhikhu Parekh, eds., *The Decolonization of the Imagination: Culture, Knowledge, and Power* (London: Zed Books, 1995), 176–203. Spivak's escape clause of "strategic essentialism" was developed in "Subaltern Studies: Deconstructing Historiography," in Ranajit Guha and Spivak, eds., *Selected Subaltern Studies* (New York: Oxford University Press, 1988), 3–32, which itself was an elabo-

ration of the argument of "Can the Subaltern Speak?" in Cary Nelson and Lawrence Grossberg, eds., *Marxism and the Interpretation of Culture* (Urbana: University of Illinois, 1988), 271–313.

19. We were really at a loss to see how Louise Tilly could have read our 1980 article as primarily an attack on *Alltagsgeschichte* ("a rather narrow but admonitory look at the first steps of younger German labor historians toward the 'everyday life' approach") or as a kind of preemptive strike. On the contrary, our advocacy of *Alltagsgeschichte* over a longer period speaks for itself. See, for example, Geoff Eley, "Labor History, Social History, *Alltagsgeschichte*: Experience, Culture, and the Politics of the Everyday—A New Direction for German Social History?" *Journal of Modern History* 61, no. 2 (1989): 297–43; Eley, "Foreword" to Alf Lüdtke, ed., *The History of Everyday Life: Reconstructing Historical Experiences and Ways of Life* (Princeton: Princeton University Press, 1995), vii–xiii, which was the first programmatic translation of work from the German. In *Social History,* we also sought exposure for the new work in its earliest stages. See the special German issue, including articles by Alf Lüdtke, "The Role of State Violence in the Period of Transition to Industrial Capitalism: The Example of Prussia from 1815 to 1848," and Dieter Groh, "Base-Processes and the Problem of Organization: Outline of a General History Research Project," *Social History* 4 (May 1979): 175–221, 265–83. Tilly's description ignored the main purposes of our 1980 article, which argued the relationship between social history and politics on a broad front of British and German social history. See Louise A. Tilly, "History's Noncrisis," *International Labor and Working-Class History* 46 (Fall 1994): 87.

20. The bibliography of possible illustrations is obviously much greater than can be cited here, but might include the following. In U.S. history: Lizabeth Cohen, *Making a New Deal: Industrial Workers in Chicago, 1919–1939* (Cambridge: Cambridge University Press, 1990); Gary Gerstle, *Working-Class Americanism: The Politics of Labor in a Textile City, 1914–1960* (Cambridge: Cambridge University Press, 1989); Earl Lewis, *In Their Own Interests: Race, Class, and Power in Twentieth-Century Norfolk, Virginia* (Berkeley: University of California Press, 1991); Robin D. G. Kelley, *Hammer and Hoe: Alabama Communists during the Great Depression* (Chapel Hill: University of North Carolina Press, 1990); Thomas Sugrue, *The Origins of the Urban Crisis: Race and Inequality in Postwar Detroit* (Princeton: Princeton University Press, 1996). In Soviet history: Stephen Kotkin, *Magnetic Mountain: Stalinism as a Civilization* (Berkeley: University of California Press, 1995). In British history: Anna Clark, *The Struggle for the Breeches: The Making of the British Working Class, 1780–1850* (Berkeley: University of California Press, 1995); Robert Gray, *The Factory Question and Industrial England, 1830–1860* (Cambridge: Cambridge University Press, 1996). In German history, the list might run from Mary Nolan, *Social Democracy and Society:*

*Working-Class Radicalism in Düsseldorf, 1890–1920* (Cambridge: Cambridge University Press, 1981), Eve Rosenhaft, *Beating the Fascists? The German Communists and Political Violence, 1929–1933* (Cambridge: Cambridge University Press, 1983), and Adelheid von Saldern, *Auf dem Wege zum Arbeiter-Reformismus: Parteialltag in sozialdemokratischer Provinz Göttingen (1870–1920)* (Frankfurt am Main: Campus, 1984), to Canning, *Languages of Labor,* Thomas Lindenberger, *Strassenpolitik: Zur Sozialgeschichte der öffentlichen Ordnung in Berlin 1900 bis 1914* (Bonn: Dietz Verlag, 1995), and Anthony McElligott, *Contested City: Municipal Politics and the Rise of Nazism in Altona, 1917–1937* (Ann Arbor: University of Michigan Press, 1998).

21. Ira Katznelson, "The 'Bourgeois' Dimension: A Provocation about Institutions, Politics, and the Future of Labor History," *International Labor and Working-Class History* 46 (Fall 1994): 18.

22. Katznelson, "The 'Bourgeois' Dimension," 9.

23. See Eugenio F. Biagini and Alastair Reid, eds., *Currents of Radicalism: Popular Radicalism, Organized Labour, and Party Politics in Britain, 1850–1914* (Cambridge: Cambridge University Press, 1991). Pelling's only monograph of any empirical density (as opposed to a series of often short general histories of the Labour Party, the British Communist Party, the trade unions, the Labour governments of 1945–51, and Britain in World War II) was his first book, *Origins of the Labour Party, 1880–1900* (London: Macmillan, 1954).

24. Katznelson, "The 'Bourgeois' Dimension," 21. However, given the relative thinness of Pelling's work apart from *Origins* and the reference work *Social Geography of British Elections, 1885–1910* (London: Macmillan, 1967), his hostility to theory, and his indifference to social contexts, Katznelson's commendation seems absurdly inflated: "[T]oday within labor history there is no single body of work as accomplished as Pelling's that takes seriously a relational approach to the ties between the state and the working class via an analysis of their institutions considered in a larger regime framework."

25. Even an extensive list of citations would only scratch the surface of the potential bibliography here. One start might be through Neville Kirk, "'Traditional' Working-Class Culture and 'the Rise of Labour': Some Preliminary Questions and Observations," *Social History* 16 (May 1991): 203–16, which contains a critical survey of recent literature, as of that time.

26. Eugenio F. Biagini, *Liberty, Retrenchment, and Reform: Popular Liberalism in the Age of Gladstone, 1860–1880* (Cambridge: Cambridge University Press, 1992), 2.

27. We're thinking of Ernesto Laclau, *Politics and Ideology in Marxist Theory* (London: Verso, 1977); Stuart Hall, "Notes on Deconstructing 'the Popular,'" in Raphael Samuel, ed., *People's History and Socialist Theory* (London: Routledge, 1981), 227–40, and the essays in Stuart Hall, *The Hard Road to Renewal: Thatch-*

*erism and the Crisis of the Left* (London: Verso, 1988), especially 123–73; Ernesto Laclau and Chantal Mouffe, *Hegemony and Socialist Strategy: Towards a Radical Democratic Politics* (London: Verso, 1985); and the essays in Gareth Stedman Jones, *Languages of Class: Studies in English Working-Class History, 1832–1982* (Cambridge: Cambridge University Press, 1983).

28. The argument for status and culture as the decisive referents for later nineteenth-century politics descends from Peter F. Clarke's classic article, "Electoral Sociology of Modern Britain," *History* 7 (1972): 31–55. See also his *Lancashire and the New Liberalism* (Cambridge: Cambridge University Press, 1971).

29. Gareth Stedman Jones, "Anglo-Marxism, Neo-Marxism and the Discursive Approach to History," in Alf Lüdtke, ed., *Was bleibt von marxistischen Perspektiven in der Geschichtsforschung?* (Göttingen: Wallstein Verlag, 1997), seems to be making this move. For more measured discussions of holding "the social" and "the political" together, in the interests of a better social history of politics, see Rohan McWilliam, *Popular Politics in Nineteenth-Century England* (London: Routledge, 1998); James Epstein, *Radical Expression: Political Language, Ritual, and Symbol in England, 1790–1850* (New York: Oxford University Press, 1994); James Vernon, ed., *Re-Reading the Constitution: New Narratives in the Political History of England's Long Nineteenth Century* (Cambridge: Cambridge University Press, 1996). For the most careful and challenging study produced from *inside* the new revisionist skepticism about the relationship of "politics" and "class," see Jon Lawrence, *Speaking for the People: Party, Language, and Popular Politics in England, 1867–1914* (Cambridge: Cambridge University Press, 1998).

30. In contrast, Katznelson's foregrounding of the institutional forms of politics, no less than the "postmodernist" advocacy of Joyce or some recent statements by Stedman Jones, *do* appear to be inviting us to go down that road. In particular, Katznelson recommends as models the exponents of a political history (Biagini and Reid) who appear to be rejecting social historical explanations as such.

31. Stedman Jones, "Anglo-Marxism," 205.

32. Robert Gray, "Class, Politics, and Historical 'Revisionism,'" *Social History* 19 (May 1994): 211.

33. The main peaks of intensity will be familiar. They include the British conflicts of the later 1970s, brought to a head in Edward Thompson's anti-Althusserian diatribe *The Poverty of Theory and Other Essays* (London: Merlin, 1978) and memorably staged at the Ruskin History Workshop in December 1979; debates around Stedman Jones, *Languages of Class;* the reactions to Joan Scott's poststructuralist theorizing of gender history, represented most angrily by Bryan D. Palmer's *Descent into Discourse: The Reification of Language and the Writing of Social History* (Philadelphia: Temple University Press, 1990); and

most recently, the hostilities around Patrick Joyce's advocacy of postmodernism.

34. Here we'd see Richard Johnson's doubled critique of "structuralism" and "culturalism" (and the larger rethinking of ideology, subjectivity, and identity associated with Stuart Hall and the Birmingham Center for Contemporary Cultural Studies), Stedman Jones's *Languages of Class,* and Scott's appropriations of poststructuralism as the three moments of this trajectory. In addition to the references already given, see especially Joan W. Scott, "The Evidence of Experience," in Terrence J. McDonald, ed., *The Historic Turn in the Human Sciences* (Ann Arbor: University of Michigan Press, 1996), 379–406.

35. For a good guide through the pitfalls of theorizing identity, see the now-classic article by Linda Alcoff, "Cultural Feminism versus Post-Structuralism: The Identity Crisis in Feminist Theory," in Dirks, Eley, and Ortner, eds., *Culture/Power/History,* 96–122.

36. This formulation is indebted to Ernesto Laclau, "The Impossibility of Society," in Laclau, *New Reflections of the Revolution of Our Time* (London: Verso, 1990), 89–92.

37. For a detailed account of the success of the socialist tradition in these terms since the later nineteenth century, see Geoff Eley, *Forging Democracy: The History of the Left in Europe, 1850–2000* (New York: Oxford University Press, 2002), 47–118, 384–404.

38. Our reference here is to Eric Hobsbawm and George Rudé's *Captain Swing: A Social History of the Great English Agricultural Uprising of 1830* (London: Lawrence and Wishart, 1968), which in its time was an inspiring materialist account of a popular uprising, using structural analysis and quantitative techniques. The other reference of the couplet is to Joan W. Scott's prescriptions in *Gender and the Politics of History* (New York: Columbia University Press, 1988) and "Evidence of Experience."

39. However, in dealing with the exclusions attendant upon race Western European working-class historiography still has an enormous way to go. In Joyce's Oxford Reader *Class,* any discussion of empire or race is notable for its absence. Likewise, David Cannadine's *The Rise and Fall of Class in Britain* (New York: Columbia University Press, 1999) entirely ignores the importance of empire, decolonization, immigration, and race for the shaping of working-class identities during the nineteenth and twentieth centuries. For succinct counterstatements, see Stuart Hall, "Ethnicity: Identity and Difference," in Geoff Eley and Ronald Grigor Suny, eds., *Becoming National: A Reader* (New York: Oxford University Press, 1996), 339–49; Paul Gilroy, "One Nation under a Groove: The Cultural Politics of 'Race' and Racism in Britain," Eley and Suny, eds., *Becoming National,* 352–69; Catherine Hall, "Histories, Empires, and the Post-Colonial Moment," in Iain Chambers and Lidia Curti, eds., *The Post-Colonial*

*Question: Common Skies, Divided Horizons* (London: Routledge, 1996), 65–77, and "Re-Thinking Imperial History: The Reform Act of 1867," *New Left Review* 208 (November–December 1994): 3–29; Antoinette Burton, "Thinking Beyond the Boundaries: Empire, Feminism, and the Domains of History," *Social History* 26 (2001): 60–71.

40. The first two of these phrases are from titles by Neville Kirk and Patrick Joyce, who are among the most polemical advocates of the respective positions. See Neville Kirk, "In Defence of Class: A Critique of Recent Revisionist Writing upon the Nineteenth-Century English Working Class," *International Review of Social History* 32 (1987): 2–47; Patrick Joyce, "The End of Social History?" *Social History* 20 (January 1995): 73–91. For "realism" versus "postmodernism," see Neville Kirk, "Class and the 'Linguistic Turn' in Chartist and Post-Chartist Historiography," in Kirk, ed., *Social Class and Marxism: Defences and Challenges* (Aldershot: Scolar Press, 1996), especially 93–100, 119–26, 128 n. 22; Joyce Appleby, Lynn Hunt, and Margaret Jacob, *Telling the Truth about History* (New York: Norton, 1994). For "redistribution" versus "recognition," see the exchange between Nancy Fraser and Iris Marion Young, provoked by Fraser's "From Redistribution to Recognition? Dilemmas of Justice in a 'Postsocialist' Age," in Fraser, *Justice Interruptus: Critical Reflections on the "Postsocialist" Condition* (New York: Routledge, 1997), 11–39: Iris Marion Young, "Unruly Categories: A Critique of Nancy Fraser's Dual Systems Theory," *New Left Review* 222 (March–April 1997): 147–60; Nancy Fraser, "A Rejoinder to Iris Young," *New Left Review* 223 (May–June 1997): 126–29. Fraser's admirably lucid exposition converges with our own political position. See also another important exchange: Judith Butler, "Merely Cultural," *New Left Review* 227 (January–February 1998): 33–44; Nancy Fraser, "Heterosexism, Misrecognition, and Capitalism: A Response to Judith Butler," *New Left Review* 228 (March–April 1998): 140–49.

41. Here U.S. social history is way ahead of work in Europe. See Cohen, *Making a New Deal;* Dana Frank, *Purchasing Power: Consumer Organizing, Gender, and the Seattle Labor Movement* (Cambridge: Cambridge University Press, 1994); Kathy Peiss, *Cheap Amusements: Working Women and Leisure in Turn-of-the-Century New York* (Philadelphia: Temple University Press, 1986). Work in German history has taken more of a cultural studies turn. See Erica Carter, *How German Is She? Postwar West German Reconstruction and the Consuming Woman* (Ann Arbor: University of Michigan Press, 1997) and "Alice in the Consumer Wonderland: West German Case Studies in Gender and Consumer Culture," in Robert G. Moeller, ed., *West Germany under Construction: Politics, Society, and Culture in the Adenauer Era* (Ann Arbor: University of Michigan Press, 1997), 347–72; Ina Merkel, "Consumer Culture in the GDR," in Susan Strasser, Charles McGovern, and Matthias Judt, eds., *Getting and Spending: European and American Con-*

*sumer Societies in the Twentieth Century* (Cambridge: Cambridge University Press, 1998), 281–99; Uta G. Poiger, "Rock 'n' Roll, Female Sexuality, and the Cold War Battle over German Identities," in Moeller, ed., *West Germany under Construction*, 373–410; Katherine Pence, "Schaufenster des sozialistischen Konsums: Texte der ostdeutschen 'consumer culture,'" in Alf Lüdtke and Peter Becker, eds., *Akten. Eingaben. Schaufenster. Die DDR und ihre Texte. Erkundungen zu Herrschaft und Alltag* (Berlin: Akademie Verlag, 1997), 91–118. Work on Britain has tended to focus on organized consumers' movements. See now Peter Gurney, "The Battle of the Consumer in Postwar Britain," *Journal of Modern History* 77 (2005): 956–87; Matthew Hilton, *Consumerism in Twentieth-Century Britain: The Search for a Historical Movement* (Cambridge: Cambridge University Press, 2003).

42. Joyce, "End of Social History?" 76 n. 7.

43. This description comes from a speech by Peter Mandelson, then the Secretary of State for Trade and Industry and Tony Blair's right-hand adviser. See *Independent on Sunday*, 4 October 1998.

44. Stuart Hall, "The Great Moving Nowhere Show," *Marxism Today*, November–December 1998, 14.

45. Katznelson, "The 'Bourgeois Dimension,'" especially 7–11.

## Chapter 6

1. The confrontation in question was staged at the final plenary of the Thirteenth History Workshop in Oxford on 1 December 1979. The three prepared contributions by Stuart Hall ("In Defence of Theory"), Richard Johnson ("Against Absolutism"), and Edward Thompson ("The Politics of Theory"), were subsequently published in Raphael Samuel, ed., *People's History and Socialist Theory* (London: Routledge, 1981), 376–408. See also Martin Kettle, "The Experience of History," *New Society*, 6 December 1979, reprinted in Raphael Samuel, ed., *History Workshop: A Collectanea, 1967–1991. Documents, Memoirs, Critique, and Cumulative Index to History Workshop Journal* (Oxford: History Workshop, 1991), 107; Susan Magarey, "That Hoary Old Chestnut, Free Will and Determinism: Culture *vs.* Structure, or History *vs.* Theory in Britain," *Comparative Studies in Society and History* 29 (1987): 626–39.

2. For a rapid introduction to the range of these literatures, see R. J. Morris, *Class and Class Consciousness in the Industrial Revolution, 1780–1850* (London: Macmillan, 1979); Robert Gray, *The Aristocracy of Labour in Nineteenth-Century Britain c. 1850–1914* (London: Macmillan, 1981); Alastair Reid, *Social Classes and Social Relations in Britain, 1850–1914* (Cambridge: Cambridge University Press, 1995); Mike Savage and Andrew Miles, *The Remaking of the British Working Class, 1840–1940* (London: Routledge, 1994).

3. See Richard Johnson, "Reading for the Best Marx: History-Writing and

Historical Abstraction," in Richard Johnson, Gregor McLennan, Bill Schwarz, and David Sutton, eds., *Making Histories: Studies in History-Writing and Politics* (London: Hutchinson, 1982), 153–201.

4. This was the entire burden of Edward Thompson, "The Poverty of Theory: or an Orrery of Erros," in *The Poverty of Theory and Other Essays* (London: Merlin, 1978), 193–397.

5. For example, Patrick Joyce, "Introduction," in Joyce, ed., *Class* (Oxford: Oxford University Press, 1995), 8: "In social history . . . the basic repertoire of concepts is still essentially Marxist."

6. Stuart Hall, "The Problem of Ideology: Marxism Without Guarantees," in Betty Matthews, ed., *Marx a Hundred Years On* (London: Lawrence and Wishart, 1983), 57–85.

7. William H. Sewell, Jr., "Toward a Post-Materialist Rhetoric for Labor History," in Lenard R. Berlanstein, ed., *Rethinking Labor History: Essays on Discourse and Class Analysis* (Urbana: University of Illinois Press, 1993), 16.

8. Sewell, "Toward a Post-Materialist Rhetoric," 17, 18.

9. The idea therefore seems without foundation that something to do with class, its consciousness and its periodization, was permanently fixed in British historiography by the innovations of Thompson and others in the 1960s and 1970s. Yet, writing in 1991, Patrick Joyce proposed for social history since the sixties a unitary theoretical grounding of such exclusionary centeredness as to amount to a collective fixation in the field: "Until relatively recently," he wrote in the opening sentence of his book, " 'class' in British history was a settled matter. The periodization given to the 'class consciousness' of workers had assumed fairly distinct lines. Despite the large amount of subsequent scholarship, the work of E. P. Thompson and E. J. Hobsbawm remained, and remains, central, fixing the historical sequence of past development." See Patrick Joyce, *Visions of the People: Industrial England and the Question of Class, 1840–1914* (Cambridge: Cambridge University Press, 1991), 1.

10. Gareth Stedman Jones, "The Determinist Fix: Some Obstacles to the Further Development of the Linguistic Approach to History in the 1990s," *History Workshop Journal* 42 (Autumn 1996): 19.

11. See Bryan D. Palmer, *E. P. Thompson: Objections and Oppositions* (London: Verso, 1994), 159, 194 n. 5.

12. Perry Anderson, *Arguments within English Marxism* (London: Verso, 1980).

13. Karl Marx, *Capital: A Critique of Political Economy*, vol. 1 (Harmondsworth: Penguin Books in association with *New Left Review*, 1976), 340–416.

14. See sequentially: Andrew Ross, *The Failure of Modernism: Symptoms of American Poetry* (New York: Columbia University Press, 1986); *No Respect: Intel-*

*lectuals and Popular Culture* (New York: Routledge, 1989); *Strange Weather: Culture, Science, and Technology in the Age of Limits* (London: Verso, 1991); *The Chicago Gangster Theory of Life: Nature's Debt to Society* (London: Verso, 1994); *Real Love: In Pursuit of Cultural Justice* (New York: New York University Press, 1998). Ross also edited one of the early benchmark volumes of commentaries on postmodernism, *Universal Abandon? The Politics of Postmodernism* (Minneapolis: University of Minnesota Press, 1988), and two further volumes within cultural studies, *Microphone Fiends: Youth Music and Youth Culture* (New York: Routledge, 1994) and *Science Wars* (Durham: Duke University Press, 1996), the former coedited with Tricia Rose.

15. Andrew Ross, ed., *No Sweat: Fashion, Free Trade, and the Rights of Garment Workers* (New York: Norton, 1997), was followed by *No-Collar: The Humane Workplace and Its Hidden Costs* (New York: Basic Books, 2003) and *Low Pay, High Profile: The Global Push for Fair Labor* (New York: New Press, 2004). See also *The Celebration Chronicles: Life, Liberty, and the Pursuit of Property Values in Disney's New Town* (New York: Ballantine Books, 1999).

16. This type of politically engaged scholarship, which sought to explore possible horizons of collective agency and aspiration by empathetically reconstructing past forms of locally derived community, solidarity, and resistance, was the characteristic genre of the annual History Workshops during the 1970s and supplied much of the élan for the journal's early years. Among its many other discussions and features, the inaugural issue, *History Workshop Journal* 1 (Spring 1976), included articles on railway workers (Frank McKenna, "Victorian Railway Workers," 26–73); local museums of ordinary life (Ian Rodgers, "Village History in Brill," 114–16; Alessandro Triulzi, "A Museum of Peasant Life in Emilia," 117–20); workers' libraries (Hans-Josef Steinberg, "Workers' Libraries in Germany before 1914," 166–80; Stan Shipley, "The Library of the Alliance Cabinet Makers' Association in 1875," 181–84); the presentation of a nineteenth-century miner's autobiography (Edward Allen Rymer, "The Martyrdom of the Mine, Part I," introduced by Robert G. Neville, 220–44); and a programmatic reflection, "Local History and Oral History," by Raphael Samuel (191–209). The commitment to seeing historiography as a social movement was most apparent perhaps in the "Noticeboard" feature at the back of the journal, which collected calendars of events, annotated listings of local publications, publishers, bookshops, journals, archives and museums, "fraternal groups," and regional History Workshops.

17. Founded in 1960, the national Society for the Study of Labour History built its important network through annual conferences and the *Bulletin.* It was followed in 1967 by the Scottish Labour History Society and its journal, *Scottish Labour History;* the Society for the Study of Welsh Labour History (1971) and its journal *Llafur* (from 1972); the Irish Labour History Society (1973) and its jour-

nal *Saothar* (1975). Regional groups were formed in the North East (1967), with its own *Bulletin* (transmuting later into *North East History*); and the North West (1973), with its *North West Labour History Journal* (from 1974); by 1979 there were also groups in Sussex, Yorkshire, Humberside and North Midlands, West Midlands, Sheffield, and North Staffordshire. In the United States, MARHO: The Radical Historians Organization was founded in 1973, with its journal *Radical History Review*.

18. See especially Joan W. Scott, *Gender and the Politics of History* (New York: Columbia University Press, 1988).

19. We are thinking especially of Joan W. Scott, *Only Paradoxes to Offer: French Feminists and the Rights of Man* (Cambridge: Harvard University Press, 1996).

20. Eley and Nield, "Farewell to the Working Class?" 18. In that particular discussion at least, our appeal fell on deaf ears.

# INDEX